BOY GENIUS

Boy Genius

Karl Rove, the Architect of George W. Bush's Remarkable Political Triumphs

Carl M. Cannon, Lou Dubose, and Jan Reid

PublicAffairs
New York

Composition by Mark McGarry, Texas Type & Book Works,
based on a design by Jennifer Dossin.

Library of Congress Control Number: 2002116766

ISBN 1-58648-336-6

10 9 8 7 6 5 4 3 2 1

To Raymond D. Strother, a Texan and a friend,
who opened my eyes to the rowdy ways
of political consultants

CMC

To Jeanne Goka, Michael, and Emiko

LD

To Dorothy Browne, Mark McKinnon,
and a genial patron saint of politics and writing,
the late Billie Lee Brammer

JR

Contents

Part 4: The Plan Comes Together

A Note on the Text

Lou Dubose, Jan Reid, and Carl M. Cannon acted as the co-authors for this book. Messrs. Dubose and Reid wrote Parts 1 and 2 and Mr. Cannon wrote Parts 3 and 4.

Prologue

Consider this tableau.

Fifteen flags posted along the back of a speakers platform provide the backdrop for a former secretary of state, a former chairman of the Republican Party, a former member of the National Security Council, the governor of Michigan, the senior U.S. senator from Georgia and four members of the U.S. House of Representatives. All their eyes are fixed on a figure as central to this scene as Christ was to Leonardo da Vinci's "Last Supper." The point of focus is George W. Bush, standing behind a lectern bearing the Seal of the Great State of Texas. He looks right and left, at the dignitaries flanking him. Then he turns his attention to the press pack that represents eighty-seven news outlets.

Seated among the reporters so he can watch the spectacle from their perspective is the strategist who directed both of Bush's campaigns for governor, as well as today's event: Karl Rove.

The figure at the center of Rove's set piece is neither a seasoned campaigner nor a practiced political tactician. Twenty years earlier George W. Bush lost a race for Congress in Amarillo, Texas. Five years earlier he was elected governor of a state where the governor cuts the ribbons while the lieutenant governor cuts the deals. And his foreign policy pronouncements about "Grecians," "Kosovarians" and "Timorians" are driving his poll ratings down even as they drive Jay Leno's Nielsen ratings up.

All this is momentarily forgotten by the reporters who sit transfixed before the Presentation of George W. Bush.

Bush is announcing only that he has formed an exploratory committee and will consider running for the presidency. Yet Robert Bryce of the *Texas Observer* writes of "an air of inevitability." *The New York Times* describes "a grand pageant of political might." To the reporters gathered in the Austin Convention Center ballroom, Bush already looks like a president, though the first primary is a year away. When Miriam Rozen of *The Dallas Observer* asks Rove why no reporter at the event has challenged Bush's limited understanding of national and foreign policy issues, Rove grins and responds: "Why didn't they do it? Because they were spellbound."

After the 2004 presidential election, the nation should be spellbound. Not only with President Bush, but with the man Texans have come to know as "Bush's brain" and whom the president himself calls "boy genius."

Karl Rove spent a quarter-century in Texas as a political consultant. But ask a politically aware Texan to name the one person who most altered the political landscape of the state over that same time period, and it's not likely that Karl Rove's name will come up. Pose the question in the form Rove himself might have, polling a random sample of potential voters, and it's even less likely that Rove's name will appear in the polling data. To most Texans—and now to most Americans—Karl Rove is a name they may have heard, without really knowing what he's done. But ask the same question of the 1,500 lobbyists who muscle their clients' bills through the Texas Legislature every two years, and Rove is at or near the top of every list. He also polls high with the capitol press corps in Austin, the bureaucrats who do the real work of government on legislative committees and regulatory agencies, and with elected officials.

Karl Rove is now in a category of major figures in American politics notable because the people in it are often relatively unknown. Rove is to George W. Bush what Kenny O'Donnell was to John F. Kennedy, what Michael Deaver was to Ronald Reagan, what Lee Atwater was to George H. W. Bush, and what James Carville was to Bill Clinton. As is true of most aspects of modern life, being behind the scenes these days is a lot more visible than it used to be. That's how James Carville got to be a national figure; now the same thing is happening to Karl Rove. The Boy Genius of Texas politics emerged from the tangle of the 2000 presidential contest to become an important figure in the White House. But it wasn't until George W. Bush's 2002 midterm election triumph that Rove became a celebrity of the first rank. Who is this fellow who guides the Republicans to such victories?

The role political consultants play in the shaping of American politics and public policy is enormous. Their ascendance could have been predicted forty years ago by a careful reading of Jane Jacobs' classic book, *The Death and Life of Great American Cities*. Jacobs lamented several technological changes that were transforming social life in America. Television and air conditioning were moving Americans away from their porches and public places and into their living rooms. Affordable cars and cheap gas were moving them out of the cities and into the suburbs.

Jacobs' book had nothing and everything to do with modern American politics. The changes she describes also created a new way of doing politics. Conversations about elections began to occur in living rooms, where they involve a television and a viewer. If political candidates could no longer talk to the voters of the suburban diaspora in labor unions and civic clubs, they could always catch them in front of their televisions. Or they could reach them through targeted mail drops, whose messages had been "polled and focus-grouped."

The immediate effects of those "conversations" are tested by overnight tracking polls, as close as you get to a real-time measure of how well a particular message resonates. Taken together, that all adds up to a sophisticated political conversation. Add a huge influx of money to the mix of television, direct mail, and polling, and the power of the professionals who master those media is evident. Political consultants are today's political bosses. They don't use the same means, but the ends are the same.

In the world of major league consultants today, Karl Rove has no peers. Just as no professional basketball player has ever performed at the level Michael Jordan reached when he was at the top of his game, no political consultant has ever played the high-stakes game of electoral politics like Rove does. Not Michael Deaver, not Lee Atwater, not James Carville. None of these "legends" was ever the dominant force in politics and policy that Karl Rove is today. His mastery of every aspect of modern politics—mail, television, polling, money, message, opposition research, electoral demographics—distinguishes him from others doing the same work. Other political professionals inevitably describe Rove through one of two martial metaphors. It's either war or chess. Rove either sets out to "conquer and destroy and takes no prisoners," or "sees the whole board and thinks twenty moves ahead." Like George Patton and Bobby Fischer, he has not been afraid to take risks with bold moves.

Karl Rove is the kind of political sage who knows how to make his candidate look good. George W. is a meet-and-greet master. But his grasp of the details of policy is often shaky. What Rove can do is figure out what Bush can say and to whom. Even more important, he understands how to move the pieces around on the chessboard so that the candidate on the attack is his and the one on the defensive is the other guy's, preferably a Democrat. George W. Bush has moved from a beginner in politics to the pinnacle based on a mix of things: luck, natural political skill, a conservative political tide, and shrewd strategic planning. The victory in Florida in the 2000 post-election added another component: outmaneuvering the opposition. But if Bush is the virtuoso, then Rove is the composer.

Looking back over Rove's career, a pattern emerges in which he focuses on the opponent and through a mix of the out-front and the underhanded, is able to win. Unlike Atwater who was mean and Carville who knew folksy, Rove is actually relatively low-key. He likes to remain behind the scenes, and underestimated. In the past, his opponents tended to overlook him until it was too late. But now, the candidate who Rove first helped in a losing campaign for a West Texas congressional seat is the Commander in Chief, and neither Rove's opponents nor the American public can afford to overlook him.

* * *

Rove got to where he is through a twenty-two-year political campaign of his own design. It was a campaign that began in Texas, and involved taking from the Democratic Party every statewide office and both houses of the Texas Legislature, and then redrawing the political map of the state to ensure that the Legislature remains in the control of the Republican Party.

When Rove first answered the call of George H. W. Bush to come to Houston and work for his political action committee, Texas was completely controlled by the Democratic Party. Every statewide office was held by a Democrat. Of the 181 seats in the Legislature, Republicans held only twenty-one. It had been over one hundred years since a Republican was elected governor.

But Rove saw the future, and it was "conservative white Democrats who are fed up with the liberal Democratic leadership at the state and national level, middle-class Hispanics who have become more independent and more conservative, and the migration to Texas of Republicans from other states."

Certainly, Texas was already changing when Rove got there in 1977. When Lyndon Johnson signed the Civil Rights Act in 1964 he said he feared that he had just delivered the South to the Republican Party. And so he had. But Rove anticipated that change before many Democrats in the state got wind of it. He became the agent of that change. He accelerated it. And he worked to ensure that the change was so profound that it is now almost structural.

Rove remade Texas in a way that observers of the 2002 midterm election victory will find familiar. He didn't wait for the right candidate for office to reveal himself; he recruited and created candidates. When the wrong candidate for a critical office revealed himself, Rove saw that the right candidate got the nomination.

Rove remade Texas in a way that observers of George W. Bush's defeat of John McCain in the South Carolina primary in 2000 will also find familiar, where it was alleged he used whispering campaigns conducted by surrogates to raise questions about an opponent's character.

In short, Rove remade Texas by methodically and ruthlessly eliminating the Democratic Party from the top down. He targeted Democratic candidates he believed he could defeat. He undermined them to make sure they would be defeated. He recruited Republican candidates who would win and remain in office. He lured conservative Democratic members of Congress into the Republican Party, with bankable promises of support in races for higher office.

And he delivered.

Rove learned his political skills in Texas, and Texas was a good place to practice. It's a state that comprises twenty media markets. If the state were an independent country—an idea that holds considerable appeal right now to Al Gore, John Kerry, John Edwards, and the other Democratic presidential losers—it would be the eleventh largest economy in the world. Texas also defines the Wild West of campaign contributions. Any individual can contribute any amount to any candidate, as long as the contribution is declared with the proper agency in Austin. In 2002, the Democratic candidate for governor spent $64 million to lose the election—to a lieutenant governor who twelve years earlier had been recruited from the Democratic Party, repositioned, and run as a Republican—by Karl Rove. If there is a state in the nation in which to cultivate the fundamental political skill of raising and spending political cash, Texas is that state.

Rove has moved from state politics to the national stage. So what might we continue to expect of him? It is axiomatic to political journalists that the best method to predict what a politician will do is to look at the record. Rove's record is writ large on the state of Texas and America.

We need to understand where Rove came from, how he got so smart, what his relationship with Bush is about, what he stands for, what he wants, and what all this means to the people of the United States, because now it is us he is in charge of. Behind-the-scenes operatives are unique for their power in a democracy. None of us has any real voice in who they are or, unless they mess up, in getting rid of them.

This is Karl Rove's time.

PART 1

YOUNG REPUBLICAN

1

Gone to Texas

One morning in Austin in 2000, at a time when Karl Rove was just becoming a national political player, he stood in the airport holding a briefcase, awaiting a flight to Chicago. George W. Bush had a habit of assigning people nicknames, and he called the architect of his political career "Boy Genius" or "Turd Blossom," depending on his mood and the moment. It was a winter day, and the Republican master strategist—this was becoming his third moniker—was splendidly attired for the blast of cold that awaited him up north. Over his suit, white shirt, and tie he wore a beautiful cerulean wool overcoat that must have cost two thousand bucks and matched the blue of the Jaguar he drove. Rove was a stout figure, his blond hair combed straight back from a large gleaming forehead, and he wore tortoise-shell glasses. It was the hairstyle and affect of none other than John Dean, that snitch and betrayer of Rove's first and lifelong hero, Richard Nixon. Within the surplus pounds Rove possessed the same kind of baby-faced handsomeness. He was at ease among his fellow travelers but was also remote from them. He reeked of power, and carried himself like a man who knew he was making history.

Traveling with Rove was Mark McKinnon, one of his many admirers. Though nominally still a Democrat, McKinnon had fallen under the spell of Bush and had signed on, as long as the team would have him, as producer of the Republican candidate's TV ads. Once a liberal hellion and country-western songwriter on the staff of Kris Kristofferson, McKinnon had worked as a young press aide and speechwriter for a Democratic governor of Texas named Mark White. Rove's first big success in Texas politics had been at the helm of the gubernatorial campaign of Bill Clements, the roughneck Republican who trounced White in 1986 after having surrendered the office to him four years before. "Karl wiped the floor with us," McKinnon joked of that misbegotten race. Four years later, McKinnon was the campaign co-manager in the first leg of Ann Richards' winning campaign for governor. George W. Bush's surprising demolition of Richards in 1994, of course, vaulted Rove to national prominence and positioned his candidate to seek the White House. McKinnon had seen first-hand what Rove brought to a political campaign—from the losing side. Now he wanted to be on Rove's team.

McKinnon observed Rove's pose of hauteur with a smile, as he asked a friend and colleague from the Richards days (at the airport to catch a different flight) if he would like to meet the famous consultant. The man's body language answered for him: not particularly. Bush might be a decent and charming fellow, but Rove had a nasty reputation among the liberal Texas Democrats he had for years put to rout.

McKinnon countered that working with Rove the politico was like watching Bobby Fischer play chess. Rove saw the whole board and was always several moves ahead. "He is a master of everything," McKinnon said, exploring other metaphors. "Most great political minds can understand strategy, media, and polling, but not all the little parts—budget, scheduling, mail, fundraising. It's the difference between driving the car and being able to take apart the engine when something goes wrong." McKinnon surmised: "When the President was growing up, he wanted to be Willie Mays. But when Karl was growing up, he wanted to be senior adviser to the President."

Once, during a panel discussion hosted by a conservative think tank, the American Enterprise Institute, the moderator asked Rove when his obsession with being on the inside of presidential power and history began. Rove's comeback was unhesitating: "December 25, 1950." It was the day he was born.

Karl Christian Rove was a Christmas child, born in Denver. When the doctor whacked him, he probably yelped "I Like Ike!" Rove was Republican as soon as he could formulate the thought, though Dwight Eisenhower may have been a little soft around the edges for him. As a little boy Karl was always thinking, always reading, ever the eager student. That could be a burden in Sparks, Nevada, and other towns out West where he grew up. Rove was hardly born to country clubs. A grandfather had labored on a highway crew during the Depression; his mother once lived in a tar paper shack with walls patched with newspaper and flour paste. His dad was a geologist prospecting for zinc, lead, uranium, copper, and molybdenum, so they moved around a lot. Then, as now, the West was largely Republican. Rove was born into the cold war, to the menace of world communism, and he seemed to comprehend at once the importance of knowing one's enemies and how their minds work.

As a grade-schooler he wrote a paper on dialectical materialism. "A complete nerd," he described himself, many years later, when it was not so painful. With burr haircut and glasses, he would put on a white shirt and tie and hurry off to grade school carrying his first briefcase. He had a brother named Eric, and a sister, Reba. Reba said the three of them used to play a game called "See if You Can Stump Karl." His brother would read a passage from a book Karl had consumed the week before. The trick was for Karl to guess which word his older brother left out. One of the first books he read was titled *Great Moments in History*. For a long time, he always kept his worn and cherished copy of the book with him.

"My parents were totally apolitical," Rove said. "I have no idea why I was not." In 1960, in Arvada, Colorado, young Karl announced that Richard Nixon ought to be president. Eisenhower's vice president was a Californian, and he was intense in a way the old general was not. He thrust his chin out and shook his finger in impromptu debate with the Soviet leader Nikita Khrushchev. Khrushchev was a frightening man whose anti-American belligerence had driven him to pound a podium at the United Nations and threaten the West by stating that "We will bury you." Rove spoke up for Nixon to a girl who lived across the street and who preferred John F. Kennedy. She let go a roundhouse and decked Karl. She was older and bigger, which perhaps soothed his wounded pride.

At age eleven, according to his dad, he was visiting an aunt in Minnesota and dashed through a police barricade at a parade so he could get an autograph of a governor. He dreamed of being president, and was elected class president in junior high and high school. He had a big poster above his bed that said, "Wake Up America." The Western states were spawning a militant far-right conservatism, and groups like the John Birch Society perceived in socialist ideology a danger to the country that was traitorous and omnipresent. Kennedy's glamour was lost on teenagers like Karl.

After Nixon lost the 1960 presidential race and went on to lose the governor's race in California two years later, he was replaced as the unblemished star of the right by a jut-jawed U.S. senator from Arizona named Barry Goldwater. Goldwater had written a book called *The Conscience of a Conservative* that would become an American political classic. "Extremism in the defense of liberty is no vice," he proclaimed. Goldwater cast aside the Republican establishment, then personified by the progressive New York govenor Nelson Rockefeller, and rode a crest of emotion to the party's presidential nomination in 1964. His campaign slogan was "In your heart you know he's right." Goldwater was a hero to young conservatives; his ideological purity was an inspiration. But the world had tottered on the brink of nuclear war during the Cuban Missile Crisis, and then Kennedy had been assassinated in Dallas, a hotbed of the far right. By 1964 right-wing extremism had lost some of its allure. The Democratic nominee, President Lyndon Johnson, successfully cast Goldwater as a loose cannon who might lead the nation to a nuclear apocalypse; by contrast, Johnson appeared reasonable and restrained, a steady leader in a troubled time. When the sun set in the mountain time zone, the 1964 presidential election was already over; Johnson had buried Goldwater's far-right campaign.

Rove went to Olympus High School in Holladay, Utah. One friend recalled him fondly as "the biggest dweeb" in school. A teacher and LBJ Democrat named Evan Tolman recognized Rove's intelligence and talent and told him that to get an A in social studies he would have to volunteer for the campaign of his choice. He became a youth coordinator in the 1968 reelection campaign of Republican Senator Wallace F. Bennett. He worked as a volunteer at the campaign office and mobilized crowds of like-minded teens at rallies.

Across the country, protesters were taking to the streets, screaming obscenities about the Vietnam War; urban ghettos were erupting in anarchy and flames; the guns of assassins were ringing out. In the midst of this turmoil, Republicanism was a rock of steadiness. Richard Nixon might not have had the charisma of Barry Goldwater, but he proved to be a much better politician. This time Nixon got it right and he was elected president, which made the fall of 1968 doubly sweet for Rove: Senator Bennett won as well.

In a state dominated by Mormons, Rove grew up in a household without religion. His best friend and debating partner later said that this seemed to bother Rove, but for whatever reason, religion never took with him—despite its importance to his politics and many of his candidates.

Rove's father traveled a lot for his work, and the marriage of his parents was rocky. Just as the A-student and class president was about to leave home and make his way in the world, his dad walked out for the last time on Christmas, Karl's birthday. His mom got a divorce in Reno. Years later, when the children were grown, she committed suicide.

Rove was like a character in a Charles Dickens novel. At much too young an age he had to start living by his wits and designing his own future. In the spring of 1969 he was admitted to an honors program at the University of Utah in Salt Lake City. He had a $1,000-a-year scholarship from the William Randolph Hearst Foundation. That wasn't enough to live on, of course. He waited tables in a dorm and got a gun stuck in his face one night while working in a convenience store.

For a while, he later said with amusement, he manned a cash register in a shop thick with that perfume of hippies, patchouli oil. The period's wild ride of sex, drugs, and rock 'n' roll wasn't for him. He escaped the Vietnam draft, but loathed everything those anti-war protesters on TV stood for. If this was an ideological inconsistency, he never dwelled on it; and it was one he would share with hawks like Dick Cheney and Paul Wolfowitz. "I came from a relatively conservative state, Utah, and it was hard to sympathize with all those Commies," Rove explained.

Rove loved American presidential history. He devoured tales about Andrew Jackson and Theodore Roosevelt. His college mentor, a political scientist named J. D. Williams, said of Rove: "He could write well. He had good organizational skills, and he had a very clear love of victory. Politics was his varsity sport."

Rove might have gone on to the academic career that seemed to beckon, except that electoral politics was a lot more fun. By 1970, Rove had dropped out of college and moved to Illinois. The decision to leave school was a measure of his rise in young Republican politics, signaling no loss of intellectual ambition. Everett Dirksen, Illinois' colorful, gravel-voiced U.S. senator, had just died, and Rove was hired to organize young Republicans for Dirksen's appointed successor, the soon-to-be-forgotten Ralph Tyler Smith. Bob Kjellander, then president of the College Republicans at the University of Illinois and prominent in the national party, described the Westerner's arrival for *The Boston Globe*: "He was incredibly energetic and full of ideas. He was a ball of fire. He could get kids motivated, and you have to remember that was the height of the Vietnam War.

Being a Republican on a college campus in 1970 was not popular, but Karl motivated people and got them working."

Rove also picked up some "down-ballot" work—that is, work for candidates for lesser offices, which are listed below the presidential and gubernatorial races on a ballot. A Democrat named Alan J. Dixon, who would later make it to the U.S. Senate, was running for Illinois state treasurer that year. Pretending to volunteer for the campaign, Rove got into Dixon's office and swiped some letterhead. He wrote a letter and mailed 1,000 copies, even distributing it among skid-row bums, inviting them to Dixon's campaign headquarters for "free beer, free food, girls and a good time for nothing." It was just a dumb prank, he insisted when his authorship of the letter was exposed. It was a youthful indiscretion, he said, but the episode would hound him.

Rove headed for Washington in the summer of 1971 and got a plum job, considering that just two years earlier he had been a broke student working a cash register. He was hired as the paid executive director of the College Republicans, which was run by the national Republican party. The following year, Nixon destroyed George McGovern in the presidential race, using dirty tricks to do so even when they weren't necessary, and then embarked on a strategy of paying his enemies back. The loyal Republican Rove absorbed one of Nixon's guiding convictions: The end always justified the means. In Washington Rove ran with a GOP firebrand from South Carolina, Lee Atwater, who would later rise to fame as a renowned strategist—and attack dog—for Ronald Reagan and the elder George Bush. They talked politics, endlessly, but then Atwater would be at the center of a social hubbub, listening to blues music on the radio and collecting phone numbers from young women, as the shyer Rove held back. "I guess I'm more cerebral and lack his great people skills," Rove would say of his friend. "And I'm more of a nerd. Lee was a nerd in high school, but then he learned to play the guitar and talk to girls, and I never did. That's serious."

Rove was always self-deprecating, in that way. But David Tyson, another of the young Republicans then in Washington and later a crucial Rove ally in West Virginia, remembered their crowd: "This was a group of people who were conservative, sharp, and aggressive, but Karl stood out. He was more mature, more poised, than the rest of us." Tyson elaborated: "Even at that stage of the game, he had command of what was going on. Some of the College Republicans were just there to socialize, but Rove was there to work."

Rove was twenty-two now. The lack of a college degree on his résumé nagged at him, and he took courses at George Mason University, in a Virginia suburb of the capital. Still, he was on a fast-track in GOP politics. In 1973 he ran for national chairman of the College Republicans. His opponent was Terry Dolan, who would later found the National Conservative Political Action Committee, the direct-mail and soft-money machine that helped vault Ronald Reagan to the presidency. Rove always said the contest for head of the College Republicans was one of belief and direction, not just intra-party ambition. Rove was heir to the pragmatic Nixon, who would break with traditional Republicans to seduce the Teamsters and establish diplomatic ties with Red China. Dolan was the rigid ideologue who wanted to ban abortion and coddle the Christian right. The choice for voters on college campuses was a stark one.

In the contest for the chairmanship, Dolan's allies included Charlie Black, Paul Manafort, and Roger Stone, all of whom rose to power as whiz kids, policy advisers, and fundraisers for Reagan. But Rove had Atwater as his chief strategist and manager of the South. They raced around the country in Rove's brown Pinto; Atwater turning on the charm with the girls. In the end it was no contest. Rove beat Dolan, 63 votes to 5.

But an ugly thing called Watergate was loose in the land, poisoning the atmosphere—especially in Washington. George H. W. Bush had been a Houston congressman, a failed U.S. Senate candidate, and an ambassador to the United Nations. Now he took on the thankless task of directing the Republican National Committee as the accusations worsened, John Dean sang, and the Nixon presidency came apart. A then-little-noted sidebar of *The Washington Post*'s Watergate coverage maintained that a young politico named Karl Rove had conducted training sessions for College Republicans on the nuance and technique of Nixon-style dirty tricks. A scandal involving collegiate Republicans was all George Bush needed. Nixon by then had been forced to resign the presidency—an extremely bitter pill for Rove to swallow—in part because of similar allegations. The *Post*'s story carried enough weight that Bush felt compelled to send an FBI agent to question the young man. Rove was horrified by the public stain on his reputation. He owned up to the childish prank he'd pulled in Illinois, but swore that the alleged training sessions were a foul lie planted by his rival Terry Dolan. Out West, Rove's sister Reba remembered her brother making long and frequent phone calls to their mother, assuring her of his innocence: "He just kept telling her and Dad that he didn't do it." After a month of internal inquiry, the national party cleared Rove and ratified him as the collegiate chairman, but Reba believed that the incident permanently spoiled her brother's appetite for being the candidate himself.

In 1974 Rove got his first job as a real campaign manager, directing a congressional race in Nebraska. But he was quickly back in Washington, where Bush put him to work. Watching Nixon go down had been painful for Bush, whose Republican ties ran deep. The GOP needed to be rebuilt, and if Rove's résumé suggested anything, it was loyalty and a willingness to work for the party, no matter how tarnished its image. Rove took a job as special assistant to Bush.

After Gerald Ford was defeated by Jimmy Carter in the 1976 presidential election, Bush cast his eyes on the White House, knowing that Ronald Reagan, the former governor of California, would be his strongest rival. In Houston, Bush's master strategist, the sleek attorney James A. Baker III, had formed The Fund for Limited Government. It was a political action committee—a new type of organization proposed by Congress as an antidote to the abuses of Watergate. But for Republicans as well as Democrats, PACs had quickly become fronts for raising vast campaign war chests, and Bush and the Texans didn't mean to be outspent by Reagan and his Californians. Impressed by Rove's work for the party, Bush picked him to go to Houston and direct his PAC.

Rove left Washington and the verdant Virginia countryside for the Southwest in 1977, his future bright before him. For an avid student of American history, the move was rich in precedent: Sam Houston, Davy Crockett—all the intrepid souls who had gone out west to find their fortunes, in rattling wagons painted with the letters "GTT." *Gone to Texas.*

2

The Future in Plain Sight

When he was still working at Republican party headquarters, Rove was sometimes called upon to run errands for the party bosses. Though his political talent was obvious, he was still young, and such dues-paying was a part of the routine for even the most ambitious. So there was nothing particularly unusual about Rove being asked to deliver a set of car keys to the son of a party functionary. The dashing young bachelor who would be driving the purple AMC Gremlin with denim-blue seats was visiting from Harvard, where he was getting his MBA.

Years later, Rove would still vividly remember the first time he handed a set of keys to George W. Bush: "Huge amounts of charisma, swagger, cowboy boots, flight jacket, wonderful smile, just charisma—you know, wow."

In 1978, as Rove was joining James Baker III and the senior Bush's political action committee in Houston, George W. was in the West Texas town of Midland. His father had made his first million dollars in the oil field there, and Bush returned hoping to do the same. He had been working as a landman, a class of oilpatch deal-makers who pore over deed records in search of mineral rights to purchase for oil and gas leases. In fact had gone as far as incorporating his own small oil exploration company, when a veteran Democratic congressman announced his retirement. Bush, who had recently married a Midland school librarian named Laura Welch, decided to run for the open seat. He told friends who were surprised about his sudden interest in politics that he feared that under President Jimmy Carter the "United States was heading for a European-style socialism."

Bush entered the Republican primary runoff to face Jim Reese, who had been the mayor of Odessa, the blue-collar twin city that provided drilling company executives in Midland a steady supply of roughnecks and roustabouts. Reese had since become a stockbroker. He attacked Bush for his father's association with the CIA and the Trilateral Commission, an organization of government and business leaders from the United States, Europe, and Japan, whose existence stirred the suspicions of many conservatives. He also went after Rove, mailing out a letter warning that Bush had "Rockefeller Republicans such as Karl Rove" working on his campaign. Bush denied it, telling the *Midland Reporter-Telegram* that Rove was "a young twenty-seven-year-old guy who works in my Dad's office in Houston. He has nothing to do with my campaign. I doubt if he even supports Rockefeller." It would be many years before Bush would admit that Rove was in fact involved in his campaign—albeit in a limited way.

Bush won the primary to face Democratic state Senator Kent Hance in the general election. Hance made an issue of Bush's huge fundraising advantage ($400,000 to $175,000), claiming that much of the money came from outside the congressional district. He painted Bush as a child of privilege who had attended prep school in Andover, Massachusetts, and had graduated from Yale and Harvard. His stump speech included an elaborate story in which he described the driver of a car very similar to Bush's asking a local resident for directions to a nearby ranch. He is told to go about a mile, turn left, and then look for the cattle guard. Wanting to make sure he won't miss it, the driver asks one further question: "Now, what color uniform is this cattle guard wearing?" In addition to being funny, the story painted a vivid picture of Bush as a clueless, carpet-bagging Yankee.

For his part, Bush misread his constituents and supported the grain embargo that blocked the sale of Texas High Plains wheat to the Soviet Union. Sure, the locals were against communism, but bidness was bidness. Then, on the eve of the election, Bush was blindsided by a mailing sent out by a Hance supporter criticizing a "Bush Bash" at Texas Tech University in Hance's hometown of Lubbock. "Dear Fellow Christians" the letter began. It went on to detail an ad in the Texas Tech newspaper that promised "free beer" at a Bush political rally. Hance won 53 percent of the vote.

It was a textbook example of how to lose an election. Bush's campaign was hastily put together and made poor use of the money advantage it enjoyed. Bush allowed his opponent to define him, and he did a poor job of defining himself. Ads of the candidate jogging suggested that Bush was out of touch with the Texas Panhandle in 1978, where pedestrians of any sort were viewed with suspicion, if not alarm. Rove, whose involvement in the campaign was limited to a volunteer role as an adviser, but who watched the race intently, must have winced when Hance "went negative" on Bush late in the campaign, inadvertently echoing the fake "free beer" flyer Rove had used to tarnish Alan J. Dixon eight years earlier. But no Rove campaign would ever again make the blunders made in Bush's 1978 congressional campaign. In fact, with the exception of running against a much-better-funded opponent, Hance's winning campaign looked much like the campaigns Rove would run in the future.

Bush learned his lessons from the campaign as well. After losing, he told his opponent, "Hance, you had a message and you stayed with it." That the "message" had less to do with policy than it did with personal attacks might not have escaped Bush's attention.

Not long after his loss to Hance, George W. Bush was unwinding at a backyard dinner party in an Austin neighborhood north of the University of Texas campus—geographically speaking, the very heart of Texas Democratic liberalism. Bush and his wife, Laura, had come as guests of one of her oldest friends from Midland, who now made her home there.

Bush was no doubt pleased and proud of the obvious stir his attractive young wife caused in the group, which included reporters, professors, and trial lawyers. Most of these people were Democrats, but Bush was relaxed, friendly, and nonchalant about his defeat by Kent Hance in the West Texas race for Congress.

"What's your dad doing now?" one man asked politely.

"Running for president," came the genial reply.

The man blinked. Slight smiles and eye rolls were exchanged among the other guests.

George Bush? President of the United States?

Texas Democrats might not have felt the ground shifting beneath their feet, but Karl Rove was convinced he did. Working in Houston for Bush and Baker's PAC, Rove was emerging in Texas GOP circles as a wizard of the political technique known as direct mail. He crafted letters with underlined zingers that fired up parti-

sans to get involved, sign up, and write fat checks. Just as important, he had an instinctive and highly-developed gift for knowing to
whom to send those letters. At the same time, Rove was building
the foundation for a political consulting firm that he hoped would
enrich him as well as bring him power. Tom Cole, a major player in
the national GOP party structure, later said: "He had the idea that
someday Texas would be a Republican state, and he wanted to be
there at the beginning. That was a brilliant political insight, but it
was an even more brilliant business insight. He got himself ready
for something he saw was coming. He planned from the start to be
the dominant guy in the emerging Republican Party in the second
biggest state in the country. That's the political equivalent of deciding to be Microsoft."

Texas certainly seemed to be moving his way. Though the
younger Bush had lost his impulsive run for Congress, that same fall
saw the diminutive U.S. Senator John Tower, a state Republican
pioneer, win a tough reelection race.

Liberals had been apathetic about the Democratic nominee, a
professorial congressman named Bob Krueger, and turnout was
low. But Tower was pulled across the finish line by a new partisan
fervor, rallied by an effective phone-bank operation that had also
fired the governor's race. The Republican candidate for governor,
Dallas oilman Bill Clements, had launched his campaign by flinging
a toy chicken across a banquet table at his startled opponent, the
overconfident attorney general John Hill, and declaring that he,
Clements, was going to tie Jimmy Carter around Hill's neck like a
dead rooster tied to a dog. Clements delivered on his boast.

Bill Clements had built his oil company around friendships with
men who had been his teammates on a state champion high school
football team in Highland Park, the lily-white enclave of old-Dallas

wealth and privilege. That season had been played a long time ago, when football helmets were still made of leather, but even after all those years, the old-timers' loyalties and estimates of each others' abilities never wavered. Clements would use his own wealth and the support of his friends to underwrite his campaign, and it was a formidable combination.

Clements was everything the genteel Yankee George H. W. Bush was not. Unapologetically unrefined, he was a Texcentric worthy of a cameo in a Larry McMurtry novel: rich, rough-hewn, outrageous, outspoken. He drove a blue Mercury station wagon with imitation wood paneling, and his sartorial signature was a windowpane-plaid sports jacket. And he was a Republican in a predominantly Democratic state. Any political consultant could have bent your ear for an hour explaining why there was no way to elect Bill Clements governor.

And yet Karl Rove did it. Twice.

Clements was Rove's first client as an independent political consultant, and it was Clements' first campaign that anticipated the rise of the Christian right. In 1978, Texas was a Democratic state, and a dull Democratic attorney general named John Hill was the odds-on favorite to win the governor's race. But Hill had shut down a Christian boys' home in South Texas, after discovering that the boys living there had been subjected to beatings with pine paddles, enforced kneeling for hours on hardwood floors, and solitary confinement while listening to hours of their pastor's recorded sermons. Though he was only doing his job, Hill's civil suit cost him the election.

Lester Roloff, the Baptist preacher who ran the home, began urging evangelicals to vote for "Brother Bill" Clements, making appeals on his radio program and barnstorming the state in the small Cessna he would later pilot into the hereafter. Christian crossover voters provided the 18,000-vote margin that defeated the Democratic attorney general. After his election, Clements took Brother Roloff's side in the lawsuit, describing Hill's legal action against the Christian boys' home as "nitpicking."

Rove was in transition from working for Bush in Houston and running his own campaigns in Austin. He worked on Clements' campaign but was not nearly as central to it as he would be to his subsequent runs for governor. But Rove saw the future in Bill Clements' 1978 win.

Clements was the first Republican governor since Reconstruction, elected in a state that had been a Democratic Party franchise for more than a century. At the time, Republicans held one of the state's two U.S. Senate seats, two of its eighteen U.S. House seats, and eighteen of 150 Texas House seats. Only three of the thirty-one state senators were Republicans, and none of the twenty-two statewide offices was occupied by a Republican. Until Bill Clements defeated John Hill.

After several Texas Republican Party funders saw what Clements had pulled off in 1978, they decided to begin raising money for his second election campaign. Like Clements, Bum Bright had played high school football at Highland Park. And like Clements, he had gone to work as an oilfield roughneck and later built a company, or several companies, that made him a millionaire. Bright was putting his money into two Texas institutions: Texas A&M University and the Republican Party. In 1979, he called Rove and offered him a job raising money for Bill Clements.

Rove would later recall that at the time, Texas Republicans didn't recognize the potential for raising money in the state: "I still have the piece of paper that Bum Bright gave me on the budget. They wanted $200,000 in two years from direct mail because they had 5,000 donors in the '78 campaign. And they were very dubious about direct mail."

By the end of the first year Rove had expanded the donor list to 44,000 names and raised $1 million for Clements. The state was a huge pool of conservative money that hadn't been explored or exploited.

American electoral politics were changing, and old-style political operatives like George Parr, the South Texas political patrón who helped Lyndon Johnson steal an election from Coke Stevenson two years before Karl Rove was born, had all but disappeared. Voters were moving away from the political organizations that had once been influential in the cities and were most easily reached by two types of media: direct mail and television. Computerized databases made targeted direct mail a powerful political tool, and Rove—always an autodidact—was quickly teaching himself how to use direct mail, mail that raised money and got a candidate's message into homes.

Rove even walked a business journal through the process: "Write the plan, position the client, write the copy, secure the list, design the package, supervise and (or) generate some of the production here and then we set up a system to analyze response to understand what worked and what didn't." It was a pared-down description of the complex process that has become such a science that direct-mail consultants can predict within a fraction of a percentage what the return on a particular mailing will be.

It was not quantum physics. But Rove achieved a success with it that had not been previously seen in Texas. "Karl was the right guy at the right time," said Bill Miller, an Austin political consultant who has worked with and against Rove. "He was here in the late seventies, with Bill Clements. He was the guy who began collecting the names of the people who gave the money."

In 1980, Rove accepted a job as Clements' chief of staff and threw himself into the complicated work of legislative redistricting, sometimes working in alliance with conservative Democrats. But most of what the Republicans gained would be lost in a court challenge of the new districts. Another disappointment came in his personal life. That same year, his marriage of four years to Valerie Wainwright, the daughter of a prominent Houston family, ended. And when Clements asked Rove for a five-year commitment, the young politico balked, telling Clements he wanted to start his own business. Karl Rove + Company opened its doors in Austin with one client: Bill Clements. In raising money for Clements, Rove saw a more important function than working in the administration of a governor restrained by a Democratic House and Senate and nine Democratic justices on the nine-member state Supreme Court.

Rove had several backers in his business venture. The most important, because of his deep pockets and commitment to the Republican Party, was a polo-playing millionaire rancher named Tobin Armstrong, whose wife Anne had been the national Republican party co-chair when Rove worked at the Republican National Committee. Anne Armstrong had been elected Republican National Committeewoman from Texas in 1968, when the party was still a small elite group of intruders in a territory controlled by Democrats. By 1971 she was co-chair of the RNC and had worked in the Nixon White House. Tobin Armstrong's backing gave Rove's fledgling business the imprimatur of the state's monied Republican aristocracy.

With Rove handling his direct mail, Clements was in even better political shape for his 1982 reelection bid against Mark White, the tall, drawling, centrist attorney general who had replaced John Hill. White was hardly an electrifying campaigner, and Rove and his fellow strategists had every reason to believe they would have four more years of a governor around whom they were building a Republican Party that could at last compete with the Democrats for statewide offices. But Clements' election had shocked Texas Democrats and gotten their attention. Lyndon Johnson, after all, was not too long dead. The establishment Democrats who learned the ropes and wielded power during the LBJ years might move easily in country clubs with Bush, Baker, or Clements, but they weren't just going to roll over and hand the prize to a bunch of Young Republicans. The patrician U.S. Senator Lloyd Bentsen was up for reelection in 1982, and so was the popular Democratic lieutenant governor, Bill Hobby, a Houston newspaper owner and son of a distinguished Texas governor. Cut from another mold but spoiling for the brawl was Jim Mattox, a pugnacious, labor-backed Dallas congressman running for attorney general.

Another force for the Democrats was Bob Bullock, the rambunctious comptroller. He came out of a milieu of roadside beer taverns, jukebox suppliers, and streetfighters in small towns south and east of Dallas, roots he shared with the aspiring country singer and sometime Bible salesman Willie Nelson. Bullock graduated from the Texas legislature to lobbying for car dealers to an appointment as secretary of state—a patronage post doled out as a reward for political service to the governor, in this case Preston Smith. Bullock told a story about Archer Parr, heir to the political machine that delivered the legendary mystery box of votes to LBJ in 1948, saying Parr offered Bullock a $5,000 donation to Governor Smith in the form of a check from the local school district. A careful bagman, Bullock insisted on cash, whereupon Parr walked into a bank, cashed the check, and handed Bullock the stack of bills.

Bullock ran for comptroller and won in 1974. The comptroller ran the tax-collecting agency, an obscure office that few Texans seemed to be aware existed. Bullock set out to make it the agency that drove fiscal policy in Texas, and by the end of his first year in office there was no doubting its existence. He personally led raids on businesses that were delinquent on their taxes, after conscientiously alerting the press. The pictures of state employees carting away the ill-gotten gains of tax scofflaws made for entertaining journalism, and Bullock made headlines crowing about how much money he was recovering for the taxpayers of Texas. Bullock modernized the agency, hauling in computers and buying planes, which he used to fly to other states for the ostensible purpose of seeing how other tax agencies worked. He opened offices in towns far from the capital, which served the legitimate purpose of pursuing the agency's business across the state and which also served as the infrastructure of his nascent political machine. Bullock understood that knowledge is power, and in the manner of Lyndon Johnson he had the goods on everybody, keeping a meticulous system of card files on both allies and enemies.

Bullock hired the best and the brightest and paid them better than anyone else in state government, and they earned every penny. He was notorious for what one state senator referred to as "drive-by ass-chewings." These often climaxed with the on-the-spot firing of the offending employee, who would inevitably be awakened the next morning by a phone call from Bullock demanding to know why the hell he wasn't at work. Bullock chain-smoked and worked hard and drank hard, and his inner circle of favorites were expected to keep his hours, which involved long days and longer nights.

One night early on in his career, Bullock wandered out of an Austin bar and, thinking to catch a quick nap before driving home, climbed in the back seat of what proved to be the wrong car. He woke up in bewilderment to find himself being driven through the dark city streets by a total stranger. Rallying, he thrust a hand over the seat and introduced himself to the driver, scaring the poor man out of his wits: "Hi there!" he boomed. "I'm your secretary of state!"

Another backseat tale, perhaps apocryphal, had a Manhattan cabbie zooming through stoplights and traffic, deaf to Bullock's sozzled protests from the back seat. Exasperated, the comptroller was said to have finally produced a pistol and stuck it in the cabbie's ear, roaring "I told you to slow down!"

A larger-than-life figure, Bullock cajoled and bullied people in equal measure, depending on his mood and what he needed from them, and his generosity and meanness were equally outsized. In Texas, Bullock was legendary. And he was feared.

These were the veterans aligned against Clements and the GOP recruits that fall of 1982. In their confidence and resolve to prove the state had turned Republican, party strategists ditched the strategy of picking just a few races and concentrating on them. They put up candidates for races up and down the statewide ballot, and even recruited opponents to San Antonio's veteran Democratic congressman Henry Gonzales and Houston's charismatic two-term congressman Mickey Leland, who were shoo-ins for reelection. Hardly cowed, ambitious Democrats battled each other for chances to get in the fight. One was Garry Mauro, who had upset a West Texas state senator in the Democratic primary and was running for land commissioner at the age of thirty-two. Curly-haired, handsome, and full of himself, Mauro had carried the bags and driven the car in the last campaign of the old liberal warhorse and LBJ nemesis

Ralph Yarborough, and in 1972 Mauro had befriended Bill Clinton and Hillary Rodham when Gary Hart sent them over from Arkansas to run George McGovern's doomed presidential campaign in Texas. Another Democrat was Jim Hightower, the Stetson-wearing candidate for agriculture commissioner. Bone-thin and a fount of one-liners, Hightower could be a skillful demagogue, when that was useful. He too had worked for Yarborough, and in the leftward presidential campaign of Oklahoma U.S. Senator Fred Harris; as editor of the liberal muckraking *Texas Observer,* he had railed against establishment banking, industry, and agriculture. The Democrats' candidate for treasurer, Ann Richards, was then married to a prominent civil rights and labor lawyer; she had been among the luncheon crowd of Dallas supporters John F. Kennedy was riding toward when he was assassinated in 1963. After her family moved to Austin, Richards emerged as the chief aide to state representative Sarah Weddington, the attorney who successfully argued *Roe v. Wade* before the U.S. Supreme Court. Richards had first won office as a county commissioner in Austin. Liberals and the local press loved her.

Texas was booming in 1982. The price of oil shot toward $30 a barrel, and the state sat on vast reserves of natural gas. A popular bumper sticker crowed: "Freeze a Yankee in the Dark." With the overflow energy money, instant real estate tycoons were flipping land, putting up high-rises. They thought boom times would never end. Instead of getting symbolic credit for the good times, the oil-patch millionaire Clements began to look like a stodgy figure stuck in the past. Impressed by data-bank work that had helped Fort Worth congressman Jim Wright survive a close race, an Austin political consultant named Jack Martin put the computer wizards to work for the Democratic slate. For once the Democrats ran as a team: They coordinated their schedules and in a rare show of discipline said only nice things about each other. The money and the heft that Lloyd Bentsen and Bill Hobby brought to the Democrats exposed the weakness of the Republican candidates who were down-ballot from Clements.

That October Karl Rove experienced the tremors underfoot and the sudden desperate free-fall that he would later engineer so often for enemies and rivals.

If Mickey Leland and Henry Gonzales had been unopposed, their supporters might have stayed home. Instead they voted, and they didn't split tickets for the Republicans. Turnout reached 50 percent—extremely high in Texas—and when it was over the GOP takeover of the state lay in shambles. Running behind a flood of money unleashed by the pro-business Senator Bentsen, White beat Clements going away. Bullock and the other old-guard candidates brushed their opponents aside; it was a Democratic sweep from top to bottom. In a parade on inauguration night the following January, a photographer caught Garry Mauro, with a mane of hair like an Italian playboy; Jim Hightower, with his boots, mustache, and sly country boy grin; and Ann Richards in high heels, looking like she was dancing a country two-step, hand flung in the air. Three aspiring stars of a kind never before seen in Texas, each of them aware of the rivalry of the others.

For a Republican drawn into party activism by the presidential candidacy and conservative philosophy of Barry Goldwater, the Democrats' heralded Class of '82 must have been horrifying.

It took Rove a while, but one by one, he picked them off.

3

Whatever Happened to the Class of '82?

Texas Democrats would never again see anything similar to the sweep of 1982—the state party's last great year. Rove was fiercely loyal to Bill Clements, whom he considered a real trailblazer and who had put his personal wealth into a race he was not supposed to win. Though Rove worked hard to reelect Clements, the 1982 loss was not entirely unexpected. Rove understood the power of money, incumbency, and organization in an election, and he knew that Bentsen was a formidable force in Texas politics. He was a wealthy Anglo patrón from the Lower Rio Grande Valley who had served in the U.S. House and had defeated liberal U.S. Senator Ralph Yarborough in the 1970 Democratic primary—a campaign as aggressive in tactics and in issues as anything Rove had yet put together. Flush with campaign cash, Bentsen carried the Democrats' 1982 ticket into office with him.

But the tide of electoral politics in Texas favored Rove. In 1983, Democrat Phil Gramm switched parties and was bold enough to resign his U.S. House seat and run again as a Republican. Gramm got a little help from his political consultant, Karl Rove, who ushered him into the Republican Party and then organized his successful reelection campaign against liberal humorist John Henry Faulk. Gramm became the only member of Congress in the twentieth century to resign and then successfully seek reelection as a member of another party. The Reagan landslide of 1984 helped Rove elect Gramm to the U.S. Senate seat opened up by John Tower's decision not to run for a fifth term. Rove ran a bruising, negative campaign against liberal Austin state senator Lloyd Doggett, whom Gramm easily defeated. Rove also managed to get another Karl Rove + Company client into office: Dallas-area Congressman Joe Barton. Joining Gramm and Barton in the state's Republican congressional delegation was West Texas Congressman Kent Hance, who as a Democrat had defeated George W. Bush in a race for congress six years earlier. "Karl was instrumental in my changing parties," Hance said. "He said, 'Look, the Democrats are never going to help you, you're too conservative. You'll find a warm welcome in the Republican Party.' I don't think he was acting as an emissary of the party; he was just giving me his opinion."

By 1985 the Rove + Company client list that once included only Bill Clements had grown to eighteen. And the staff in the office northwest of the Capitol complex had grown from three to ten. The Texas Republican Party was a growth industry.

Rove admired Clements because he had been first. "His personal resources made it possible for him to promise victory-starved Republicans that he wouldn't run out of gas like Republican candidates had done in the closing months of other campaigns," Rove said in a speech quoted in the *Austin American-Statesman*. Yet when Clements talked about running again in 1986, Rove wasn't among his early supporters. The Dallas oilman was sixty-eight. He had a bad hip—"a hitch in his get-along," he called it—which aggravated his congenital bad temper. He was not an easily managed candidate, nor so attractive that he was an easy sell to voters. Rove saw the future of the party in younger politicians like Gramm and Hance, who Rove believed should be the party's next candidate for governor. Hance was closer in age to Governor Mark White, eager to run for statewide office, and Rove had told him he would run his campaign. But when Clements announced his intention to run, Rove found himself conflicted. "He's a loyal person," recalled Hance. "I was going to run for governor and he had agreed to help me. He had been with Clements and he came to me and said 'I've gotta go back to Clements; Clements gave me my start.'"

Chinks were starting to show in White's armor. He had enlisted H. Ross Perot to put together an ambitious education reform program, which was now in effect across the state. To improve the quality of instruction, all teachers were now required to pass competency tests. To improve student performance in the state's secondary schools, all students participating in extracurricular activities were subject to a "no pass, no play" rule, under which students who were failing classes were barred from participating in nonacademic school activities. In a state where football is the focus of small-town social life and an annual rite of passage for young men, valuable players who didn't make the grade were suddenly spending their Friday nights in the stands with the losers from the National Honor Society. High school coaches in the state's 1,000-plus independent school districts pasted red stick-on dots to their wristwatches as reminders to vote against White, and complained to their booster clubs that Governor Mark White and H. Ross Perot were destroying Texas football.

The incumbent governor faced more than angry coaches. The price of oil had plummeted at a time when the state was still heavily dependent on the oil and gas severance tax. The recession had settled in far beyond the oilpatch. Unemployment was hovering at 10 percent, the highest in the nation. It was no time to run as an incumbent. So Rove's client, the old oilman setting out to recapture the office he'd lost four years earlier, began the race with a double-digit advantage.

But White summoned the legislature to Austin for a special session and passed a temporary sales-tax increase that would allow the state to meet its obligations and would expire when the economy recovered. If it wasn't Solomonic, it was as good as governing gets in a state where the governor has extremely limited powers and the absence of an income tax imposes drastic limits on government services. White's poll numbers turned upward so quickly that one Austin political consultant compared the comeback to Lazarus' return from the dead.

A month out, the race was a dead heat and anyone not focused on the Division 4A state football championship was wondering if the one big debate between the two candidates would decide the governor's race. The younger Democratic governor was expected to dominate the cranky old oilman. Clements had served a term as governor, but White was the candidate who better understood policy and politics. Clements' experience was in the Texas oilfields. Political handicappers predicted he would be embarrassed in a debate with White. Even if he survived, the trend in the polls favored the incumbent—as did the public perception that White had resolved the fiscal crisis in Austin.

But a funny thing happened on the way to the forum in Houston, where the two candidates were scheduled to meet. On the morning before the debate, Karl Rove held a press conference and announced that an electronic eavesdropping device had been discovered in his office. Clements' deputy campaign director, John

Weaver, described the incident as "Texasgate" and lamented that politics in the state had become so degraded that these "irregularities" could become commonplace.

Suddenly, an acrimonious debate about clandestine bugging displaced the news coverage of the debate. Stories about the incident overshadowed campaign issues like education, taxes, and crime, and shifted the media's attention away from White's comeback in the polls. Rove accused no one. But he told reporters that the only one with anything to gain from knowing what was said in his office was Mark White or the political operatives running his campaign. "Obviously, I don't know who did this," Rove said. "But there is no doubt in my mind that the only ones who would benefit from this detailed, sensitive information would be the political opposition."

There was something odd about the crime. Usually, when someone discovers their office has been broken into, they call the police. Rove called a press conference.

Rove and his campaign staff began to tell the story that they had hired a private security firm to sweep their office after *Dallas Morning News* reporter Sam Attlesey asked a question that included information so specific it could only have come from inside the campaign. Rove was certain that one fact the reporter referred to had been uttered only once, while Rove talked on his office telephone four feet from the framed red-white-and-blue needlepoint Republican elephant behind which the bug was discovered.

When the FBI finally got involved, the *Morning News* reporter told agents that the source of information about the Clements campaign was Washington Democratic consultant Harris Diamond. A political reporter at the competing *Dallas Times-Herald* got the same information from the same source. The openness with which

Diamond was talking to the press did not suggest he was a conduit for information obtained by a hidden listening device. Diamond said no one had to go to the extreme of bugging an office to find the information he'd been feeding to reporters, which had to do with the Clements campaign's television advertising budget. Most of it was readily available in a weekly media report released in New York.

The other piece of highly sensitive information that supposedly got loose via illicit electronic means was that Lee Atwater—Rove's friend and political mentor—was being asked to come to Texas. Atwater had earned a reputation for vicious attack ads aimed at "driving up the negatives" of his opponents, and for devious campaign tactics. Rove wondered how anyone outside his office could know about Atwater's plans.

As it turned out, Atwater would never make it to Texas. But Rove's plan to bring him in, according to another Clements aide, was a "closely guarded campaign secret." Rove had been talking to the Alexandria, Virginia, consulting firm of Black, Manafort, Stone & Atwater. But, Rove alleged, no one outside his office could have known that. Diamond laughed at the notion that such information could be kept under wraps in the tightly-knit world of political consultants in the nation's capital. "It's all over Washington," Diamond said. Everyone in the business knew that Clements was not satisfied with the work of his national media consultant and had approached the firm Atwater worked for.

To the White campaign media director, the bugging looked like a setup. "I am absolutely confident that our campaign had absolutely nothing to do with this," said Mark McKinnon. "I think by thinking this would be a news story, they thought strategically that they would have something to gain from this." McKinnon complained that the "whole thing stinks and the wind is blowing from the Clements campaign." Rove had blown his early twenty-point lead in the polls and the race was even, McKinnon said. Someone in the Clements campaign operation had resorted to a stunt to provide cover for their collapsing campaign.

And then the story broke the day before the debate.

No one ever proved who planted the listening device. But it was not, as Rove had implied, the White campaign. "We were first on the scene and concluded that Rove had hired a company to debug his office and the same company had planted the bug," said a source in the Travis County District Attorney's office. The *Dallas Morning News* used the Freedom of Information Act to obtain FBI memos that also pointed to Rove's private investigators. The FBI had concluded the firm hired to sweep the office planted the listening device there.

Yet no charges were filed and, after the private investigator Rove hired received a "target letter" advising him a federal grand jury was considering charges against him, the investigation ended. Democrats complained that the investigation disappeared into the Reagan Justice Department. They argued that Rove's relationship with Vice President George Bush made it unlikely that the Justice Department would take any further action.

Did the news coverage of the bugging and the public perception that the White campaign was responsible turn the election in the direction of Rove's client? "It got a lot of play in the newspapers the month before the election," said White campaign director Dwayne Hollman. Hollman said he would have preferred to see the focus kept on the candidates and the issues at a critical moment in the campaign when White was pulling ahead.

Close to the end of the race, the Clements campaign mailed out what appeared to be a newspaper to voters in certain parts of the state. It included an account of Mark White's arrest for driving while intoxicated—years earlier, when he was a college student. Jim Hightower, the Democratic Agriculture Commissioner, tried to find some humor in it. "Clements is guilty of DWI today," Hightower said. "Driving while ignorant." Maybe the laughter eased the pain for White. He came into the election knowing it would be a fight. He never expected that someone would dig up an ancient DWI. Nor did he think someone would imply he had bugged his opponent's office.

The story about the bugging stayed on the front pages of the state's dailies until a week before the November 1986 election—which Clements won by a margin of 56 to 44 percent.

"You have to put this in the context of Karl Rove," said an Austin political consultant. "Rove equates politics with war. And in war, you do whatever you have to do in order to win. You take calculated risks in order to win. It's a totally different way of looking at an election. That doesn't mean he did it. But in war, you do what you have to to destroy your enemy."

In the spring of 2000, after Rove had destroyed John McCain in the South Carolina primary and secured the Republican presidential nomination for George W. Bush, he referred to the 1986 bugging in a conversation that nagged at the reporter interviewing him. Melinda Henneberger wrote in *The New York Times Magazine* that when she looked into the 1986 bugging, she asked herself if Rove would "really have gone that far for a client." She described the bugging as "the weirdest story about Rove-related intrigue." She initially concluded that Rove would not have done it.

Then she rented *Power*—a movie Rove recommended while she

was working on the story. *Power* is a Sidney Lumet film about a political consultant played by Richard Gere. "I thought of myself as the Gere character," Rove had told Henneberger when he suggested she see the film. "He has the fabulous office and the New York high-rise and he gets paid $25,000 a month by everybody. You got to rent this. It's so unbelievably stupid. He's working for this total schlump, and of course they get the schlump elected governor."

Rove thought the plot was unrealistic because guys like him weed out the schlumps. In the end, they don't get elected. That's not what Henneberger found so fascinating. What struck her as she watched the film was that in the heat of the gubernatorial race, Gere's character discovers his office had been bugged. The film was released in 1986.

She mentioned the coincidence to Rove and he laughed. "Then he stopped laughing and kind of cocked his head. Then he said, 'I don't have any recollection of that.'"

Was Karl Rove directing a writer to a fictitious representation of himself? Or was he so secure in his new position of power that he was reminding this Washington reporter from a national daily that had been unkind to his boss that he was now in charge? So much in charge that he could tease the reporter by alluding to something he had been accused of sixteen years earlier?

What Henneberger called "Rove-related intrigue" about the 1986 office bugging didn't end when the FBI filed its report in 1986. In the aftermath of the discovery of the bug, an FBI agent named Greg Rampton interrogated Clements campaign staffers about the bug. Four years later, in almost perfect synchronicity with the beginning of the 1992 election campaigns, Rove and Rampton were again brought together in Austin, where the FBI agent was working a case.

One of Rampton's contacts was Karl Rove. All of Rampton's targets were Democrats. Two of them would end up in federal prison.

Rove had been quick to grasp the structural weakness in the "plural executive" put in place by the Texas Constitution. If an election to the American presidency is, as Rove would remind reporters ten years later, "fifty separate elections," a race for governor of Texas is six separate elections. The constitution divides the powers associated with a chief executive among the governor, lieutenant governor, attorney general, comptroller, land commissioner, and agriculture commissioner. New York elects a governor. Texas elects a cabinet.

The result of this division in a party whose candidates were accustomed to settling their scores in the primary before going on to defeat weak Republicans were evident to Rove. In 1990, the Democratic Party in Texas was Ann Richards and her consultant and mailing list; Bob Bullock and his consultant and mailing list; Jim Mattox and his consultant and mailing list; Jim Hightower and his consultant and mailing list; and Garry Mauro and his consultant and mailing list.

One of the advantages Rove realized working for a small but growing party was that Karl Rove + Company had the Clements mailing list. The same list Rove started putting together when Bum Bright had hired him to raise money. The same contacts with big Republican funders that Rove used to build his direct mail firm, where Clements was his first client. As Austin consultant Bill Miller saw it, Rove was there first: He knew where the money was in the state's Republican community, and he knew where the voters were. Republican party discipline also helped. The Republicans had an organizing principle: They were out of power and they wanted in. Democrats believe Rove used more than direct mail and smart campaigns to get them in.

Among the stars of the Democrats' Class of 1982, Land Commissioner Garry Mauro was the brash one, always in a hurry. The grandson of Sicilian immigrants, briefly an undersized, walk-on lineman for his beloved Aggies at Texas A&M, he grew up wanting to be the governor of Texas and didn't mean to wait until his hair turned gray. There were other campus politicos of note in College Station in those years—John Sharp, Rick Perry, Henry Cisneros. Mauro figured he was the measure of any of them. He organized Aggies for Bobby Kennedy in the 1968 presidential race and worked for liberal icons Ralph Yarborough and George McGovern.

Mauro had many teachers in the Democratic Party, but none meant as much to him as Bob Bullock. When Bullock won the comptroller's race in 1974, he hired Mauro and made him a senior deputy. He would send Mauro around the state to execute his on-the-spot firings of employees. Mauro didn't have the temperament to bully and hector like his mentor, but employees in the comptroller's office called him "Little Bullock," and he tried to live up to the honor.

After Mauro won the 1982 race for land commissioner, he and Bullock talked by phone almost daily. Cocky as Adonis, Mauro created image problems for himself almost at once. He got creamed, as had Bullock, for overindulging the novelty and luxury of having a state-owned plane at his call. Environmentalists thought he was much too friendly with developers. Mauro put his face on billboards advertising benefits for veterans. And like Bullock, he was tainted by his association in treacherous Duval County with an oil-patch hustler named Clinton Manges, who had long been a source of money for Democratic candidates. They laughed about the shots being fired at them, most days.

Then one day Bullock called and said they had to talk, and not by phone—he was coming over. Bullock drove the short distance between their buildings, and he came by himself, which was not his style; he almost always had aides with him. Bullock was not the kind to be frightened or intimidated by anyone, but as they rode around central Austin, Mauro could tell that he was badly spooked. According to Mauro, Bullock said, "Garry, Karl Rove is in league with a guy in the U.S. attorney's office in San Antonio. He's an FBI agent named Greg Rampton. Their sole job right now, their mission in life, is to figure out a way to indict you, me, Jim Mattox, Jim Hightower, and Ann Richards. They're out to get us all."

Mauro knew Rove slightly. Before Mauro graduated to the state pool fleet, they had been fellow regulars on Southwest Airlines commuter flights between Austin, Dallas, and Houston; rival pols and consultants saw each other and mingled all the time. Apart from the land office, Mauro had a dormant law practice with Ed Wendler, a veteran Democratic consultant. Wendler practiced local politics, as well as the statewide variety. He had been trying to help unseat a city council member in the suburb of Round Rock. "There was a very nice woman involved in that," Wendler recalled. "She was a Republican, a neighborhood organizer. She called me one day and said, 'We have this young man, a political consultant, who'd like to help us. Would you talk to him?' I said, 'Sure, I'll talk to anybody.' That was my introduction to Karl. We worked together on that. Every suggestion he made was right on the money. But the thing that struck me about him was that he was emotionless. All that counted to him was winning. I told Garry then, 'This guy exists, and he is a threat.' It wasn't very long before we started hearing about Karl and the FBI agent. Bullock was consumed by that."

In the years Rampton was in Texas, he cut a swath that left several careers and reputations in ruin, and he never went after Republicans. (His first victim had been an ambitious Waco district attorney named Vic Feazell.) Following Bullock's warning, Mauro began to hear from veterans and contributors that an FBI agent was calling them. He told his general counsel at the land office to call Rampton and tell him they'd provide any records he wanted. Mauro thought the trouble had gone away, but in June 1984, as he was preparing to make a speech at the state Democratic convention in Houston, a reporter with leaked information called and asked him to comment on the FBI's subpoena, half an hour earlier, of 70,000 land office documents. Mauro was suspected of overseeing a land appraisal scheme associated with the veterans' programs.

"There were fourteen of them," he recalled of the guys in black. "They showed up first thing in the morning, and we had rows and rows of boxes waiting. They'd demanded that we provide two computers, and they installed their software and started looking. They must not have found much, because by ten o'clock they were gone. Rampton's thesis was that any contribution from a veteran or a developer had to be quid pro quo." Mauro had a two-year-old son; Bullock was the child's godfather. Mauro found himself being thankful his son was too young to read. The press was brutal; Rampton did not always observe the FBI custom of declining comment on an active investigation. Mauro thought he was going to be indicted and hired a top criminal defense lawyer, Gerry Goldstein of San Antonio. In the argot of Texas courthouses, he feared he was about to go off to the big rodeo.

"I saw Rampton one time after that," he said. "I walked out in the hall, and he was just standing there. He handed me his card, and I asked him into my office, and we had a little chat. I never found out what he was doing there. I just assume he was trying to intimidate me."

The federal indictment never came. No charges were ever filed. Nor was Mauro ever cleared. There was just an FBI letter to Goldstein saying vaguely that the investigation was suspended. Mauro served two more terms as land commissioner, refusing to give up his dream of being governor. But those headlines would always be there, ready-made for any opponent's admaker. What was the political damage? Long afterward, Mauro chuckled at the question. "Well, let's just say I was no longer the Boy Wonder."

If Mauro was the boy wonder, Jim Hightower was the *enfant terrible*. By 1990, the folksy Texas Agriculture Commissioner represented a real threat to the Republican Party in Texas—and perhaps even beyond Texas. He had led his party's ticket in 1982 and 1986, winning by 60–40 margins. He had considered, then backed away from, making a run for the seat of one of Rove's star clients: Senator Phil Gramm. Hightower had worked for Ralph Nader in Washington in the 1960s, then joined the staff of liberal Democratic Senator Ralph Yarborough. He had a blue-collar message that combined Nader's pro-consumer politics with Yarborough's fiery populist oratory.

Before Hightower's election in 1982, the agriculture commission had been a sleepy service bureau for Texas farmers and ranchers—with a growing focus on the big agribusiness combines displacing the state's small ranchers and farmers. Hightower had decided that everyone who eats is somehow involved in agriculture and had opened the agency up to consumer advocates, organic farm consultants, a marketing and small-business-development office, a farmworkers outreach program, a regional farmers market program, and environmental analysts who cast a cold eye on pesticides. He had alienated the big ag-chem and pesticide companies, Republican Governor Bill Clements, and the Texas Farm Bureau. He used his office as a pulpit to rail against the Reagan and Bush administrations' class-based politics. He made the political economy the message, made the message clear and understandable to everyone, and punched it up with lines like: "George Bush was born on third base and thinks he hit a triple."

With the domestic policy stage dominated by Republican budgets that favored the rich over the poor, the plunder of the country's savings and loans, and the public's concern about toxic waste dumps and a safe food supply, Hightower's message seemed pitch perfect. He was unapologetic about his embrace of progressive populism, proclaiming, "There's nothing in the middle of the road but yellow stripes and dead armadillos."

In *The Washington Post* David Maraniss was suggesting that Hightower's moment had arrived. The *Post* reporter sang the agriculture commissioner's praises while quoting Hightower quoting singer and songwriter Bob Wills: "The little bee sucks the blossom, but the big bee gets the honey; the little man picks the cotton but the big man gets the money." Hightower was as relentless in his support of the little man picking the cotton as he was in his attack on the "bullies, bankers, and bastards" running the country.

The contentious ag commissioner from Denison, Texas, might as well have painted a target on his back. It required little of a Republican consultant to recognize that Hightower was a problem for the state and national party. It took considerable skill, on the other hand, to realize he could be beaten. Rove set his sights on the target.

To find an opponent for Hightower in the 1990 election, Rove went to the source that had provided him Phil Gramm: the Democratic Party. It was there that he found Rick Perry, an unremarkable two-term Democratic House member from Central Texas. Perry worked a family ranch with his father, was possessed of youthful good looks, and was as conservative as most Republican members of the House. Rove recruited Perry to the other side of the aisle and began to groom him to run against Hightower. His broader target, beyond the one on Hightower's back, was Perry's constituents: rural Democrats. Rove believed at the time that Republicans were getting all the votes they could out of the cities. Texas was an urban state, so the ballot boxes outside the state's cities no longer made an election—but they could swing one. In Perry, still something of an empty suit, Rove saw a candidate who could defeat Hightower and perhaps draw some rural and small-town Democrats in to the Republican Party. Perry was designated as the candidate who would take on Hightower. He could be marketed to the public as a cowboy, an image that still sells in Texas.

"Some political consultants measure their success by the number of clients they have," said Austin political consultant Bill Miller. Rove, he said, measures his success by the races he wins. Miller also described Rove as the most focused, disciplined, and organized consultant he had ever worked with or against.

Texas Democrats were not prepared for the political campaign Karl Rove could put in the field. Rove raised more than $3 million to sell the name of Rick Perry while tarnishing the name of Jim Hightower. Perry's campaign office established a press presence, putting out scores of press releases in a format similar to wire-service dispatches.

Hightower faced another problem in the campaign. Greg Rampton, the same FBI agent who had been digging around the offices of Garry Mauro and Bob Bullock, had turned his sights on Hightower. In the summer before the general election, while Rove was at a fundraiser in Washington, he announced that Hightower was under investigation and that indictments would be handed down. Hightower cried foul: The U.S. Department of Justice had made no such announcement. Yet the political consultant for his opponent was announcing it to reporters in Washington.

The money Rove raised through direct mail and high-dollar fundraising events paid for the television spots that made Rick Perry a household face in Texas—and Hightower's name synonymous with corruption. And with liberalism. Television ads claimed "Mr. Hightower was under investigation by the F.B.I.," and asked if he was "too liberal for Texas" because he had supported the presidential campaign of Jesse Jackson. Hightower's modest budget confined his message—and his attempts to respond to Rove—to radio spots.

Tracking polls followed Rove's targeted ad campaigns, measuring their success. Democrats, turned on by a governor's race that pitted Ann Richards against West Texas rancher and banker Clayton Williams, were giving their money not to Hightower but to Richards, who was known to be in a tight race. By the weekend before the election, though, independent pollsters knew what the Perry campaign's internal pollsters already had in hand: The seventeen-to-twenty-point lead Hightower had enjoyed was gone and the race was a dead heat.

In the weekend before the election, Perry ran newspaper ads that had Hightower burning flags and shaking hands with Jesse Jackson.

(He was innocent of the former and guilty of the latter.) Another ad was built over clipped headlines that referred to corruption within the Texas Department of Agriculture. The Perry campaign even put out a press release when Hightower carelessly cut off the tip of his finger with a power mower.

The ag commissioner who had won more than 60 percent of the vote in two previous elections lost his bid for a third term by 51 to 49. For a down-ballot statewide office, Rove had put together a campaign with all the intensity and sophistication (and negative campaigning) associated with a senatorial or gubernatorial race. Jim Hightower was left trying to explain how someone with his national following could lose to a newcomer like Rick Perry. He was philosophical about it. Politics, he said, pumped you up until you strutted around like a peacock. "Today," he said, "I stand before you a feather duster."

Although Rove is often described as a "take no prisoners" campaigner, this campaign was an exception. Two years after the election, three of Hightower's assistants were indicted, convicted, and sentenced to short terms in federal prison. They had misused department funds and raised campaign money from agency clients. The federal judge who sentenced them, Sam Sparks (an appointee of President George H. W. Bush), observed that the ag department employees had broken the law. But he was bothered by the fact that they had inherited a corrupt system that had been in place in the Department of Agriculture long before Hightower was elected, and perhaps also by the fact of his presiding over a politically driven prosecution. The sentence he handed down was so light that he was scolded by the U.S. Court of Appeals for the Fifth Circuit for violating federal sentencing guidelines.

It wasn't until after the fact that the connection between Rampton and Rove was established. In March 1991 Rove was summoned to appear before the Texas Senate's Nominations Committee. The format was as familiar as a C-SPAN capitol news feed. The witness is sworn in and faces his inquisitors sitting on an elevated dais. It's the perfect setting for what an East Texas senator once described as "a ritual ass whipping." On this occasion, Rove was going to get one. Governor Bill Clements had nominated him to the East Texas State University's board of regents. The appointment had gone unconfirmed and Clements had since been succeeded by Democrat Ann Richards.

A Democratic senator from the Hill Country began with questions about the bugging of Rove's office while he was directing the Clements campaign for governor in 1986. Then the questioning abruptly turned in another direction. "How long have you known an FBI agent by the name of Greg Rampton?" Rove was asked. Caught off guard, Rove responded much as Bill Clinton did when asked about his relationship with Monica Lewinsky. "Ah, Senator, it depends. Would you define 'know' for me?"

The senator pressed on, determined that "know" could be defined in the context of Rove's relationship with the FBI agent. "Ah, I know, I would not recognize Greg if he walked in the door. We have talked on the phone a var. . . —a number of times. Ah, and he has visited me in my office once or twice. But we do not have a social or personal relationship whatsoever."

The senator kept boring, pressing Rove about the agent who four years earlier had investigated the bugging of his office. But this wasn't about the bugging of Rove's Austin office. It was about Rove's 1990 Washington announcement of the FBI investigation of the Texas Department of Agriculture—at a moment when it could most harm Hightower's campaign.

Rove's only defense was to inform the senator that his characterization of what had happened in Washington was incorrect. The senator had asked Rove if he had issued a news release. "We did not issue a news release," Rove said. "I talked to a member of the press." Rove said the story had already been reported in the *Dallas Morning News.*

The Democratic senator pressed Rove for dates on his contacts with Rampton and Rove admitted they had indeed spoken—in June or July 1990, in October 1990, and then early in 1991. The information came too late to help Hightower. He could get mad but he couldn't get even.

Republicans seized upon Perry's election as agriculture commissioner as the advent of a new approach to electoral politics. Ag commissioner's races had been dull affairs run on the ground in what remained of the good-ol'-boy courthouse network that helped Lyndon Johnson steal a U.S. Senate race in 1948. Rove had elevated the process and made of it a sophisticated multimedia campaign that happened simultaneously in every one of the state's media markets. In doing so, he had taken a smart, ambitious popular statewide official and "drove up his negatives," replacing him with a rural legislator who had achieved nothing of great distiction in two terms in the state house.

He was now free to move on to another member of the Class of '82 dream team that was supposed to dominate the state's politics for twenty years.

4

The End of Democratic Texas

George Herbert Walker Bush couldn't be denied the 1988 Republican nomination, but the vice president was not perceived as a shoo-in candidate for the general election. The favored Democrat, Colorado senator Gary Hart, self-destructed extravagantly and early, going off on a yacht with a groupie and then daring the press to scrutinize his sex and married life. The governor of Massachusetts, Michael Dukakis, took advantage of Hart's stumble and captured the nomination. In the run-up to the conventions, the Democrats wanted to undercut Bush's strength in Texas as much as they could, and the Texas Class of 1982 still had currency in the national party. Texas Democrats jockeyed to get in the limelight at the convention. Jim Hightower, who was then harboring notions of a populist challenge to right-wing Senator Phil Gramm, hoped that he might be given prime time for a funny, rousing, give-'em-hell speech, but the Dukakis team wanted to energize feminist voters, and in the fading art of political oratory, Ann Richards was as good as anyone the Democrats had. The Texas state treasurer was given the keynote at the convention, and by the time she was through, she was a national sensation.

Provided drafts by the party's big-name speechwriters in the frantic preparation for her speech, Richards closed her eyes and pushed away the pages like they were spoiled food. With time running out, she started talking it through with the only speechwriter she'd ever used, Austin's Suzanne Coleman. Finally the cameras came on, the anchormen paused, the lights came up, and Richards appeared, stunning in her mane of silver hair and sleek, blue dress. "Twelve years ago," she began, "Barbara Jordan, another Texas woman, made the keynote address to this convention, and two women in 160 years is about par for the course. But if you give us a chance, we can perform. After all, Ginger Rogers did everything that Fred Astaire did. She just did it backwards and in high heels!" In half a dozen breaths she had called up civil rights, reminded her audience of the moral high ground that Jordan had held during the Watergate hearings, and inspired the hopes and pride of Democratic women; the crowd was swept up, roaring.

Richards talked about sitting on a pallet with her small granddaughter and thinking about what the future in this country ought to hold for her. But her language was barbed as well. She attacked the Republican vice president with down-home mockery and ridicule, tearing into one Bush policy by saying "That old dog won't hunt." But the speech would be best remembered for her grinning delivery of one tart line: "Poor George. He can't help it. He was born with a silver foot in his mouth!"

Unfortunately, few people would be able to recall what Dukakis said when he took his turn at the podium to accept his party's nomination. Even so, the Dukakis team did make one more astute move, naming Texas' senior U.S. senator, Lloyd Bentsen, as the candidate's running mate. Bentsen was the man who had defeated George Bush in the 1970 Senate race, and he played tennis regularly with Bush's most trusted adviser, James Baker. "Interesting," Bush responded when told the news. "That's interesting."

The Bush team stumbled when it came time to select a running mate. The conventional wisdom was that Indiana Senator Dan Quayle was chosen because he was young and attractive—and therefore appealing to women and to younger voters. But "light-weight" was the press epithet that at once caught hold.

At the Republican convention the GOP's most skillful speech-writer, Peggy Noonan, got the speech of his life out of Bush. Nobody knew what Bush meant by a thousand points of light, but he seemed to imagine and believe in them, and he at last emerged from the shadow of Ronald Reagan as his own man. Dukakis' seventeen-point lead in the polls evaporated, and the rout was on. In the debates, the Democratic nominee proved to be his own worst enemy. When Dukakis, who opposed the death penalty, was asked how he'd feel if someone raped and murdered his wife, he gave a bland, unemotional answer that confirmed his image as a cold fish. The sole bright spot for the Democrats was the performance of Lloyd Bentsen. He embarrassed Quayle in their debate when, in the context of youth, the Republican likened himself to John F. Kennedy. Bentsen was ready for that one. "Senator, I served with Jack Kennedy," he replied. "I knew Jack Kennedy. Jack Kennedy was a friend of mine. Senator, you're no Jack Kennedy."

But the Democratic glee over Bentsen's rhetorical victory was short-lived. Not long after, Dukakis was traveling in Texas, where he asked his convention keynote speaker to fly with him. He asked Richards how she thought the campaign was going. She responded by yelling, "*What* campaign?" and lighting into him in characteristic fashion. They did not communicate closely after that.

What campaign, indeed. While Dukakis micromanaged his campaign into the answer to a Trivial Pursuit question, the Bush campaign was rampaging across the nation under the direction of Rove's old buddy Lee Atwater.

At the outset of the campaign Bush had called his children to Houston to meet the campaign staff. It was there that Atwater found himself confronted by the vice president's curly-haired eldest son, who was not much older than the boy-wonder strategist. George W. Bush had one question for Atwater: "How can we trust you?"

Atwater, taken aback, was speechless.

"Listen, pal," the son continued in his slightly acidic drawl, "if you go to war for our family, we want you completely on our side. We love George Bush, and you better bust your ass for him."

Atwater busted ass for George Bush, and as the campaign wore on he and George W. could increasingly be found in each other's vicinity, laughing and hooting over some shared joke. It was the apotheosis of Atwater's career. Rove's old friend from the College Republicans of the seventies changed the culture of presidential politics by putting a face—especially a mouth—on the consultant. As he saw it, his job was to take flak aimed for the candidate and keep up an outrageous, distracting patter. (James Carville, among others, owes a great debt to Lee Atwater for his celebrity status.) But Atwater was also a disciple of Richard Nixon's gospel of dirty tricks. Atwater dug up the story of a murderer named Willie Horton, who had committed rape and assault while on furlough from a Massachusetts prison, and in ads that clanged like cellblock doors made the name synonymous with Dukakis' record. Atwater's attack ads were criticized as racist, but that charge was harder to pin on George Bush, who maintained a discreet distance from the ads themselves (which were produced by an independent advocacy group). Atwater also had great fun with Dukakis' description of his state's suddenly faltering economy as "the Massachusetts Miracle," and Bush was sent out on a watercraft to cluck at all the dreadful pollution in Boston Harbor. The final nail in the coffin, though, was Atwater's interception of a videotape that showed Dukakis going for a photo-op spin in a tank, his foolish grin and ill-fitting helmet conveying the acuity of a turtle. Atwater didn't really need to run the campaign like General Sherman's march to the sea, but that was his style, and by election day Dukakis the politician had been reduced to ashes.

Karl Rove's closeness to Atwater and the elder Bush's growing fondness for him gave him a limited but important role in the campaign: His reputation, once more, was for painstaking data assembly and effective direct mail.

In the sweep, Bush carried Texas easily. He was about to become the most powerful man in the world; he would preside over the fall of the Iron Curtain and the breakup of the Soviet Union. Under his watch America at last won the cold war, and then crushed the supposed Iraqi might of Saddam Hussein. Yet back in Texas, the 1988 convention speech had made Ann Richards the political darling of the season. First the lieutenant governor, Bill Hobby, and then the telegenic mayor of San Antonio, Henry Cisneros, decided to get out of the way for whatever race she chose in 1990.

The attorney general, Jim Mattox, was another member of the Democratic class of '82, and Richards had been a close ally when he was an anti-establishment state representative and congressman from Dallas. Richards' husband, David, from whom she was now separated, was a labor and civil rights lawyer and had come into the government fold for the first time to direct litigation for Mattox. The attorney general's strong-arm fundraising got him indicted, but a state jury acquitted Mattox, and he immediately started huffing and puffing that no one had better get between him and the governor's mansion.

Richards ignored him. She talked longingly of running for lieutenant governor, the office that controls all Senate appointments and legislation through presiding over the Senate. But she had to make a living. The Texas constitution provided that the lieutenant governor received a salary of just $7,200 a year, the same as everyone else in the state legislature. Salaries in the executive branch, on the other hand, were livable, if not generous, and Richards needed a regular paycheck; she wasn't wealthy. Just as significantly, the more she talked to her core supporters, the more she realized the depth of their feeling. It was time for a woman governor, they believed, and she was the one. They expected her to run.

Richards kicked off her 1990 campaign by chartering a yacht and making a port-by-port tour of the long Texas coast. Local officials, activists, and business people came aboard during the days and briefed her on issues as capitol bureau reporters dozed, and the imagery of a yacht might easily have turned on her. But compared to Mattox's angry demeanor, it was a media feast. On free television all over the state, she was seen piloting the craft as dolphins leaped and cavorted in her wake.

Meanwhile, the scutwork of the campaign was being done in her campaign office in Austin, which was as seedy, disordered, and down-and-dirty as that of any of the other Democrats. One of her campaign managers was the young consultant Mark McKinnon, who was smooth, literate, and patient with the caustic outbursts she tended to unleash when she got tired. But the most impassioned and skillful worker in the Richards campaign was a young state legislator named Lena Guerrero. Demographics were changing Texas politics as much as anything Democrats or Republicans had done; the time was soon coming when Hispanics would be the state's most numerous ethnic group. Karl Rove and other astute Republicans knew they had better be ready to ride that wave of change. Guerrero personified the Democrats' determination to make sure this particular power base continued to vote Democratic. The youthful state rep was the best utility player on the party's farm team, an aggressive campaigner who had clawed her way into the statehouse when she was twenty-five and barely out of the University of Texas. She had proved to be a capable legislator, revealing herself as a natural floor tactician, someone who could muscle votes into place and hold them there when they threatened to slip away. And she was completely and genuinely bilingual and bicultural.

Her political résumé was almost too good to be true and offered the outline of a dramatic American success story. Born in the Lower Rio Grande Valley, as a child she had worked as a migrant farmworker, following the harvest season with her family. She left the poor, dusty Mission Acres *colonia* to attend the University of Texas, where she graduated with a degree in communications and a Phi Beta Kappa key.

Karl Rove read all this carefully.

In those days, the Texas AFL-CIO convention was tantamount to a Democratic caucus. Jim Mattox expected labor to come through for him with an endorsement, for he had been their champion for years, but Richards wasn't going to let him walk away without a tussle. The Austin convention rapidly turned into a heated floor fight between the Mattox and Richards camps as they maneuvered for support from the assembled delegates. Few people in that hall had ever seen a cell phone before, but Guerrero was all over the hall with one, barking orders at her colleagues, sweet-talking crusty old refinery and dock workers, making Mattox aides so angry some observers wondered when she was going to get punched. It was a phenomenal performance. Labor chose to remain neutral in the Democratic race, a crucial setback for Mattox and a win for Richards.

Guerrero did everything but throw her body in front of a truck to deny Mattox the Democratic nomination. One reporter observed that Richards owed her improved chances to the resilience of Guerrero's bladder, wondering, "Does she ever have to pee? She never left the floor. She was out there with that portable phone all day."

As other constituent groups met to consider who they would endorse in the campaign, Guerrero (whose surname in English means "warrior") would attend to spar on Richards' behalf. At the Mexican-American Democrats convention in Corpus Christi, Guerrero stood *frente a frente* with Mattox, staring down an opponent who had all the advantages of height, weight, and gender.

Far behind in the polls, Mattox went negative, as everyone expected he would. He jumped on Richards' rowdy past and social ties to Austin musicians and hippies. He accused her of using marijuana and cocaine, and the press did not give Richards the same pass it would later grant George W. Bush when the same subject came up. "Answer the question! Answer the question!" reporters screamed at Richards as she walked out of one debate. Richards and many of her supporters thought the race was over. Former governor Mark White jumped into the contest, hoping for a comeback,

and Richards' backers began to fear that she might not even make
the run-off.

But Richards survived the primary, and the run-off with Mattox,
though she was a battered candidate. A Democratic primary was
often described—especially by Rove and other Republicans—as the
last place in Texas where liberals could have their way. The Texas
electorate was no less conservative just because Ann Richards had
won the nomination. Knowing this, Richards replaced Mark Mc-
Kinnon's campaign team with one headed by her old friend and chief
of staff at the treasury, Mary Beth Rogers, and she prepared to take
on the Republican candidate, oilman and rancher Clayton Williams.

Clayton Williams was a true outsider. He was a West Texas
Aggie with money to burn, but unlike Bill Clements he didn't pay
much attention to advice from young folks who made their living in
politics. In the Republican primary, he had overwhelmed a Dallas
attorney named Tom Luce, the favorite of the country club crowd,
and Kent Hance, the West Texan who had beaten George W. Bush
in the 1978 congressional race and then switched parties to get in
step with Ronald Reagan. Hance was Rove's client in the race and
would later recall how bad Rove felt about losing the race. "He
does not take losing easily," Hance said. "We got outspent by Clayton Williams five-to-one. The one thing I liked best about Rove: It
became obvious it was going to be a miracle if we won, but he
stayed focused and committed. He stayed hitched."

Clements seemed to have run for another term in 1986 because
he was ornery and vain and just wanted to get even with Mark
White. Under Texas law he could have sought a third term, but he
had accomplished what he set out to do. Poor health and the resulting physical discomfort had become bothersome to him, and as a

regent of Southern Methodist University, he had let himself get sucked into a hush-money scandal involving football players, coaches, and big-shot Dallas alumni. At the time, the SMU Mustangs boasted future NFL great Eric Dickerson and had played two fine seasons that stirred memories of Doak Walker and Dandy Don Meredith, but the payoffs that Clements admitted to sanctioning were so outrageous that the NCAA imposed the "death penalty" for the first time, canceling all football scholarships and kicking the school out of intercollegiate competition for a season. From afar, the football recruiting scandal—which ultimately involved all the major schools in the state but one—looked like an exotic barn dance of Texans who had too much money and too little to think about. But within the state it was a huge story. Clements still had plenty of juice and vigor, but it was time for him to head for the sidelines of GOP politics.

Karl Rove's focus in the 1990 elections was Rick Perry, whose campaign against Jim Hightower would successfully dethrone this prominent member of the Class of '82. Another significant change of regime was occurring in the office of the lieutenant governor. Bill Hobby was retiring, and after sixteen years as comptroller, Bob Bullock had decided that he wanted to cap his career by ascending to the powerful lieutenant governor's office. To a much greater entent than the other Democrats running statewide that year, Bullock had friends and donors in both parties, in addition to a reputation that would cause any would-be challenger to think twice. He drew only token Republican opposition.

In the governor's race, Clayton Williams seemed to think that he could just spit and grin and good-ol'-boy his way into office. And he might have. There were a lot of fellow good ol' boys in Texas.

Richards' own polls had her twenty points down at Labor Day. But Williams' uncalculated crudeness made Bill Clements look like a French dancing instructor by comparison. When he encountered Richards at their debate, the old cowboy refused to shake Richards' hand, an unchivalrous moment caught on film and reproduced on televisions across the state. He said he was going to "head her and hoof her," an expression rodeo calf ropers use to describe roping and tying a calf. He told reporters visiting his ranch a crude joke about the thunderstorm that was descending on them: Bad weather, he said, is like rape. "You can't do anything about it, so you might as well lay back and enjoy it." As the campaign came down to the wire, he casually allowed as how one year he hadn't had to pay any federal income taxes.

Early in the afternoon on election day, anticipation and excitement among the Democrats began to race through Austin. One of the party stalwarts was a former county judge from West Texas named Bill Young. He said he always got a haircut on election day, and his barber was the most accurate pollster he knew. Young said he came out of the shop convinced that Jim Hightower was in big trouble, but his barber also said that he couldn't bring himself to vote for Williams: "I looked at that ballot, and the face of that ignorant son of a bitch just swum up at me," he said. Young's barber wasn't alone. Middle-class wives and mothers who had never voted for a Democrat in their lives were thronging to vote for Richards.

The two candidates' election-night parties could have been scripted by a Democratic consultant. Williams' thwarted victory celebration was an invitation-only affair, and as the grim results of the day's voting trickled in, the roomful of Williams' big-money, big-hat, big-hair supporters became noticeably boisterous and inebriated. By the time the candidate appeared onstage to attempt a concession speech, he had trouble making himself heard above the crowd that had ostensibly gathered on his behalf. When he spoke Richards' name, a torrent of catcalls and shouted slurs drowned him out, and he had to raise his hands quiet the room, to no avail. "Now . . now . . you *owe me that courtesy,*" he hissed, visibly angry. The effect was striking: a roomful of millionaire yahoos who wouldn't even let their own candidate speak. The good-ol'-boy system was breaking down, live, on camera, and only the caterers would know how ugly it had really gotten.

Across town, at the Richards party, euphoria was in the air, and it was catching. Richards' celebration was open to anybody who wanted to walk in off the street, and as the poll results swept across Austin, people were getting up off their couches and going downtown to help celebrate the victory. Grizzled political veterans and true-believer campaign workers mixed with supporters who had never thought of themselves as being particularly political before. Over and over the same remark was heard: "I can't believe Ann won." That was how she was referred to, even by people who had never seen her in person before: *Ann*. It was as though everyone in the room was celebrating the triumph of a personal friend, and her appearance was greeted with unrestrained displays of emotion.

The larger significance wasn't lost on the grizzled vets nursing their drinks in the back of the room watching the Richard's celebration. A woman who had made her political career with a tongue-lashing of President Bush had been elected governor of Texas. When Williams' West Texas supporters descended on Austin restaurants the next day for pricey and joyless lunches, resentment of the capital and everything it stood for was etched plainly on their faces.

In the closing weeks Richards had taken up a refrain that when she won, she was going to lead a people's march up Austin's Congress Avenue—the people were going to take the government back. Inauguration Day in January 1991 was clear, cold, and blustery. Hundreds of supporters gathered that morning at the Town Lake bridge, and with Richards in the lead and Lena Guerrero close by her side, in blue jeans and sneakers and windbreakers they came up the broad street laughing, hollering, arm in arm. In offices above the ground level, businessmen could be seen at the windows, smiling at the spectacle, charitable for the moment. Few people heard Richards' inauguration speech on the Capitol steps, because of press helicopters hovering close overhead. After it was over, a group of her new aides ran to the Sam Houston Building to occupy their offices. The elevator doors opened on a group of well-groomed white men in suits, all carrying briefcases. They absorbed the rabble's appearance and blanched. They cut their eyes and slipped through without speaking. They were the outgoing staff of Governor Bill Clements, people who were used to getting orders—unofficially, of course—from Karl Rove.

The suburban women who would be described as soccer moms a few election cycles later had thronged to the polls to vote for the outspoken grandmother who promised a government as open to women as it had been to men. "The rooster crows, but the hen delivers," Richards had said. In her political appointments, she promised to award talent, intelligence, and loyalty, and one of her most talented, smart, and loyal lieutenants was Lena Guerrero. "Lena Guerrero won the primary for Ann Richards," said state legislator Irma Rangel, a savvy South Texas lawyer who easily shifts from English to Spanish. She then punctuated her declaration: "Pues, así es." Well, so it is.

Richards repaid Guerrero when a seat opened up on the Texas

Railroad Commission, appointing her to fill out the remainder of the departing commissioner's term. The post may sound like a bureaucratic backwater, but it carries real power, and has long served emerging Texas candidates as a springboard to higher office. The state's three railroad commissioners regulate railroads, trucking, oil, and natural gas. But it's the oil and gas regulation that put the commission on the map. Years earlier, a group of oil-rich countries had used the Railroad Commission as a model to form their own price-control cabal—today known by the acronym OPEC.

The appointment was more than a political payback. Of course Richards was rewarding Guerrero for her talent, intelligence, and loyalty. But she also perceived that Guerrero was ambitious and tough enough to run for statewide office. ("They're going to pick through your innards when you run," Richards warned her.) With President George Bush, a nominal Texan, at the top of the ticket in 1992, voters might well cast straight-party ballots that started with the Republican presidential candidate and carried down-ballot to the Republican candidate for justice of the peace. Richards saw Guerrero as a firewall who could stop voters from pulling that straight-party lever—and as a vote-driver in cities on the Texas-Mexico border and in the growing Hispanic communities in Houston, Fort Worth, and Dallas.

Guerrero moved into the offices of what had been a three-man agency and became the Commission's good ol' girl. She mastered arcane oil and gas regulation and traveled the state visiting local Railroad Commission offices. She connected with funders (one of the advantages of holding statewide office) and prepared to campaign to retain her seat on the Commission in 1992. Guerrero had no opposition for the office in the Democratic primary, and when the campaign for the general election began, she was trailed by a Republican lawyer who had run the Minerals Management Agency for President Bush. In little time she had moved from *Texas Monthly*'s "Top Ten Legislators" list to *USA Today*'s list of women to watch as possible future presidential contenders.

Ann Richards had begun her 1988 Democratic convention speech with the line: "Buenas noches, mis amigos." At the 1992 convention in New York, delegates heard the same line with a far more authentic accent. Guerrero wasn't a big enough star to get the keynote, but Richards helped her secure a primetime speaking slot. Guerrero delivered a pitch-perfect *del barrio salí yo* speech that read like a treatment for an Edwards James Olmos miniseries. If "hope flutters on broken wings" was bad poetics and she had to compete with baseball's All-Star Game, Lena was no less a star.

But not for long.

While political reporters in Austin were calling the race for Guerrero, Rove was quietly working to ensure that the speech in Madison Square Garden was the end of her political career. Before her name was even listed on the program for the Democratic National Convention, he had received a call from the spouse of one of his clients, who told Rove that according to information obtained from a University of Texas alumni group, Guerrero was not a graduate. Student transcripts are not public records, but it's often impossible to keep them private. *The New Yorker*, after all, informed the world in 2000 that George W. Bush was a C student at Yale. But at least Bush graduated. Guerrero did not. Nor was she a C student. In fact, the number of Cs, incompletes, and Fs on her transcript dropped a broad hint to Rove that she had never been inducted into Phi Beta Kappa, either. As did the fact that Phi Beta

Kappa keys are awarded only to arts and science graduates, not to graduates of the College of Communications.

Once the transcript was delivered to Rove, there was little doubt that it would become part of the public record. Rove was ever the colleague and disciple of Lee Atwater, who had elevated smear tactics to an art form. Atwater had died in 1991 of a brain tumor (he was only forty years old), but his approach to politics lived on through Rove. And there was little imagination required here; an Atwater intern could have done this deal. But not as skillfully as Karl Rove. Ann Richards' "New Texas" was a place (or at least a concept) where gender-blind meritocracy would replace the good ol' boys' bureaucracy. Fresh new faces would bring new ideas to government. The New Texas had captured the imagination of voters. Now its brightest young star was a fraud who had lied about her degree and claimed academic honors she never earned.

If "location, location, and location" sells real estate, "timing, timing, and timing" wins elections.

Rove waited. He waited until after the Democratic primary, when Guerrero was the only viable Democratic candidate. He waited until after Guerrero delivered the commencement speech at Texas A&M University, and told students: "I remember well my own commencement." He waited until after the Democratic convention, when Guerrero's profile was higher than it had ever been. And he waited until after his own candidate for the Railroad Commission, Barry Williamson, gave his midday speech to the Republican National Convention.

When a reporter from the *Dallas Morning News* called and asked Guerrero about her degree, she claimed there was an error and she would check with the university. In fact, she was buying enough time to release the information herself—a practice political consultants call "inoculating" a story. Days of bad political theater and partial corrections followed. The three credits Guerrero lacked became nineteen. More details trickled out. The star legislator had failed a course on the Texas Legislature. The Latina role model had failed a course on Mexican Americans in the Southwest.

"Karl had Lena's transcript," said an Austin political consultant. "But he held it until the right moment. The perfect moment. Then he screwed her."

Guerrero tried to redeem herself by resigning from the Commission so she would face Williamson as a candidate and not an incumbent. She had made a mistake but had done a good job in the Legislature and on the Railroad Commission. She would "let the voters decide."

They did. Williamson won by a thirteen-point spread. He even beat Guerrero in South Texas, where the majority of registered voters are Hispanic.

"The First Chink in Richards' Armor" was the *Houston Chronicle*'s headline on Guerrero's loss. In her first two years in office, Richards had seemed invulnerable. The collapse of her protégée altered that image.

It was a prelude to November 1994.

Ann Richards' press secretary was a tall, wry ex-political beat reporter named Bill Cryer. An aide to Bob Bullock had first ushered Cryer out of the press and into the fold of politics, but initially he had landed among the Republicans, getting a job in the 1982 re-election campaign of Governor Bill Clements, and for three months he worked elbow-to-elbow with Karl Rove. Cryer greatly enjoyed the collegiality in the campaign office, and coming from a newspaper press room, he couldn't believe the digs. "They had so much money," Cryer reminisced. "The office was in a swank Austin highrise, and anytime we needed to go anywhere, some rich guy had a plane waiting at the airport. Karl struck me as the consummate Young Republican. Well-spoken and funny—a great story-teller. They were all like that. Karl was the direct-mail whiz, but he was enraptured by what they were learning to do with computers. They were kids with new toys."

The Democrats also had computers, of course. Cryer recalled the election day that turned into a nightmare for Clements and his young hard chargers. "The exit polls started looking shaky, and it was raining hard over in East Texas. We got a call that blacks and refinery workers were standing in line outside the polls in a downpour. Something was happening out there, and it did not bode well for the governor. Karl and the others were blindsided; they didn't see it coming. They felt terrible for the old man, wondered how they'd let him down and all that, but they were pros. Karl in particular had this gallows humor about it all. That was the end of my dalliance with the Republicans. Ann Richards won the race for treasurer, and she hired me to do the press there. When that was announced Karl sent me a nice short note, and as time went by, and she was elected governor, he and I corresponded occasionally. His notes were always hand-written on very classy stationery. Some little anecdote, thought for the day. He could be a very charming fellow. What's the word for him in those days? Puckish. He had a puckish sense of humor."

Rove was more than mischievous in the way he went after Mark White, Jim Hightower, and Garry Mauro, but he was careful about playing hardball with the head of the Class of '82. Richards' election as a Democrat in Texas might have been a demographic fluke and beneficiary of a poor Republican candidate, but she was a popular governor and much-admired person. After the 1992 presidential election, which sent George Bush home to Texas, the former president's eldest son began testing the waters, just thinking about running against her. A Republican women's group in Dallas asked George W. Bush to participate in a comedy skit. A Republican consultant who was helping the women with the event told *The New York Times* that he got a stern call from Rove: "He said Bush would make fun of himself, his mother or whatever," he recalled, "but he would not under any circumstances make fun of Ann Richards and would appear only on that condition. It's a year out! Bush hasn't even said he's running. This is a skit for the faithful. But Karl has decided that they're not going to run against Ann's personality, because she has a great personality, so he's on the phone, all serious."

Rove knew the Democrats still had a formidable team. Through election or appointment, they controlled all but two of the state agencies. They had strong majorities in both chambers of the legislature, an able house speaker and small-town champion in the Panhandle's Pete Laney, and, above all, in the state's most powerful office, the lieutenant governor, Bob Bullock.

Bullock had been leery of Rove since the FBI investigations of the 1980s, but through intermediaries Bullock was approachable and could be flattered. He had never been a party stalwart, except in the rare times he thought it was in his self-interest to be. Neither had Bullock ever been tempted to get much involved in national politics. In the run-up to the 1994 elections, Republicans began to lay the groundwork for an accommodation with Bullock, giving him a freer hand in the Senate. Rove knew that if an adversary could be co-opted, he didn't have to be defeated.

Richards' relationship with Bullock was long, complicated, and testy. They had been friends, allies, and drinking partners, before they realized, about the same time, that their lives were out of control and went off to "drunk school," as Bullock put it. But they were rivals, too. Richards never fully trusted her lieutenant governor—and especially his staff—and in her office she used to laugh about how he tried to manipulate her. Richards came in as governors often did, promising that she was going to follow her best instincts and advice, let the dice roll, and not worry about getting reelected. That bravado was thrown out at once. She had to lead a conservative state while tamping down her reputation and past history as a liberal. She was photographed dove-hunting in the Panhandle so she could push through legislative priorities like drug treatment programs in the prisons. As governor she continually had to play to Texans' comfort level, and that became difficult, for unlike Bullock she enjoyed being a national celebrity.

A *Houston Chronicle* dispatch from a party hosted by Richards at the 1992 Democratic National Convention in New York began, "You would have thought it was a movie premiere." Among Richards' 1,200 invitees were Dan Rather, Bob Strauss, Barbara Jordan, and Hillary Clinton; Bill Cosby sent her fifty yellow roses. "In the flash of a rose-colored evening suit and sparkling rose-colored earrings," the reporter enthused, "the governor dashed back into The Supper Club, only to emerge once again hand-in-hand with Clinton for the photo opportunity of the night."

After the 1992 election, George W. Bush was mystified at how his father's presidency had just slipped away. How could you win a war and have a 90 percent approval rating and in just a few months get bounced back to Houston? George W. could never really admit that Bill Clinton beat his dad. The damage, he thought, had been done by Pat Buchanan, nipping away at the president in New Hampshire and then making that scary and offensive speech at the GOP convention, and then by Ross Perot piling on. George H. W. Bush carried Texas in 1992, but the Democrats pinned him down and made him spend unplanned millions to avoid the embarrassment of losing his home state. "The death of a thousand cuts," the son would say, stretching his mouth and shaking his head. For the sake of his dad and the pride of the family, he wanted to get even.

After his father's crushing loss, George W. Bush, by now the managing partner of the Texas Rangers baseball team, distracted himself by training to run a marathon, averaging under nine minutes a mile. This was a guy, Rove saw, with tremendous discipline and energy. Rove had had a good run in Texas himself. He'd picked Rick Perry as a presentable candidate who knocked Hightower off his high horse as agriculture commissioner, and in the same year got Kay Bailey Hutchison, an ex-University of Texas cheerleader and former television reporter, to run for the treasurer's office vacated by Richards. But those were down-ballot races, and Rove was past forty now. If he was going to become a bigger player—even a national player—and really know power, this was his chance. George W. Bush was his star.

When Bush announced that he was going to challenge Richards in the 1994 race, she had a 70 percent approval rating—and yet at the very start, polls had him only eight points down. "If his name was

George Smith," Richards aides grew fond of saying, "nobody would take him seriously." But this was actually a tremendous gift to his campaign manager—first, George W. *was* George W. Bush, with national name recognition, and second, he was constantly being underestimated. Rove also had run a governor's office and had a mind for policy, as well as political ideology. He saw not only that issues determined electoral outcomes, but that, because of this, the campaign was never-ending. Rove was a master at keeping his candidates "on-message." At the outset, he persuaded Bush to run on four issues: juvenile justice, improvement of public education, relief from property taxes, and tort reform—the last a euphemism for cutting the legal legs out from under plaintiffs' trial lawyers, who were among the Democratic Party's largest contributors. Over and over, Bush made the same pitch. Rove kept him on a continual circuit of small and mid-sized towns, where he visited courthouses and talked to small radio stations and weekly newspapers, his Midland drawl tuned to perfection. While Richards hobnobbed with Cybill Shepherd and Lily Tomlin, her challenger would run into Dallas Cowboy great Roger Staubach, a devout Republican, and joke with the quarterback: "Hey, Roger, I want you and Nolan Ryan"—recently retired from the Rangers' pitching staff—"to campaign with me in the fall. We'll call it the Old Farts' Tour."

Message was everything with Rove. And Bush was notoriously bad when speaking on his feet. At one point early in the campaign when Bush began to deviate from his script, Rove pulled him off the campaign trail for a brief retreat in the seclusion of East Texas. "All we'd heard about was Bush the playboy," said Bill Cryer. "Undisciplined in his personal life. We thought he'd get out there and start popping off, and the press would just cream him. But Karl had him almost on this mantra—Governor Richards called him a windup doll. And Karl very effectively kept him insulated from the press. Any dealing he had with a reporter was on a personal level." One such reporter was Ken Herman, the beat reporter for the *Austin American-Statesman*. Herman had won a Pulitzer as a small-town investigative reporter, and he went after Bush the candidate on occasion. But he loved baseball, and appreciated a funny story. Bush knew how to get him laughing. He would call Herman at home and ask him for advice on what to do with a major league baseball player. The disarming charm was hard to resist.

Apart from the personal qualities a politician brings to the governor's office in Texas, his or her greatest power lies in making appointments. "The Lena Guerrero episode hurt us more than anything," Cryer believed. "Here was a governor who said she was going to make a point of naming women and ethnic minorities to these powerful positions, and she picks one who's unqualified, and lies about it. That was really when we began to feel the estrangement of independent white males."

Some of the Bush-Rove team's advantages were simply gifts. Richards had already served up an easy target soon after Bill Clinton was inaugurated as president in 1993. Lloyd Bentsen was slowing down, and he accepted Clinton's offer to leave the Senate and join his cabinet as treasury secretary. For the life of her, Richards couldn't find a strong Democrat who would accept an appointment to fill Bentsen's seat, and then run in the special election to serve the remainder of his term. Democrats had been so proud of the Class of '82 that they hadn't built a bench, much less a farm system. Democrats who looked at the senatorial race had a strong premonition of what was about to happen to them and shied away, but the public perception was that Richards was just inept. Henry Cisneros and John Sharp—Bullock's successor as comptroller—turned her down. Finally, in exasperation, Richards turned to Bob Krueger, a Shakespearean scholar from Duke University who was by then a two-time loser of U.S. Senate races in Texas. Richards wouldn't have crossed the street for Krueuger during his brief heyday as a conservative Democratic candidate, but she was desperate. After accepting the appointment, Krueger carped about Clinton's presidency—which was the reason he was finally in the Senate. Meanwhile, Rove talked Kay Bailey Hutchison into running against Krueger in the special election. Toward the end of the campaign, Democratic admaker Roy Spence and Garry Mauro talked the usually dignified Krueger into donning shades and a leather jacket in an Arnold Schwarzenegger *Terminator* routine. It was embarrassing—arguably the worst political ad ever aired in Texas. Hutchison won easily, which meant that two of Rove's past clients, Hutchison and Phil Gramm, now held the Texas seats in the U.S. Senate.

Once George W. Bush began his gubernatorial campaign in earnest, Karl Rove and his team proved themselves masters at scrambling Richards' message. Karen Hughes, a former Dallas TV journalist who was now head of a campaign fund called the Associated Republicans of Texas, kept up a steady barrage of attacks against the governor. Rove's team filed an open-records request for over 5,000 employment applications for state jobs filled by Richards and demanded photocopy machines; the governor's counsel trudged off to fight the thing in court. Richards was continually on the defensive. Cryer fended off incoming fire in the governor's press office; a consultant named Chuck McDonald handled the campaign press and lobbed his own shells at Bush and Rove.

"Karl plays as fair as anybody else in politics," McDonald said later. "But he plays for keeps. I always knew where I stood with Karl. I knew he was trying to kill me." On another occasion, McDonald reflected, "He approaches everything as life or death. He does not give off the vibes that you can go and have a beer with him when the game is over."

The ruthlessness and risks he was willing to take for his candidate were captured in a story that *Dallas Morning News* reporter Anne Marie Kilday told her friend Melinda Henneberger of *The New York Times*. Kilday said Rove called her one day during the '94 race and said he was looking at the telephone records of a state official and reputed lesbian, adding that he found it interesting that the official in question made repeated calls to Kilday—"at your residence," he added. Kilday went on: "He said, 'You've just got to be careful about your reputation and what people might think.'"

Rove denied that such a conversation could ever have taken place. "The official's sexuality," he claimed, in any case, "would have had nothing to do with it."

Well, perhaps.

Rove knew he could intimidate reporters on occasion. If Rove thought a reporter had gotten a story wrong or was unfair to Bush, he would call with a loud angry rebuttal. He wasn't always looking for a retraction, but he knew the reporter would write other stories in the future and he wanted to get his message across. (Later, as the presidential campaign got in gear, editors would sometimes hear from the campaign press office about a story Rove considered editorial in tone.)

Meanwhile Bush was as nice to Richards as he could possibly be. He came off in the race as a well-bred young gentleman. Bush had also learned from his dad the peril of ignoring the Christian right; he talked about faith-based social services and the right to life. But neither Rove nor Bush wanted any part of the Hispanic immigrant-bashing espoused by Pat Buchanan and California's Republican governor, Pete Wilson. "Hell, if they'll walk across Big Bend, we want 'em," Bush would say privately about undocumented Mexican workers.

Bush didn't have to do anything to win over one important block of voters. In Richards' first session, legislators had pushed through a bill that would permit Texans to get a license to carry concealed handguns. Richards vetoed it, and law enforcement groups were urgent in their support of her position, but the thing came right back at her. Before one group she answered a question about the bill by saying, "Well, I could support it if they had to wear them around their necks. Everybody would know who's packing. 'Uh-oh, look out for that one—he's got a gun.'" She also ridiculed the idea that women would be safer if armed, saying that as a woman she understood that there was no way any woman would be able to find a gun in her handbag. Gun owners did not find these jibes funny. Bush talked about the sanctity of the Second Amendment and said that he would sign a concealed handgun bill, and he won the votes of angry voters who were spoiling to punish Richards.

Reporters marveled at the efficiency and the detail of George W. Bush's campaign and the skill of the man running it. The 1994 race was when Karl Rove shed his reputation as another hatchet man and became the Boy Genius. He could say he admired Richards as a person and her character was not the issue. But no potentially damaging detail was left unattended. Democrats complained that it was no coincidence when Bill Ratliff—a Rove client and Republican state senator from East Texas, who was known for his principle and integrity—held a press conference in Mount Pleasant and raised the specter of lesbians working for Ann Richards. The story seemed to die among urban sophisticates in Austin, but not among more conservative voters in Longview or Tyler. Push pollsters began to place calls and wonder aloud if people would vote for Richards if they knew she moved in social circles with lesbians, and might be one herself. Reporters were wary of that rumor, and wouldn't touch it. But it was out there.

Though Richards' popularity ratings continued to be high, the mood of her staff revealed the fear that had set in. They stopped sharing information with Bullock and his staff, convinced that he had crossed over and was feeding every tidbit to Bush and Rove. In Richards' debate with Bush, the challenger once more benefited from underestimation. He was polite and respectful. "Thank you, Governor," he said with a nod, when she dismissed a reporter's question about his military service during Vietnam, and then scored the point of the night when he said her expressed reasons for wanting to be governor hadn't changed one bit in four years. There was a day of excitement in her office when Ross Perot, forever trying to pay back those Bushes for some perceived wrong, endorsed her, but the polls didn't move.

That election day in 1994, the Democrats experienced what Rove had felt in the Clements campaign twelve years earlier. They knew. There was a national race, too, the midterm congressional election. Hillary Clinton's health care plan had been a disaster, and Newt Gingrich was coming to power in Congress. After two years the Clinton presidency appeared to be a cinder. That night, with

Bush ahead by more than 300,000 votes, 53 to 47 percent, Richards made her concession speech early. She almost looked relieved.

Stunned commentators attributed her loss to the nationwide repudiation of Bill Clinton, but Richards and her aides knew that wasn't how it happened. They recalled her announcement of her campaign for reelection at a birthday celebration. The country singer Jimmie Dale Gilmore performed, and she had made one of her colorful and fiery speeches, yet the event didn't have a pulse. Neither would her race. The soccer moms who had supported her against the insulting cowboy Clayton Williams went back to being Republicans. She was tired and adrift, and the marathoner Bush just kept coming, always on message. Richards loyalists were left with regrets and the belief that this was a race not just lost but blown. "Karl deserved all the credit he received," his onetime co-worker Bill Cryer said with a sigh. "It was a masterful performance; they did everything right. But let's hear it, too, for the Ann Richards campaign. If it hadn't been for us, George W. Bush wouldn't be president of the United States."

With the election of Bush as governor, the Democrats were finished in Texas, though they could not yet admit it to themselves. With Texas effectively conquered and with a candidate of limitless confidence and possibility, Karl Rove could now turn his sights on the rest of the nation.

PART 2

RISING STAR IN THE LONE STAR STATE

5

Kiss Me First

The roar of approval and adulation that greeted Bush as governor was instantaneous, and it carried him along with hardly a flutter or dip. He had the advantage of being Republican in a state whose electorate had turned that corner, probably for good. The power of the governor's office was extremely limited, had been designed that way and had stayed that way for more than a century. Texans felt they had been abused by the scalawags and carpetbaggers whom the federal government had authorized to serve as governor during Reconstruction, and once that was over and the occupying federal troops were withdrawn, a new constitution had been enacted, in 1876, that would keep any governor from wielding such power again. A legislative attempt to modernize and rewrite the state constitution had collapsed in the mid–1970s, so the Texas government creaked along, changing in small increments. Many ballots contained a list of arcane constitutional amendments, which only a popular vote could authorize, just to keep the government working.

The governor still had power, of course. Education, utilities, insurance, transportation, the environment, the state parks system, and many other areas were overseen by commissions whose boards the governor appointed. There was some overlap between the boards of each governor, so the lurches in policy and direction, wouldn't be too sudden, but in making those appointments, the governor charted the path of the bureaucracy. The state senate and house of representatives met every other year in 140-day sessions, and that was all the time they had to jam legislation through— unless the governor called a special session over some emergency, and most governors were reluctant to do that. Legislators were paid such a ridiculously low sum, $7,200 a year as previously mentioned, that unless the senator or representative had some very lenient and supportive employers, only rich people could hold the office, at least for very long. In this way the rule of the establishment was assured.

The speaker of the house was chosen by pledge of the individual legislators, just as it's done in the U.S. Congress. The lieutenant governor, though, was elected by the people of the state to preside over the senate, and since there were just thirty-one senators, his power was less dispersed. The senate defined the lieutenant governor's power by writing the rules of the body; if the lieutenant governor was well-liked, or much-feared, then the senators designed the office in ways that gave their leader great power. The conventional wisdom was that the lieutenant governor had the real power in Texas.

The balance of power between governor and lieutenant governor was also measured by personal style and charisma. A John Connally or Ann Richards came to have substantial power as governor; a Preston Smith or Dolph Briscoe served his term and was soon forgotten. George W. Bush could be arrogant, defensive, and full of himself, but those facets seldom caught the public eye. He had enormous magnetism and charm; he was a good ol' boy without being smarmy in the way of other notable GOP Southerners like Trent Lott or Haley Barbour. Bush was a relative stranger in Austin, but he was immediately appreciated. He was personable and sophisticated; he and Laura were soon noted and admired for their taste in chefs and restaurants. And in Texas the new governor was buoyed always by a deep reservoir of affection for his dad and mom. Now living in Houston, the elder Bush was immersed in writing his memoirs and building his presidential library in College Station, on the campus of Texas A&M.

The Democrats still had majorities in both houses of the legislature. Some Democrats believed that Bob Bullock had made an open secret of helping Bush's campaign because he was tired of being adored less than his old drinking pal Richards—that Bullock believed this rich kid knew nothing about state government and would be more easily bent to the lieutenant governor's will than Richards had been. There was a story that Barbara Bush had asked Bullock to look out for her son, and he was charmed by her personal request. Whatever the source of their chemistry, Bush and Bullock carried on like soulmates from the start, and Bush was no less adept at swapping yarns about West Texas and small-town life with the house speaker, Pete Laney. The governor got anything he wanted from his first session of the legislature.

Bush also began the seduction of Bob Bullock, which would pay off later. The lieutenant governor had a sinecure at an Austin law firm, but he was not a wealthy man by any means. Bush invited him to fly along and join the family on hunting leases Bullock could never afford—all the while flattering the older man's sense of importance. On one occasion Bush's courtship of Bullock seemed more than a metaphor. The lieutenant governor once complained to Bush, after the governor refused to support him on a particular issue, "If you're going to fuck me, you're going to have to kiss me first." To disarm Bullock, Bush kissed him. Bush would make the mistake of retelling this story during the 2000 presidential campaign to Tucker Carlson, who was writing a profile of him for *Talk* magazine.

A *Texas Monthly* writer asked Karl Rove when it was that he first realized Bush might be presidential timber. "Sometime during the '95 [legislative] session, it dawned on me," he said. "He was a fabulous candidate, but I didn't know how he was going to govern. To see him walk onto a stage with such a complicated cast of characters—Bullock, Laney, Democrats in all the major positions—and difficult personalities and win them over was a revelation."

In many ways Bush's first term as governor of Texas foretold his style and agenda in the White House. There was no way to anticipate the defining moment of his presidency, of course. Governors have no military and foreign policy—no moment in history, as Rove would often put it, that predict that capability as commander in chief. But the Texas agenda proved to be a blueprint for Bush's domestic policy.

There were some housekeeping items and promises to be kept. An early priority was to let Texans have their licenses to carry concealed handguns. Fine—make sure they went to some kind of safety school first. More important to Bush was a tax cut. As comptroller, Bullock had voiced the heresy that Texas was never going to steady its finances unless it instituted a state income tax. Scorched by the political fireworks that went off as a consequence, he retreated from that position, and as lieutenant governor, seemingly in a fit of pique, he maneuvered through the legislature a bill that prohibited the imposition of a state income tax unless voters approved a constitutional amendment. It was vintage Bullock logic—if he couldn't personally chart the state's fiscal future, and institute a change that was needed, then by God nobody was going to. The state collected sales and franchise taxes and increasingly passed the buck to cities, counties, and school districts, so property taxes soared. Tax relief was a middle-class issue. Bush wanted a big tax cut on his record, and with Bullock's and Laney's help he pushed one through. A $7.6 billion surplus on the state's books whistled toward a record deficit as high as $12 billion by 2002. But he delivered on his promises; he was true to his word.

Rove said the angriest he ever saw Bush was that first year. An education bureaucrat came to brief the governor and staff and remarked in passing that 43,000 third-graders in Texas couldn't pass minimal tests for reading skills. Rove described the conversation: "The governor said, 'What happened to the forty-three thousand?' The guy said, 'Well, thirty-nine thousand went on to the fourth grade.' The governor went through the roof." Education reform, universal testing, became his legislative crusade, and the house and senate gave him that as well.

Bush was an oilman, albeit an unsuccessful one; not much was expected of him on the environment. Still, his father had offered the Clean Air Act as one of the intellectual high points of his administration, remarkable coming from a Texas oilman. Apart from what the muck was doing to Texans' lungs, Houston, Dallas-Fort Worth, El Paso, San Antonio, Austin, and smaller urban centers were in continual danger of falling out of compliance with that federal law, and the law had teeth—states that did not ensure compliance could lose billions of dollars in highway funds. The EPA issued a periodic toxic release inventory of contaminants spewed, leaked, or dumped into the environment; in every announcement, Texas ranked first or second to Louisiana. Weeks after he had been elected governor, Bush acknowledged that he had never heard of a toxic release inventory. Bush, his staff, and his advisors blithely ignored the matter of Texas and the Clean Air Act. They would rely on incentives for industry and voluntary compliance.

Bush dismantled Richards' ambitious program of drug and alcohol treatment in the prisons, and Bullock, who had helped her build it, chose not to fight for the program. Such an approach rankled Bush. He didn't need a twelve-step program to overcome *his* drinking problem. He just woke up one morning with a bad hangover and years of guilt, and he quit drinking. Bush said he did it with discipline and faith, and that's what he wanted to see in the prisons. He invited Charles Colson, the Watergate heavy who was born again in federal prison, to introduce his program of prayer in the yards and cellblocks.

The governor had a reputation and air as a moderate. He shunned the Christian Right and disdained the immigrant-bashers in his party. Bush was accepted, even by Democrats who would never vote for him, as a decent country-club Republican, rather like his dad. But he was much more of an ideologue than he let on. People invited to his office to talk about jobs came away stunned by his obsession with privatization. Bush remarked to a South Texas Democratic legislator that he'd love to privatize the University of Texas, though he doubted he would see that in his lifetime. Privatize a public university with 50,000 students on just one of its campuses and an oil-based endowment rivaling those of Harvard and Yale? If Bush could imagine that, why not Social Security?

In taking from the legislature, the governor knew when to give a little in return. Like Arizona and California, Texas had a problem of long-term water supply. The problem was complicated by the state's relative vastness—the state is the size of France or Spain—and by its range of climates, from mosquito-laden swamp in the east to bone-dry desert in the west. The weather was prone to ruinous droughts, and legally, Texas is one of the few states that still subscribed to the right of capture—water, even groundwater, is a private property right. Bob Bullock said the arguments had scarcely varied since he was a legislator in the 1950s, and he wanted a system that would give local communities a way to plan for and protect their water future. He called his proposal Senate Bill 1, a pointed way of stressing its importance to him. Bush helped him find common ground with the rural and industry interests who had gone after Richards with a vengeance when she proposed a similar plan.

From the start Rove was described as a pillar in Bush's "Iron Triangle" of advisors, along with press aide Karen Hughes and chief of staff Joe Allbaugh. But Rove did not go on Bush's state payroll, as he had with his first elected governor, Bill Clements. A few blocks from the Capitol, the consultant spent the days in a windowless Karl Rove + Company office, identifiable by the "Labor for Nixon" bumper sticker on his door. Direct mail specialists are pleased with a 2 percent response rate. Three percent is exceptional and anything over 5 percent is spectacular. When a reporter asked Rove about his response rates, he pulled out a sheaf of papers. "Here's one where we got a 24.24 percent response," he began. "Here's one where we raised about $300,000 on a 24.81 response with an average gift of $57." He continued reading off the list: "Ten percent. . . . Here's one with 4 percent, here's one with 18 percent." Rove said the key to success in direct mail is having "the right list, with the right message at the right time. It has to grab attention and it has to be based in fact and need."

The tall, articulate, ever-forceful Hughes was Bush's communications director and most visible policy adviser. Allbaugh (now director of the Federal Emergency Management Administration) was a bluff, loud man who had worked for an Oklahoma governor and who presented a startling figure to Austin slackers. He had a brush cut—not a crewcut, he stressed—that was greased and stood straight up; a "flat top" was the Texas term for the look when it was current about half a century earlier. He came on like a high school football coach from that era.

The ideologies of Bush and Rove were most aligned in the team's approach to social services. Bush and Rove had come through their youth in the war-protesting, drug-taking sixties with vastly different backgrounds and personal experiences, but they were joined at the hip in one conviction: That was a time in the nation's life deserving of revulsion, not nostalgia.

Their ideological creed was a 1993 book by Myron Magnet called *The Dream and the Nightmare: the Sixties' Legacy to the Underclass*. Magnet, a *Fortune* magazine writer and a fellow at the Manhattan Institute for Policy Research, contended that lazy minds bred by the sixties (such as that of Bill Clinton) had passed on their notions of free love and self-fulfillment to the poor, ruining their chances of pulling themselves out of poverty by their own bootstraps. Magnet wrote that the counterculture "withdrew respect from the behavior and attitudes that have traditionally boosted people up the economic ladder—deferral of gratification, sobriety, thrift, and so on—through the whole catalogue of antique-sounding bourgeois virtues." In his office Rove had a shelf full of copies of Magnet's book, and he handed them out like Bibles.

In their zeal for privatization and welfare reform, Bush and his team wanted to bury whatever remained of Lyndon Johnson's Great Society and remind the nation of its heritage of faith-based social services. That was a delicate pitch to sell, even in Texas. There was the constitutional requirement of separation of church and state, for starters. Also, Texas had a sorry past of religious schools for poor and unwanted kids that had been licensed by the state and run, to politicians' embarrassment, like concentration camps. (The Lester Roloff homes that John Hill had shut down as attorney general were only the most egregious example.) The Bush team's most tireless and vocal critic was an organization called the Texas Freedom Network. It raised a steady drumbeat of fear and antagonism toward the Religious Right. The group's founder and spokesperson was Cecile Richards, the ex-governor's daughter.

There was another issue the Bush team had to be careful with, one that would reappear during his run for the White House. Bush got less than 9 percent of the black vote in his race against Richards, and the rejection puzzled and bothered him—he described that as the one major disappointment of his campaign. Myron Magnet's disdain for hippies and draft-dodgers was easy for him to defend intellectually—in his view they were losers in a sorry time that was long past, and most had continued to demonstrate their shiftlessness and mediocrity. Outside of a diminishing slice of popular culture, such people had few defenders; all the relevance they had now was negative. But the argument that their glamorization had soaked into and contaminated the values of the underclass was a riskier jump to make—especially if Bush and Rove wanted to carry that leap into politics and social policy. At best, Magnet's value judgments implied a condescension toward people who were poor. An overwhelming majority of Texans living in poverty were black and Hispanic. The perception of being haughty white lords over poor people of color was a bogey that Republicans were trying hard to shake.

The wordsmith who could sell these concepts to the general public turned out to be right under the Republicans' noses. On the University of Texas journalism faculty was a tall, ungainly, immensely confident man named Marvin Olasky. He had grown up Jewish in New York, a doctrinaire leftist, but then underwent a crisis of spirit and came out of it born again, a philosopher of the Christian right. Olasky wrote columns for editorial pages of Texas newspapers, and they had caught the eye of the governor and his strategists. Soon Olasky was a regular in the governor's office, briefing aides on the fundamentalist philosophy and how it could be applied. He gave them the feel-good term and concept they were looking for: compassionate conservatism.

6

Two Birds with One Stone

Not every conservative Christian was as enthusiastic and effusive about George W. Bush as was Marvin Olasky, the avatar of compassionate conservatism. In fact, there was one high-profile Christian in the Texas Republican Party leadership whom Rove would gladly have banished to a Trappist monastery, where a code of silence is strictly enforced.

Karl Rove's fight with Tom Pauken began in 1994. It involved the one faction in the party Rove had underestimated: the evangelical Christians who had come into the Republican fold with Pat Robertson's 1988 presidential campaign. Nowhere had their strength been more evident than at the 1994 Republican state convention in Fort Worth. Christian Right delegates filled the convention center two blocks from the hotel where John Kennedy spent the night of November 21, 1963. Prayer breakfasts drew bigger crowds than hospitality suites. The virtuous William Bennett came in first in the presidential straw vote. Texas Senator Phil Gramm won only 8 percent of the pool because he was soft on defense of the unborn. Every winning candidate (and most losing candidates) for party office praised God and excoriated abortion. And U.S. Senator Kay Bailey Hutchison was booed when she stood up to address the convention. Not because of anything she said in her speech, but because she openly supported women's reproductive rights.

Rove could count.

He knew he had lost control of the party. But with his new candidate, George W. Bush, then starting a race for the governorship against an incumbent with approval ratings in the 60s and 70s, Rove had to control the party chairmanship. The new evangelical majority had already thrown out Fred Meyer, George H. W. Bush's handpicked chairman, and were backing Tom Pauken, a Dallas lawyer who had run the ACTION volunteers program for Ronald Reagan. Pauken was a stout, pugilistic conservative who had run two bruising if losing campaigns against Jim Mattox, a liberal Democratic congressman from Dallas. He was backed by an uncompromising faction Rove couldn't control. So Rove recruited his own candidate: Dallas-area Congressman Joe Barton, who spent three days campaigning under the rubric "Pro-Life Joe." Barton—one of Rove's first clients when he ran for the U.S. House race in 1984—showed up with an impressive list of supporters: Senators Gramm and Hutchison, both elected to office under the guidance of Karl Rove; most of the Republican delegation in the U.S. House; and the party's new marquee star, the son of the President of the United States, George W. Bush.

The Christian delegates weren't impressed.

The fight for the state chair was a rare miscalculation for Rove. Even if he was fighting within the confines of the party, the pragmatist known for picking winning candidates had picked a fight he couldn't win. It was over before the first "Grand Old Prayer Session" drew 3,500 delegates on the opening day of the convention.

But Rove and Barton wouldn't let it go. The vote was set for Saturday. By early Friday evening the beleaguered Congressman Barton was barking at his operatives: "I'm tired of hearing what I can't do. I want to see their cards. I want *them* to prove *they* can do it." Rove continued to beat the dead horse on which he had bet $100,000 in campaign cash and the political future of George W. Bush.

When Barton finally saw the Christian delegates' cards, he folded. Tom Pauken held 3,076 commitments to Joe Barton's 2,162. Instead of a floor fight on the final day of the convention, delegates embraced a platform that supported constitutional rights for the unborn, the repeal of the Clean Air Act and the Endangered Species Act, the end of the state's authority to compel children to attend school, a repeal of the minimum wage, and a return to the gold standard. Eight years later, only the quaint monetary policy seems extreme in the context of a Congress led by Majority Leader Tom DeLay. Yet Bush immediately distanced himself from his party's platform.

Rove and Bush came to an important strategic conclusion in Fort Worth. To govern on behalf of the corporate right, they would have to appease the Christian right. Both Rove and Bush were pragmatic economic conservatives. Rove would say he had no great abiding faith, and only when Bush began his campaign for the presidency would he begin to speak more openly about his religious beliefs. Neither of the men were Pat Robertson Republicans. But the 1994 convention taught them a valuable lesson. The party's economic conservatives and social conservatives had to be kept in harness.

What was learned in Fort Worth was evident in Bush's accommodation of the Christian conservatives' agenda and his zealous pursuit of the business community's agenda after he became governor. It was also evident when Rove retained the services of Ralph Reed, who had served as executive director of the Christian Coalition, as Bush prepared to enter the Republican presidential primaries.

They also concluded that Tom Pauken had to go.

Yet Pauken had fallen in line (more or less), coming to the same conclusion reached by Rove and Bush. The marriage of the Christian conservatives and the economic conservatives had to be made to work if the party was to work. This marriage, after all, defines the modern Republican Party. Pauken sparred with Rove but was well behaved during Bush's first legislative session in 1995. As Bush's second biennial session got underway in 1997, though, Pauken appeared to be testing the limits of his uneasy domestic relationship with Bush and Rove. And he was doing so at a time when Bush was preparing to use his success in managing the Texas Legislature to quietly begin his campaign for the presidency.

In January of that year, Pauken entered the race to succeed Mississippi lobbyist Haley Barbour as chairman of the national Republican Party. Rove would have been happy to see Pauken leave Texas, but not if he were moving into the national headquarters of the Republican Party. So the campaign against Pauken began. Rove's old client, Bill Clements, began calling around the country informing high-level Republicans that Pauken was damaged goods.

Pauken claimed that Clements, by that time almost eighty years old and retired from politics, had offered him a job if he would withdraw from the election for the Republican national party chairmanship. He also accused the senior George Bush of pressing Clements to nudge him out of the race for party chair. According to

Pauken, the former president feared that if Pauken were Republican National Committee chairman, he would get in the way of George W.'s 2000 presidential race.

"Nuts," Clements said. "It's just nuts."

"Baloney," he said. "All of that is just absolute baloney." Clements said he had met with Pauken for two hours, but there had been no job offer. And certainly no discussion of any presidential campaign. Pauken held his ground, saying he would not "be bought."

Colorado developer Jim Nicholson won the national eight-candidate race and Pauken kept his job as chairman of the Republican Party in Texas. But the feud continued. Rove saw to it that many big Republican funders did not contribute to the party. Pauken saw to it that Karl Rove + Company lost the Republican Party's direct mail contract. If this lacked the intensity and drama of the feud between Lyndon Johnson and Texas Senator Ralph Yarborough, it nevertheless made it more difficult for Rove to prepare for a presidential campaign.

Pauken also created a problem in the Legislature. The Texas Legislature meets every two years for 140 days, and some careful observers of the process have made the case that meeting for two days every 140 years might be preferable. The same constitutional framers who feared placing too much power in the hands of the governor also feared placing too much power in the hand of the Legislature. So sessions are biennial and salaries are laughable. The business lobby perennially includes at least 1,500 registered members, who spend approximately $250 million each session in their efforts to influence the votes of 181 legislators. Thus every two years the Texas Legislature becomes a bottleneck through which only the bills of the most powerful, most plaintive, most persistent, or most devious interests can pass.

A governor can draw up an agenda and get in line with competing interests. Or he can use his political skills and expend his political capital to get his own legislative package enacted. Bush's first session, in 1995, won rave reviews from the critics. He charmed legislators by connecting with them individually. And he delivered on his campaign promises of tort reform, more prisons, a more punitive juvenile justice system, and some education reform. "Like a knife through butter," was how lobbyist Bill Miller described Bush's run through the Legislature in 1995.

After he lost his race for the national committee chair, Tom Pauken returned to Texas and settled into the 1997 legislative process like a tropical depression. The big reform proposal Bush was delicately moving through the Legislature would have replaced the state's creaky corporate franchise tax with a tax on partnerships. (The franchise tax functioned like an income tax on corporations, but limited partnerships were exempt, so many businesses escaped taxation.) Property taxes would have been reduced. And lost revenue would be replaced by taxes on goods and services. It is a cultural imperative that Republicans don't raise taxes, so the governor's staff and the governor promised that whatever they passed would be "revenue-neutral." No new money would be raised.

To Pauken, increasing any tax or taxing something heretofore untaxed was a tax increase—even if another tax was lowered. "It's not a tax cut, it's a tax hike," Pauken told reporters at a Capitol press conference. He described Bush's ambitious proposal as a scheme to "give us something in one hand and then take it back in another." At times it was impossible to tell whether the hit sheets attacking the Republican governor's tax plan were faxed from the offices of Democratic Party Chair Bill White or Republican Party Chair Tom Pauken.

Pauken urged Republican legislators to vote against the bill. He even bought newspaper ads attacking "Governor Bush's Tax Increase." And he succeeded in persuading Republicans to vote against their governor's tax measure, which only passed in the House because Democrats supported it. The proposal finally died in the Republican-controlled Senate. Bush would have to wait two more years for a campaign sound bite describing him as "the governor who cut property taxes for all Texans."

Pauken didn't feel as if he had to wait until the current session ended. The tax bill was dead, but Pauken still tried to hang it around Bush's neck. "It's like something you would expect from a liberal Democrat," he told *Washington Post* reporter Sue Anne Pressley in May 1997.

Here was a *Post* reporter in Austin working a softball page-one story about George W. Bush. Everything was falling into place for Rove. A former LBJ aide was talking Texan, observing that Bush didn't seem to be doubled over with ambition: "The best politics is an easygoing politics. Some of these fellas overdo it when they try to run for something." A Republican legislator was cultivating the log cabin myth. "When George moved back to Midland, he bummed an office, he bummed golf clubs, bummed shoes." Even the Democratic Party's press flack was singing Bush's praises: "Some people thought he was not the brightest porch light on the block, and they were wrong about that." The lone critical voice in a national daily story that framed Bush as a leading contender for the presidency just happened to be the chairman of the Republican Party of Texas.

Rove and his surrogates couldn't get their hooks into Pauken. But later in 1997, the Texas party chairman made a move that would put him directly in Karl Rove's gunsights. He announced he would run for the Republication nomination for attorney general. It was the opportunity Rove had been waiting for. He didn't have a mechanism to move Pauken out of the party chairmanship. But he did know how to win elections.

The 1998 attorney general's election was one of the most peculiar races in a state known for its peculiar politics. And it almost requires a playbill to follow it from start to finish. Rove wanted to seize the moment and send Tom Pauken back to his Dallas law practice. But he also wanted to defeat the Democratic incumbent, Dan Morales, an attractive, unpredictable Hispanic who was often mentioned as a candidate for governor.

Morales was almost a perfect Democratic candidate. A Mexican-American from a middle-class family in San Antonio, Morales had attended preppy Trinity University in San Antonio and Harvard Law School. Out of Harvard, he worked as a prosecutor, a lawyer in a corporate law firm, and a state representative. He was a boyish-looking thirty-four when he was elected attorney general. This dapper Hispanic—trim, telegenic, and slightly dweeby—had more crossover appeal than Antonio Banderas. He turned on Mexican-American voters while turning out suburban women—and the middle-class white men who often eluded the Democrats. If his Spanish wasn't as good as that of George W. Bush, he had the surname to sell to Hispanic voters. And Morales was the only Democrat whose name would appear near the top of the ballot. His unanticipated, spectacular, vertical collapse—largely of his own doing—had all the intrigue and melodrama of a Mexican telenovela.

In the run-up to the 1998 election, Morales was the candidate who most worried George Bush. "The entire focus was on Morales. Bush did not want Dan Morales. He did not want Morales to win," said a Republican campaign consultant to the 1998 election. Morales was the last star in the Democratic Party's fading constellation, the only Democratic incumbent on the statewide ballot. If he could be eliminated—and the Democrats running for open seats defeated—the party that eight years earlier had a lock on every statewide office would hold none. And every statewide office is a power base, providing patronage, employment for campaign operatives, publicity platforms, and a farm team to develop new talent.

Eliminating Morales was a critical step in Rove's project of dismantling the party from the top down. If he could do it in 1998, a Republican sweep from the top of the ballot down would be easier to achieve in 2002. Morales had also talked about running for governor. At the top or close to the top of the ballot, a star with Morales' crossover appeal would discourage some voters from voting the straight Republican ticket that was becoming more common in Texas.

Rove also had a personal reason for targeting Dan Morales. A year into Bush's first term, the Democratic attorney general had filed suit against the nation's big tobacco companies, to recover some of the money the state had incurred in treating tobacco-related illness. To prepare for the lawsuit, the lawyers Morales hired to represent the state decided to question Rove. Pitting a strong candidate against Morales also allowed Rove to settle the score with the attorney general who had dragged him into a lawyer's office, put him under oath, and subjected him to a deposition by Democratic trial lawyers hired to represent the state in a lawsuit against the tobacco industry.

To kill two birds—Pauken and Morales—with one stone, Rove recruited to the Republican side of the race John Cornyn, a San Antonio lawyer who had once earned a living defending insurance companies, and who remained a faithful friend of the industry in the votes he cast as a justice on the Texas Supreme Court. Trim, tall, courtly, and blessed with prematurely white hair, Cornyn had more box-office appeal than the shorter, stocky Pauken. But because the Supreme Court is invisible to most voters—the Court of Criminal Appeals is the rocket-docket forum to executions in Texas—Cornyn didn't have the high profile Pauken did. So Rove's handpicked candidate entered the race trailing Tom Pauken.

As the state's Republican Party chairman, Tom Pauken was an irritant for George Bush. As the state's independent attorney general he would be a real threat. And it appeared that the underfunded Pauken, with broad-based support from hardcore Reagan Republicans and evangelical Christians, would defeat Rove's handpicked candidate, until an odd thing happened. Barry Williamson, a Republican who was leaving the Texas Railroad Commission to run for comptroller, changed his mind and joined the attorney general's race. Williamson had won his first election to statewide office four years earlier, when Rove was advising his campaign. His entry in the race, with $1 million to spend, meant that two candidates, both flush with cash and both linked to Karl Rove, were now running against Tom Pauken.

"Rove was not supposed to get involved in Republican primaries," said a source close to the Cornyn campaign. Rove was so formidable that Republican candidates didn't want him in the primaries. "But Pauken was in the race," the campaign source said. "And Bush hated Pauken. So the whole idea was that in a three-man race, Rove could see that Cornyn was elected." Williamson became the political equivalent of a *banderillero*, the bullring cape man who works on foot, sticking small barbs into the bull's neck— to provoke it and make it charge, while lowering its head to make it easier for the matador to complete the kill.

While Williamson was lowering Pauken's head, Rove was raising the profile of the real candidate in the race. "Karl was worried about Cornyn's name," the Cornyn campaign source said. "He said it was a bad name for politics. Nobody could pronounce it. And John didn't have an issue to run on. So Karl decided he should file the tobacco suit."

Here was another stone to hit his two birds. The tobacco suit that Rove had Cornyn file, according to this campaign source, was a challenge to the contingency fees that had been earned by five attorneys the state had hired to sue the tobacco industry. That original suit had been filed in 1996 by Dan Morales.

The suit had been a difficult issue for Bush. As governor, he had to support going to court to recover billions the state had spent on health care for indigent patients with tobacco-related illnesses. Yet he opposed industry-wide lawsuits like the cases several states already filed against the tobacco industry. Bush had run for office promising tort reform. "Putting an end to junk lawsuits that clog our courts," was a Rove one-liner Bush repeated like a mantra while campaigning. He was successfully pushing a package of tort reforms through the Legislature. And the tobacco companies were major Republican Party donors and underwriters of the party's national conventions. Bush also knew there was neither sufficient staff nor money for the attorney general to undertake the lawsuit. As Mississippi had done, Texas had to retain lawyers on contingency fee. This arrangement would cost the state nothing up front, but if the state prevailed, the fees would enrich the plaintiffs' lawyers hired by the state. And most (if not all) plaintiffs' lawyers, or trial lawyers, are Democrats. Derided by the senior George Bush as "trial lawyers in tassel loafers," they were the very Democratic funders George W. Bush believed had defeated his father.

The governor was in a box.

So was Rove.

As the governor's campaign strategist, Rove was the architect of the campaign Bush ran against the state's trial lawyers. He helped devise the tort reform program Bush was pushing through the Legislature. And he had a personal conflict. From 1991 to 1996, Rove worked for Philip Morris, the tobacco company with the largest market share in Texas and the nation, earning $3,000 a month. And the way monetary damages are awarded in multiple-defendant lawsuits, Rove's client would take the biggest hit if the state collected on tobacco-related health costs.

The tobacco companies had made Rove's difficult position ever more difficult. In an effort to discourage Morales from suing them, Philip Morris, R. J. Reynolds, Lorillard, and Brown & Williamson hired a political consultant to conduct a push poll targeting Morales. Rove wasn't a tobacco company executive, employee, or even a lobbyist. So he would not be named a party to a tobacco suit. But his professional relationship with Philip Morris made him a potential witness—putting him in the one position political operatives and presidents try very hard to avoid: under oath. The tobacco companies' push poll made that even more likely. Push polls test public support of candidates while measuring the effect of negative information provided by the pollster. They are sometimes used to disseminate negative information—which doesn't have to be true because it is presented as a hypothetical—to "drive up the negatives" on a candidate. In the Morales poll, a straightforward question that asked about support for Morales was followed by a question that asked if it were known that Morales supported the causes of Louis Farrakhan and the Nation of Islam. If the pollster conducts enough telephone interviews or mails out enough polls, he begins a public discussion about Morales' work with Farrakhan, which never occurred. Tobacco's push poll on Morales did in fact link him to Farrakhan, as well as to several other issues which were anathema in Texas: affirmative action, out-of-control youth gangs, and gun control. (Affirmative action was the unkindest cut of them all, as Morales had angered his own party by supporting and expanding a federal appeals court ruling against race-based admissions to the University of Texas Law School.)

Rove had been consulted in the design of the poll and several weeks later was summoned to the office of Philip Morris' Austin lobbyist, Jack Dillard, when the lobby group met to discuss the results of the poll.

A year after Morales filed suit against the tobacco companies—with the reluctant public blessing of Governor Bush—Rove was sitting in the office of a Democratic plaintiffs' lawyer. Under oath, Rove was answering questions about his work as a Philip Morris consultant—and whatever other questions the lawyer from the state's tobacco trial team wanted answered. After Rove was questioned, Morales released transcripts of the deposition to reporters.

This was not a common practice, although depositions are public record.

News accounts of the four-hour deposition were an embarrassment to Rove. Under oath he insisted that in order to avoid a conflict of interest, he never spoke with the governor about tobacco issues. Yet he was forced to admit that he delivered the results of the push poll to Bush executive assistant Joe Allbaugh. After admitting he served as a courier for the tobacco lobby, Rove backtracked. Yes, he had delivered the poll, he said, but only because he knew Allbaugh would never let Bush see it: "If Allbaugh had said let's go show it to the governor, I don't think we ought to. This is a matter between Philip Morris and Morales. I think we ought to ditch the poll."

It required a grueling thirty minutes to get Rove to the position of admitting he had done what he had done:

Q. Isn't it fair to say that you had contact with the office of the Governor on an issue related to tobacco when you said you weren't going to do that?
A. Fine. Yeah.
Q. That is correct, isn't it. Your answer is yes?
A. No.

The lawyers continued until Rove angrily agreed, or almost agreed, that he had been in contact with Bush's office on a tobacco-related issue.

It's rare that a political consultant's core beliefs are tested under oath, but pressed by the Mississippi trial lawyer, Rove even got in a riff on tort reform. He said he had crafted Bush's message about the excessive influence of trial lawyers. He referred to the "utility of frivolous and junk suits as a political issue." And when pressed to explain frivolous lawsuits, Rove responded with the anecdotal bite tort reformers routinely rely on to support their position:

> The woman from North Texas who buys her son a car or a grandson a car to drive back and forth to community college in Oklahoma and then gets sued when he has an accident. Or the guy in Lubbock who lends a ladder to his neighbor and then proceeds to get sued by his neighbor when his neighbor falls off the ladder for not having instructed him properly that the ladder is dangerous.

Suddenly, in the context of a contentious deposition, without missing a lick, the deponent shifted into the campaign mode:

> And my opinion is that there are too many lawsuits and too many frivolous claims by people against other people, that the legal system is jerry-rigged. And it's rigged in a certain way.

Gesturing in the direction of the portly lawyer interrogating him, Rove said there are health risks with certain products like saccharine, but the tradeoff is the health risks related to obesity.

In the end the state's lawyers got little they could have used in court. And Rove never took the witness stand. But the industry settled with the state for $17 billion, and $3 billion in legal fees that would be paid separately by the tobacco companies. The five trial lawyers were going to collect paychecks that would put them in a tax bracket with Halliburton's Dick Cheney, Enron's Ken Lay, or GM's Jack Welch. It was more than Rove could stomach. Billions in discretionary income in the hands of five men with a history of underwriting Democratic candidates could undo all the party-building Rove had accomplished since arriving in Texas twenty years earlier. After all, Texas is the Wild West of Campaign Finance: Any individual can give any amount of money to any candidate, as long as it is declared. The tobacco fees might mean that Democratic candidates for statewide office would have access to the kind of financial backing that had heretofore been available only to Republicans.

It was at this point that Rove pushed John Cornyn into the Beaux Arts federal courthouse that sits astride the state line in Texarkana, where the complex tobacco suit had just been settled. Cornyn—who had resigned from the Supreme Court to run for an office that would make him the lawyer for the state of Texas—stood in the courtroom and announced that he was "a private citizen" intervening in a multibillion-dollar lawsuit that all the involved parties had agreed was over. And Judge David Folsom—who over two years had presided over hundreds of hearings, ruled on the admissibility of hundreds of thousands of documents, and resolved countless disputes between tobacco company lawyers and lawyers hired by the state—suddenly must have regretted leaving a lucrative law practice to preside over a courtroom being turned into a stage for second-rate political melodrama. (And it would only get worse. Bush filed his own motion to intervene, sending staff attorneys to Texarkana to take on the attorney general and the trial lawyers. It's hard to imagine Bush would take such an action without consulting Rove. It's also a safe assumption that Rove was consulted when Bush wisely withdrew his motion after several months.)

If jumping into a settled case was an egregious abuse of the federal court system, it was also smart politics. The candidate with the name that no one could pronounce had found his issue. Though the legal fees were set by an arbitration panel acceptable to all parties, did not come out of the state's $17 billion settlement, and would revert to the tobacco companies if overturned, Cornyn could claim he was defending Texans against greedy trial lawyers.

In a bolt from the blue, Dan Morales announced in December 1997 that he was not running for reelection, and he was subsequently investigated by the feds for trying to secure a half billion dollar legal fee for an attorney he had secretly brought into the tobacco case. In the Republican race, Cornyn forced Pauken into a runoff and Williamson out of elective office and into the daily schmooze of the corporate lobby. Then, with $1.5 million provided by a tort-reform PAC and hundreds of thousands of dollars from the tobacco companies, Cornyn sent the underfunded Tom Pauken back home to Dallas.

Two years later in his law office, Pauken reflected on his defeat. "When I became party chair," he said, "Karl discouraged people from giving to the party. The whole time I was chair, we didn't get any Enron money, because Karl was close to those people and dissuaded them. It was difficult." So Pauken knew what to expect when he entered the attorney general's race. He would get little money from the party's big corporate donors. And he would campaign against a candidate selected and managed by Karl Rove. "Cornyn was Karl's candidate in the AG race," Pauken said. What Pauken didn't anticipate was a third candidate brought to serve as a spoiler. In the end he was outspent and outsmarted by Bush's Boy Genius. Pauken believes that Rove called the shots at Williamson's campaign, or at least that the political consultant running Williamson's campaign was a little too tight with Karl Rove.

"Rove was close to the Williamson campaign, to that heavy-set campaign manager from the Northeast," Pauken said. "Heavy-set" is a bit of an understatement. David Carney, brought in from New Hampshire to run Williamson's campaign, stands six-four and weighs 325 pounds. Like Rove, he was a disciple of the late Lee Atwater. His negative ads, directed at both Cornyn and Pauken, seemed to hurt Pauken most. With no money to buy TV, Pauken couldn't respond.

"I'm not mad at him," Pauken said of Rove. "I beat him. He beat me. That's life: I'm in political exile, and Karl's running the country."

Now Rove had the opportunity to dispose of the last member of the Democrats' celebrated class of '82. Running in Dan Morales' place was former Democratic Attorney General Jim Mattox, first elected to statewide office with Ann Richards, Jim Hightower, Garry Mauro, and Mark White. Rove directed John Cornyn's disciplined, well-financed, campaign against Mattox—the last of the traditional "lib-lab" Democrats—those who represented the liberal-labor wing of Texas' Democratic Party. Mattox was once known as the junk-yard dog of Texas politics because of his aggressive campaign tactics. In 1998, he met his match. With Karl Rove calling the shots, John Cornyn won the race. Four years later, he would be elected to the United States Senate, and the fight Karl Rove started over the $3 billion the lawyers earned representing the state would still be tied up in a district court in Houston.

Set in low relief in the transcript of Rove's deposition in the initial suit—the one that may have portended the end of the career of Dan Morales—is a professional résumé so extraordinary that it must be considered more newsworthy than the embarrassing accounts of Rove's four hours under oath.

In the course of questioning Rove about his background, Mississippi trial lawyer Charles Mikhail put down on paper a professional profile of the man who at the time remained largely behind the scenes. There were interesting bits of news, such as Rove's admission for the first time that he had helped on George W. Bush's 1978 congressional race—which Bush had to deny at the time because Rove was perceived to be too liberal in the West Texas district where Bush was running. And Rove's mention of filing suit against former U.S. Attorney General Richard Thornburgh—after he failed to pay a bill he incurred when Karl Rove + Company ran his failed senatorial race in Pennsylvania in 1991. But what is truly stunning is the account of Rove's work in Texas since he answered the call of the elder George Bush in 1977.

In 1981, with the financial support of one of the state's Republican aristocrats, polo playing South Texas rancher Tobin Williams, Rove founded the direct mail consulting firm, Karl Rove + Company. The list of Republican clients—and one Democrat (Phil Gramm in 1982)—defines the remaking of the political landscape in Texas:

Q. Mr. Rove, in the state of Texas other than Senator Hutchison and Governor Bush, what other clients have you had in political campaigns?

A. I'm not going to be able to remember them all, but Governor Clements in '86. Railroad Commissioner Kent Hance in '88. Treasurer [Kay Bailey] Hutchison's '90 race. State Senate campaigns at various times of Teel Bivins. Troy Fraser, Robert Duncan, Florence Shapiro, David Sibley, Bill Ratliff, Steve Ogden. I'm leaving somebody out in the Senate. State House, a number of State House races. Todd Staples, Troy Fraser when he was in the House. Congressman Lamar Smith. Congressman Joe Barton.

Q. Members of the Supreme Court?

A. Every Republican member of the Supreme Court. Railroad
Commissioner Barry Williamson. Railroad Commissioner Carole
Rylander.

Rove was working from memory and forgot Hance's 1990 primary race for governor. Six months after the deposition, the only
Democratic justice on the nine-member Supreme Court would
retire to be replaced by a Rove client. And John Cornyn might have
been counted twice; he was leaving the Supreme Court to run for
attorney general.

News is what's happening at the moment. But an accurate sub-
head to the *Austin American-Statesman* headline, "State Lawyers
Grill Bush Aide About Tobacco Role," would have pointed to a
story of far more durable news value. It might have read: "Rove
Admits to Making Texas a Republican State."

"What's your batting average?" the lawyer asked Rove.

Rove responded as if he'd been asked to state his name.

"Pretty high."

7

God Bless Texas

As the 1996 presidential race approached, George W. Bush politely and firmly voiced his support for Texas' distinguished U.S. senator, Phil Gramm. A former Texas A&M economics professor, Gramm had started his political career with an unsuccessful conservative Democratic challenge to Lloyd Bentsen in 1982. Then, with Karl Rove's help, he had won a central Texas congressional seat as a Democrat. Gramm announced next that he was switching parties and was going to resign his seat, so that people could decide if they still wanted him. Gramm had made his switch to the Republicans come off like an act of courage. When John Tower decided not to seek reelection to his U.S. Senate seat in 1984, Gramm moved in, destroying a liberal Austin legislator named Lloyd Doggett in one of the meanest campaigns ever directed by Rove. The quip, "Even his friends don't like him," dogged Gramm's angry and rather solitary march through Washington's halls of power.

Following the rout of the Democrats in the 1994 midterm elections, Gramm concluded that he was just the man to put an end to the presidency of Bill Clinton. In a speech that became the earmark of his campaign, Gramm bawled that he had "the best friend a politician can have—money," a line that Rove surely did not supply his former client.

The Gramm presidential race was a disaster: Republicans could not be persuaded to see their future in a man with the visage and mien of a snapping turtle. Whom could they turn to? Steve Forbes? Pat Buchanan? Bob Dole, the old reliable, finally got his turn, and persuaded Jack Kemp to join him on the ticket. Conservative Republicans watched the election unfold in fury and disbelief as Clinton cruised to an effortless reelection.

Amid the grumbling, the Texas governor's presidential campaign edged toward its dawn. "There's no magic moment," Karl Rove would say of how people were responding to George W. Bush, "but sometime during the '96 campaign, you know, people were saying, 'You've done such a marvelous job here. Why don't you—I wish you were the candidate. I wish you were the vice presidential running mate.' . . . It was other people coming to him and saying, 'Think about this.' And his first reaction was dismissive, and then shortly after the '96 elections there's the story about Karen [Hughes] coming in with a poll saying he was the front-runner. And somewhere in that period of time, somewhere in those passage of months after '96 he began to seriously think about it."

Rove went on: "There were three separate wars to be fought, and one of them was the preliminary for the nomination—to win the pre-primary primary. Then there was the primary process and then the general election. And, yes, there were battle plans for each one of them, and, yes, we began thinking about them. A lot of people began thinking about them relatively early, that is to say sometime in '96. Late '96, early '97 there were some discussions, but then serious work in '97 and early '98."

The first challenge, which Phil Gramm never rose beyond, was money. "There would be the primary of money," Rove said. "You know, could you raise the amount of money necessary. . . . The general conventional wisdom was $25 million by the end of the year prior to the primary season." Rove stroked the governor's ego, telling him he already knew how to run for the presidency—the 1994 campaign in Texas had been a sneak preview. "That really was the model for the 2000 campaign," Rove said. "It was, 'Okay, if I'm going to run, I've got to have a vision.' In fact that was his big issue. . . . 'Do I feel I've got something worthy to take to the country? And if I do, I'll run. If I don't, I won't.'"

The questions of capability did not just concern the candidate, of course. The Republicans had just suffered two straight disasters in presidential elections, and Karl Rove was as likely as anyone to lead them out of the wilderness. "No, I haven't run a national campaign, but who has?" he growled. "Jim Baker?" Rove was impudently biting the hand that once generously fed him, perhaps not realizing that the campaign would need to make use of Baker before it was all over. But Rove knew from 1994 that the most successful call to political action was one that looked to the future and claimed it. George W. Bush would not be elected if his campaign was perceived as a re-run of his dad's presidency, with the same aging cast of characters. "Do you populate the campaign with people from 1908?" he asked rhetorically. "No!"

Rove wanted to cultivate the impression of a spontaneous groundswell of people eager to support Bush. From Austin the call went out to issues advisers, GOP members of congress, grassroots organizers. In the meantime, the governor would win reelection in a display of his enormous popularity in Texas. Which was genuine, as Democrats knew all too well.

Someone had asked Ann Richards what she would have done differently if she had known she was going to have just one term. "Oh, I would have raised a little more hell," she replied. After her loss she made a Super Bowl commercial debating the merits of potato chips with her partner in sudden retirement, former New York governor Mario Cuomo. She embarked on a new life as a consultant and corporate board member, on the go between New York, Washington, and Mexico City. She achieved even greater fame as a guest pundit on the political talk shows, and she was making money for the first time in her life. When she was back in Austin she went to movies with her old friend and steady date, the writer Bud Shrake. She liked not having to be chaperoned by a trooper from the Department of Public Safety. And she knew the numbers in Texas. She wasn't about to seek a rematch with George W. Bush. As a candidate she was through.

Who could run against Bush, then? The smooth and urbane former mayor of San Antonio, Henry Cisneros, the Hamlet of Texas Democratic politics, was in Clinton's cabinet as the Secretary of Housing and Urban Development. But during a routine background check, Cisneros had lied to the FBI about money he had paid to his former mistress, and ultimately would plead guilty to a misdemeanor count of lying to a federal official. Bob Bullock had signaled that he wouldn't be running for any office next time around. The business-oriented comptroller, John Sharp, was ballyhooed as the Democrats' great white hope, but he wanted no part of a dust-up with Bush.

Sharp had been a state senator and claimed to love the legislative process; he wanted to succeed Bullock as lieutenant governor. Sharp was among the Democrats who believed the best politics was to concede the top spot on the ballot and make the presidential contender run against nobody. It would keep straight-ticket Republican voters at home and give candidates for other offices, like Sharp, a better chance. The argument was a measure of just how dispirited and marginalized the Democrats had become in Texas.

Sharp and land commissioner Garry Mauro had been student leaders together at Texas A&M, and in the years since they had been allies and friends and increasingly bitter rivals. Finally seeing his chance for the governorship, Mauro decided he would run.

Mauro worked hard to tidy up his image. During his travails in the eighties, reporters would smirk and speculate on who had done the perm of his signature curly locks, until Mauro and his wife had a son with the identical curly hair. Someone convinced Mauro it was time to change his hairstyle, and that may have been a mistake. Before, he at least had had a distinctive appearance, even if it was a nod to the sixties; now he looked like just another smooth-faced pol with a razor cut.

Mauro knew that in order to run he had to try to change the subject from the FBI investigation and other implications that he cut too many ethical corners. Mauro had a loyal base, especially among Hispanics on the border, but raising money was going to be a significant problem. In late 1997 he looked at his meager campaign fund and decided he would put out a book that explained himself to the electorate. *Beaches, Bureaucrats and Big Oil* was a vanity book, and he hired a team of writers to help him get it out [one of the authors of this book was the editor], but he talked the stories through until he thought every line was right. He talked about public land, oil spills, and ships' dumping of garbage in the Gulf, the wisdom of Sam Houston and Bob Bullock. From Texas political writers he got the best press of his life. He embarked on a book tour, saying he was going to let people tell him whether he ought to run.

A year out from the election, he announced his candidacy, flying by private plane to several cities in the state, and it was a great day for him. But as the plane came back to Austin Mauro fell to brooding, thinking he would be met by the same cynical gang of reporters, sneering their unpleasant questions about his character. Instead there was a rowdy crowd of people holding up signs. For a few short weeks he could almost believe he had a chance.

Mauro had convincing polls showing that managed health care was suddenly a hot issue. He rolled the dice, spent what money he had, and went on TV with the issue, early in the summer of 1998. He looked good and sounded smart, yet the polls in favor of Bush didn't move. This time, Rove had Bush running on a single issue—the governor was determined that "social promotion" of educationally deficient grade-schoolers could no longer be allowed. Democrats heard it and gaped at each other. That was all Bush had?

It was all he needed. Rove didn't even have to put the headlines about Mauro and the FBI on the air. With speculation about the 2000 presidential campaign building, Bush's campaign was going to be heavily covered by the national media, just because of who he was. And because he spent $25 million on the campaign while his opponent spent less than $3 million.

Bush and Rove wanted to prove to the national audience that the candidate had strong support among Hispanics, so they hired a San Antonio consultant and spent more money on Spanish-language radio ads than Mauro could budget for his entire campaign. The Republicans went all-out to carry even traditionally Democratic, heavily Hispanic El Paso, and Mauro was obligated to fight desperately to salvage that outpost.

Rove consented to put Bush onstage with the Democrat in one debate. It took place in El Paso, which is in the mountain time zone, ensuring that in the state's major population centers it would be seen only by political junkies. The debate was one of the few times Bush's arrogance showed in public. He was inarticulate and barely civil, and he clearly lost the debate. But it was like Walter Mondale winning a presidential debate with Ronald Reagan in 1984—so what? Mauro would hold the line in El Paso, but just barely. Bush would get 49 percent.

The final twist of the knife was applied not by Rove, but by an irascible old man Rove had once terrified by sending an FBI agent after him. Or so Bob Bullock believed. In failing health—he had continued to chain-smoke, despite being diagnosed with lung cancer—Bullock had turned his attention to the construction of a new museum of Texas history (which would eventually be named after him) and sprucing up the State Cemetery, where he would soon be buried. Bullock was a complex character—the most fascinating Texas politician of his generation, if all the stories were to be sorted out and told. Who knows what drove him? "God bless Texas" was his signature signoff, and perhaps Bullock just believed one candidate would be better for Texas than the other, as he said. But Bush's election was a foregone conclusion, which made Bullock's endorsement of Bush over Mauro seem gratuitously cruel. Mauro had been Bullock's friend, his hand-picked protégé. Bullock had been godfather at the baptism of Mauro's little boy. He didn't have to break anybody's heart.

The Rove team had timed Bush's endorsements with a rhythm that Mauro later likened to Chinese water torture, culminating in the announcement that Bullock was endorsing George W. Bush. When it came, Mauro and his people were thunderstruck. They couldn't think of anything to say.

In the end, Mauro would barely break 40 percent, giving Bush what the commentators liked to call a record-setting mandate of approval. John Sharp would lose a cliffhanger to the Republican lieutenant governor candidate, who was none other than Karl Rove's discovery and sometime star, Rick Perry. Sharp blamed Mauro for his loss, saying his weakness brought the whole ticket down. But Bush didn't waste any time on a postmortem. As the frontrunner for the 2000 Republican presidential nomination, he had people to see and places to be.

8

The Yellow Rose Garden

"The Yellow Rose of Texas" is a rousing song that celebrates the apocryphal seduction of General Antonio López de Santa Anna by a mulatto named Emily West. During the final battle of Texas' war for independence from Mexico, she kept the general occupied in his tent while Sam Houston's soldiers swept down on the Mexican army camped on the banks of the San Jacinto River. George Bush's Yellow Rose Garden campaign was an equally spectacular act of seduction, planned and executed by Karl Rove. Rove kept the American public occupied with a parade of political functionaries arriving at the Governor's Mansion in Austin to endorse George W. Bush. While the public was engaged with four months of political theater, Rove raised money, home-schooled his candidate, and created the illusion that a thoughtful but reluctant governor of Texas was pondering the many requests that he run for president.

George W. Bush was ready for neither a presidential campaign nor the presidency when the Texas Legislature convened in January 1999. His most glaring weakness was a woeful ignorance about the world beyond Texas and Washington. Although he grew up in the shadow of a father who had been an ambassador to China, the U.S. delegate to the United Nations, and the director of the Central Intelligence Agency, Bush had never demonstrated a grasp of—or even an interest in—foreign affairs. In fact he hardly demonstrated much interest in domestic policy affairs in Texas, even after his upset victory over Ann Richards a little over four years earlier. None of this was a great liability in a state whose constitutional limitations on the governor's powers suited Bush's managerial style of governing.

But Bush was running for the presidency.

Rove conceived of a campaign that would turn his candidate's weakness into a strength—perhaps a virtue. He would keep the governor under wraps, while at the same time keeping him in the public eye. The message was simple. Bush had a great deal to say about the great national and international issues confronting the world's most powerful nation. And he would speak to all those issues.

But only after he fulfilled his responsibility to the voters in Texas, who elected him and depended on him to lead and govern. The January-to-June 1999 legislative session provided Bush a perfect opportunity to avoid exposure to the media. He would campaign only after the session ended, when the demands of office were not so urgent.

Rove knew, as did the Austin press corps, that Bush was not ready for prime time in January 1999. He was possessed of neither Bill Clinton's passion for policy nor Rove's voracious appetite for books. As governor, he had governed much as Ronald Reagan had as president—disengaged from the details of legislation and the history that informed it. Keeping Bush in the Governor's Mansion and his Capitol office was not a hastily conceived response to his lack of preparation; it was a carefully designed strategy. The extra study time was helpful. Yet Rove had already decided Bush would begin to "campaign" in the summer, shortly before the Iowa Straw Poll.

Nothing, in fact, had been hastily conceived.

In 1995, as he tells it, Rove decided that Bush would be "a fabulous candidate" for president—assuming he could govern as governor. So by 1999, Rove had been thinking about the campaign for five years and planning for three. The organizational plan for a national presidential campaign was in place long before legislators arrived in Austin that January. A year earlier Rove had set up campaign offices in each state, where staffs and directors could begin their work when the campaign required it.

Not only were campaign offices in place; the "spontaneous" national movement that would urge Bush to run was ready to move. In the fall of 1998 Rove had called Mississippi lawyer-lobbyist Haley Barbour. Barbour had served as the Republican Party's national chairman and was still a big player in the party. Rove pitched his plan to Barbour, as he would pitch it to others. He intended to persuade name Republicans, mostly in their forties and fifties, to join an exploratory committee. He wanted to avoid party leaders associated with Bush's father, because he wanted to make sure the committee looked like the future of the party—the next generation of Republican leaders, not its past.

It was a bold request. Rove was asking a party leader to commit to a presidential candidate more than a year before the first caucus or primary. Barbour said he would consider it. A one-on-one conversation with Bush himself finally closed the deal. (Bush may not have been openly working on Rove's quiet campaign to make him president, but he was not uninvolved.) While waiting for Barbour to come aboard, Rove had continued to work the phones, putting together a committee of Republican leaders willing to join the Bush team.

Republican governors also joined the effort. Montana's Marc Racicot had offered Bush his services in 1997 and Rove took him up on it. Michigan's John Engler was leaning on the Republican Governors' Association, playing on the political capital he had accrued while building the organization. As Bush was modestly suggesting he would consider running if there was support for his candidacy, Engler was urging governors to support Bush's candidacy—warning them not to wait until the train left the station. Or, as Rove would tell those who were not ready to commit: "Keep your powder dry." He wanted them to be ready to join the campaign when Bush announced

As the legislative session began, so did Rove's "spontaneous" groundswell of endorsements and public entreaties for Bush to run. Reporters were summoned to the south lawn of the mansion for carefully choreographed press conferences that would begin with a dignified procession of Republican governors emerging from the governor's residence. "This was neither requested nor authorized by Governor Bush," Mark Racicot said during one such event (which did raise the question about how they had gotten onto the grounds). Racicot was speaking for twelve governors who had traveled to Austin to pledge their support to Bush. He promised three more would soon follow. Another four governors would announce at a later date. With the governors came their statewide fundraising and campaign organizations. These events spared Bush from unseemly self-promotion and allowed him the time to attend to the responsibilities of the office. The endorsement parade charade was reminiscent of the "Chinese water torture" that Garry Mauro had experienced in his 1998 campaign against Bush, when endorsements were announced at regular intervals in the months before the election.

Also traveling to Austin were members of Congress, though Rove had to manage them with discretion, since Bush was running as an outsider, against Washington. Republican House Whip Tom DeLay's reputation for crude, muscular politics, for example, kept him off the Bush exploratory committee—although he was a dedicated supporter of the governor. His surrogate, the more benign deputy whip, Roy Blunt of Missouri, signed on in his stead. One of the messages Rove had Bush advancing was that government in Texas worked because of an absence of partisan politics (a claim utterly divorced from the reality of the political campaigns Rove had run since arriving in Texas twenty years earlier). To bring in Republican Party heavies from Washington risked association with what Bush called "the partisan politics of Washington, D.C." "I'm a uniter, not a divider," Bush would say (many, many times).

Foreign dignitaries were also paraded through the Governor's Mansion. On one February afternoon, William Hague, then head of Britain's Conservative Party, stood beaming as Bush predicted that the ineffectual Hague would become a prime minister as great as Winston Churchill (a notion that no doubt provoked a laugh riot at 10 Downing Street and in the editorial offices of even the most conservative Fleet Street dailies). On another afternoon, Bush introduced former Canadian Prime Minster Brian Mulroney in the House gallery. Another caller at the mansion was Qatar's foreign minister, Sheik Hamad bin Jassim bin Jabr al-Thani. The sheik was accompanied by his country's ambassador. "I get ambassadors that come all the time," Bush said. "This presidential speculation has seemed to have caused more governments to send their ambassadors my way. So I look forward to listening."

This was hardly an "A-List" of the world's leaders. Sheik Hamad was not a household name. Hague was so ineffective as a party leader that he is now banished from the leadership circles of his own party. And the six years Mulroney had been out of office were hardly sufficient for members of his Progressive Conservative Party to forget how badly he had governed. None of that mattered. Bush's greatest deficit, his slippery grasp of foreign policy issues, was being addressed by suggesting that the world's leaders were coming to Austin and that the governor was spending his time cloistered in the mansion with them—"listening," and therefore learning.

The south lawn of the Governor's Mansion (literalists should know there's no actual Yellow Rose Garden), and at times the mansion itself, were turned into sets for carefully choreographed events that were part of a campaign that was not supposed to exist. Yet the non-campaign was already more sophisticated than anything Bush's Republican rivals would field after their campaigns hit the road. In April, as the pace of events picked up, a Bush adviser who couldn't contain himself whispered to *The Weekly Standard's* Fred Barnes that Rove was the genius behind the throne: "He's been orchestrating all this. He's done a marvelous job, yet practically no one's accused him of manipulating it."

By that time, Rove had also orchestrated the campaign's first primary victory—the one Rove refers to as "the money primary"—which occurs before any formal declaration of candidacy. In that campaign Bush easily defeated John McCain, Gary Bauer, Lamar Alexander, Alan Keyes, Elizabeth Dole, and Pat Buchanan. It was a primary contest Rove began himself, before he brought in Donald L. Evans, Bush's old friend from the West Texas oilfields, to direct fundraising. While Evans would be the face on the fundraising campaign, Rove was the brain behind it. In an Austin office that one writer described as a virtual smoke-filled room, Rove made phone calls, sent faxes and at times dealt with as many as 300 e-mail messages a day. The man with the direct-mail experience and the best lists and Rolodex in the universe of Republican Party donors was reaching out of Austin and into their pockets. He had $7 million in the bank a month after Bush announced he might run—while Dan Quayle had raised $2 million, John McCain $1.6 million, and Christian conservative Gary Bauer $1.3 million. None of the others in the crowded Republican pack had reached the million-dollar mark. In fact, the money primary might have been over on March 31, 1999, the day Bush raised $2.3 million. On that day alone Bush brought in more than what John McCain had raised in all the previous months. By the end of June (when the Iowa Straw Poll was held), Rove and Evans had raised $36.4 million—more than the aggregate total raised by all of Bush's primary opponents. The only competition Rove faced in the money primary was the $38 million check Steve Forbes wrote to cover the cost of his own campaign—if that's considered fundraising. Though the visible political battle was yet to be joined, in reality the contest for the Republican presidential nomination was over before it began.

While the façade and south lawn of the mansion served as a stage for politicians expounding on reasons for endorsing Bush, other visitors were discreetly chauffeured in and out the back gate. Experts

from across the country came to Austin to home-school Bush on the
public policy issues he had to master before being exposed to the
press and the public. Among them were the foreign policy scholar
Condoleezza Rice; Herb Stein, who had chaired Richard Nixon's
Council of Economic Advisers; former secretary of state George
Shultz; and former Swedish Prime Minister Carl Bildt, who at the
time was the UN special envoy to the Balkans.

North of the mansion, in the Capitol building, legislators faced
enormous pressure to pass laws that would shore up Bush's conservative image. (If there was one pre-primary miscalculation Rove
made, it was the assumption that the greatest threat Bush would
face in the primary was political commentator Pat Buchanan.) The
centerpiece of Bush's legislative agenda was the $2 billion tax cut,
but there were other things to accomplish as well. A lax environmental law that locked the state out of compliance with federal EPA
clean air mandates was passed to provide the campaign a model of
cooperation with industry. A welfare bill with sanctions Democrats
found too punitive was repeatedly reworked and referred to "the
political office" watched over by Rove. Equally important was that
certain legislation be stopped, such as a bill that would have prohibited the execution of mentally retarded individuals convicted of
murder.

"You have to understand that Karl Rove believes that you govern
to be reelected," said an Austin political consultant. "They were the
most politically driven government we have ever had in Texas. And
they are more politically driven now that they're in Washington."

As the pre-campaign grew into a campaign, Rove moved from
the periphery of campaign events closer to the candidate at the cen-

ter of the stage. He was more available than he had previously been, talking more to reporters, arguing the significance of polling trends, making predictions, offering reporters more than they asked for.

Bush would win the nomination, he said, because the Haley Barbours of the party, and 114 U.S. House members, and fourteen U.S. Senators, and a substantial majority of Republican governors had endorsed him. He was the candidate of the establishment, and he was ahead by more than ten points in the polls. Historically, any candidate who combined those two factors won the nomination. It was one of many predictors Rove would refer to.

When the media outlets handicapping the race got it wrong, Rove called them on it. "*Newsweek*'s bullshit," he told Austin reporter Robert Bryce in response to a question at the end of one press conference about the newsweekly's prediction that Bush was at a disadvantage in the general election. In less than a minute, Rove ran the numbers on how Bush would beat Gore in the Electoral College. "It's a rather simple equation," Rove said. "One hundred, 114, twelve, equals forty-four . . . There are 100 Electoral College votes between the Sierra Nevadas and the Missouri River—from Idaho to North Dakota and from Arizona to Texas and everything in between plus Alaska," Rove said. And all are in "good shape for Bush. Solid. In fact they [the Gore campaign] are only making a play for one of those states.

"Take 114 in the South, not including Tennessee. And they are only playing essentially for three of those states: Louisiana, Arkansas, and Florida. But we are in good shape in all three of those. Indiana gives us twelve more. That gets us to 226. That leaves forty-four more to go.

"We've got to put forty-four more to go—out of four in Maine, four in New Hampshire, three in Delaware, twenty-three in Pennsylvania, twenty-one in Ohio, eighteen in Michigan, eleven in Wisconsin, eleven in Missouri, twenty-two in Illinois, seven in Iowa, eleven in Washington state, seven in Oregon," Rove said. "We have to find forty-four out of that . . . what is it, 119? [It's 142.] And we have thirty-two of them locked up. Maybe thirty-six."

Bryce walked away a believer—although he would later recall Rove's response—"No. No. No. No. Not going to happen!"—when he said his reading of the electoral map suggested that Gore could win the popular vote and lose in the Electoral College. There were very few instances when Rove did not have an answer that stated or implied the inevitability of the Bush presidency.

In March 1999 Bush told Rove he had to sell his consulting firm if he wanted to be a part of the campaign. Rove's sister, Reba Hammond, said her family was surprised that Bush—who was being made enormously wealthy by the sale of the Texas Rangers baseball team and its taxpayer-financed stadium—made her brother sell the company he had worked so hard to build. "We all thought it was kind of odd," she said. "Why didn't he just take a sabbatical? And he told us he didn't sell it for quite the price he wanted." A past employee of the consulting business said that Rove told him Bush ordered the sale because he "wanted 120 percent of his attention. He wanted him full-time—day and night."

Rove was already fully engaged. For the past two years he had talked to Bush at least twice a day. With the sale of Karl Rove + Company, not only was he Bush's full-time employee; he was in full control of the campaign. The guy who had once handed the family car keys to a young George W. Bush was now in the driver's seat.

The fights in Texas, the bugging of the Clements campaign, the tabloid that recycled the story of Mark White's college DWI—they all seemed like the script from another play. Rove and his wife Darby, a graphic designer at his company, whom he had married in 1986, had bought and remodeled a charming home that had once been a farmhouse. Their son Andrew had been born in 1989, but in school the little boy had some learning difficulties, and the genius dad paid close attention to his son's schooling, helping him get over that hump. Then Rove was staggered a few years later when Darby was diagnosed with breast cancer. It was a terrifying time in their lives, but they had gotten through it—and now her health was good. Nearing fifty, Rove was no longer the perennial College Republican. He had grown up, just as the youthful wildseed George W. Bush had grown up.

Though Bush demanded full-time attention, it's a measure of Rove's enormous energy that during that run-up to 2002 he found time to teach a popular course on politics at the University of Texas' LBJ School of Public Affairs—a graduate program for aspiring bureaucrats. Rove had half a dozen colleges on his transcript by now, but he still did not have a bachelor's degree, and it bothered him. While finishing off the last of the state's Democrats and preparing to take on the daunting task of running a presidential campaign, he enrolled in a Ph.D. program in the university's first-rate history department. By the time he would arrive in Washington in 2001, the movers would dolly out 148 boxes of books. Most of them were about politics.

From the governor's office and the formative presidential campaign there were stories that Bush would indulge great yawns when Rove launched into one of his political monologues. "Oh, very nice point, Karl," Bush would snicker when he thought a Rove remark or proposal was off the wall. A reporter asked a Bush team insider how sensitive Rove was to these jibes. "I don't know. He takes some rough ones." In Bush's management style, what mattered was keeping all disagreement inside the tent. There was just one boss and candidate—just one star—and everyone on the team was expected to conform to his or her roles. Sometimes Rove was tempted to wax verbose and accept credit that everyone in Austin knew he deserved. According to the *Dallas Morning News*, on one occasion Bush saw some reporters gathered around his adviser and groused: "Is the Rove news conference over?" Chastened, Rove moved away from them. Darby Rove said she believed her husband's friendship with Bush was more philosophical than personal. She said Karl "has hundreds of friends and no one he's intimate with" outside their small family. As the presidential race took form, Rove told another Texas newspaper: "I have no other persona other than Bush."

Even if Bush sometimes poked fun at Rove's eggheadedness, he had to appreciate that Rove's study of politics had made him a master of political narrative. What Rove was doing, as Bush used the Legislature as a pretext to stay in Austin, was creating a story line. The elements of the story included a noble governor who wouldn't abandon his charge until it was complete, the leaders of a political party who wouldn't rest until the governor accepted the call to run for the presidency, financial backers willing to invest in the candidacy, and the inevitability of Bush's election.

It was a political narrative with its own historical antecedent. The Bush campaign was a modern-day version of the campaign of President William McKinley a century earlier. Like Bush, McKinley had been elected to a statewide office limited in its power by constitutional restraints. Also like Bush, McKinley had campaigned in 1896 from the Governor's Mansion, in his case in Ohio. As it developed, Bush's Yellow Rose Garden Campaign became more and more like McKinley's "Front Porch Campaign."

That, at least, was the narrative Rove imposed on it.

There were other historical parallels beyond the porch. McKinley tried to redefine the Republican Party, much as Rove thought he and Bush were doing in their appeal to working-class voters and immigrants. McKinley also faced a Republican Party that was threatened by internal divisions as treacherous as those faced by the modern party, as Christian social conservatives often find themselves at odds with economic conservatives. And McKinley's campaign flowed out of Ohio on a river of money.

In his graduate studies, Rove had naturally focused on Republican politics. He had an interest in and an admiration for Wendell Willkie, whom Franklin D. Roosevelt overwhelmed in 1940. Then he told two distinguished historians on the faculty, Lewis Gould and Robert Divine, that he wanted to set the record straight on the Republican race and national convention of 1896. Rather than becoming a Willkie revisionist, he would resurrect the career of William McKinley.

Rove and his young son spent many nights at the university library, photocopying documents and hauling piles of books to a carrel. Without a bachelor's degree, Rove did not have all the prerequisites for the doctoral quest, of course. The university required him to take an undergraduate course that demonstrated his writing ability, which by all accounts is considerable. He worked hard for a semester, at which point the university discovered that the course he had taken was no longer in the catalogue. His work was all for naught; if he wanted to keep going, he had to take another course of similar description. Incredibly, instead of tongue-lashing some tenure-cushioned dean as he had done to reporters who had crossed Bush, Rove signed up for the course.

After reading all the books and papers he could find, Rove concluded that William McKinley was the most underrated American president. The ballyhooed Texan political strategist Mark Hanna, who was to McKinley as Rove was to Bush, was little more than a fundraiser. The unknown geniuses of the McKinley campaign were two politicos in their thirties. One, Charles Dawes, would rise to be a vice president and ambassador to Great Britain and would win a Nobel Peace Prize. The other was Theodore Roosevelt.

Rove's love of history was evident in the enthusiasm with which he reconstructed the past, using the present tense to do so. Theodore Roosevelt, Rove would enthuse, has the most fabulous job in the world. He's police commissioner of New York. A year later, 1896, he hates it. He backs the wrong candidate for the Republican presidential nomination. He writes a wonderful letter to his sister saying "McKinley, I think he's a dolt. You know, he's just not up to it." And yet by the end of the campaign, Roosevelt has ridden a train across the country to campaign for McKinley. He has enthusiastically campaigned for his candidacy and delivered two important speeches for him before crowds of tens of thousands of people. At the end of the campaign Roosevelt is rescued from obscurity by being rewarded with the job that vaults him into his future: assistant secretary of the Navy.

How could this relic of presidential history be germane to a race that would unfold 104 years later?

"Look," Rove would explain, "the 1896 thing was interesting

only because it represented the kind of election this might be. That is to say, an election [in] which each party's agendas were largely irrelevant or in danger of becoming irrelevant, in which each party had the responsibility of trying to come to cope with a changed circumstance of the country, changed demography, changed economy, changed world situation, changed nature of the party, and the declining power of each party's elite. In the case of McKinley, all the people who fought in the Civil War were dying off, and this was going to be the last election—in fact, it was one election past the point at which the parties could fight on the slogans from the 1860s. No longer could you say 'states' rights' as a Democrat and 'vote as you fought' if you were a Republican.

"So I don't want to carry the analogy too far. But it did allow us to sort of . . . we did steal most prominently the idea of the front porch campaign from it. Only we applied it to the primary, not to the general."

To Rove, history is a flowing continuum, and it's instructive. Like all history buffs, he also enjoys a good yarn. He developed a great admiration for Teddy Roosevelt's virility and decisiveness, as well as for the assassinated president he succeeded. After he himself was one of its occupants, Rove loved to tell the story of how the West Wing of the White House came about. The center of the executive branch needed more office space, and Roosevelt was hectoring the architects, builders, and landscapers to get the project done quickly. Over the years glass conservatories had been erected around the White House, Rove would say, beaming. "People liked to see orange trees growing, that sort of thing. Roosevelt's wife found out they were going to take out the conservatories, and she told the architect, 'You can't do that.'"

Rove paused, then delivered the punch line: Roosevelt turned to the architect and ordered, "Smash the glass houses!" The historian and strategist smiled, then explained that Roosevelt's decisiveness had come at a cost. The builders, hurried by executive fiat, had done shoddy work, and after TR left office, the new addition had to be torn down and rebuilt. Rove summarized the incident with a certain bemusement:

"He got his way, but they had to clean up after him."

9

Firewall

Rove's strategy for taking the Republican nomination read like some inscrutable Taoist treatise: First, align the full power and majesty of the Republican establishment behind your candidate. Then sell him to voters as an outsider eager to upend the status quo.

Both prongs of the plan were necessary. As had been the case in George W. Bush's business career, one of the governor's biggest assets was his ability to attract the support of the wealthy and powerful to enterprises that might seem chancy to the casual onlooker. By the end of June—less than three weeks after he announced his candidacy—his campaign had raised $36.4 million. The best way to convince voters—and, more importantly, contributors—of his viability was to line up the big guns before anyone had a chance to ask questions, so that to question Bush was to question the judgment of his august supporters.

The fundraising wasn't the half of it. Rove was everywhere, setting up campaign headquarters in all fifty states, securing further endorsements, and even buying up potentially embarrassing Web site names like www.georgebushsucks.net and connecting them to the campaign's home page. From the beginning, it was a national campaign, and Rove oversaw every aspect of it. If the devil is in the details, he had found Karl Rove waiting to greet him when he got there.

But given Bush's decidedly local résumé—more than one critic was calling him the least qualified presidential candidate of modern times, and unflattering comparisons to Warren G. Harding were not uncommon—Rove had almost no choice but to run him as an outsider. An electorate fatigued by Bill Clinton's endless dance of equivocation and triangulation (and the virulent Republican reactions it provoked) was ripe for promises to "change the tone in Washington." The pledge was cast in political terms, but the moral implications were clear. Clinton had done Bush a tremendous favor by creating a political climate in which "experience" was a dirty word, or at least tainted by association.

Rove had set up most of the first part of his plan before Bush had even announced his candidacy. Now he set about introducing Bush to the people who at some point would actually have to vote for him. The candidate began to appear with increasing frequency in the states that would determine the frontrunners as the primary season got underway: Iowa, where the first party caucuses would be held in January, and New Hampshire and South Carolina, the sites of early primaries.

The idea was to appear presidential, with the dual purpose of intimidating Bush's challengers and—on some symbolic level—assuaging doubts about his fitness for the office. One staffer recalled the effect the campaign had on the communities through which it passed: "Bush—like most governors—traveled with security, which meant motorcades, cops, flashing lights; and there were always scores of press in pursuit. It was an impressive show that swept people up in its excitement. . . . When it worked, it was like a shadow government in motion. We'd hit a town and it was like nothing they'd ever seen." Bush would emerge from a car, appear before an enormous crowd, uncan his remarks, and disappear back into his motorized phalanx. While this approach minimized the retail politicking that had helped to make him popular in Texas, it also minimized the likelihood of the embarrassing verbal slips he was prone to and ensured that he wouldn't have to deal with the press, a chore he openly disliked, any more than necessary.

It helped that there wasn't much in the way of competition. Of the candidates who were already seeking the Republican nomination by the time Bush entered the race, only self-declared Christian candidate and former Reagan aide Gary Bauer could be considered a fresh face, politically speaking. The others—publishing heir Steve Forbes, Utah Senator Orrin Hatch, former Vice President Dan Quayle, commentator Pat Buchanan, former Tennessee governor Lamar Alexander—were all damaged goods to one extent or another, having attempted the race before and been squelched early on in the process. (They would be joined in September by Alan Keyes, a pro-life candidate whose unpredictable swings between riveting oratory and paranoid ranting earned him the eternal gratitude of a stultified press corps.)

They were all toast, and Rove knew it. His strategy of frontloading the money and endorsements had paid off handsomely, and although Bush would be obligated to go through the motions of a few debates to avoid the appearance of arrogance, it looked like he was on his way to the nomination without having to get out of his car too often. Rove and Karen Hughes had already begun the lengthy process of publicly lowering expectations for the debates, painting the governor as more of a big-picture kind of guy than a big-words kind of guy, an assessment that anyone who'd ever heard him talk found at least partly credible.

On September 27, one final candidate formally entered the race. Senator John McCain of Arizona did not mention the heir-presumptive to the Republican nomination once during his announcement, but every other sentence was an implied reproach to Bush: "There comes a time when our nation's leader can no longer rely on briefing books and talking points," he said. "[The president] is alone in a dark room when the casualty lists come in. I'm not afraid of that burden. I know both the blessing and price of freedom."

McCain's very existence was also an implied reproach to Bush. A Navy pilot who had been shot down over Vietnam, McCain had been held as a POW for five and a half years, during which time he was tortured so severely that thirty years later he still walked with a pronounced limp and was incapable of lifting his arms high enough to comb his own hair. McCain, whose father and grandfather were four-star admirals, was offered early release by his captors, who seemed to think that sending the pilot they called "The Crown Prince" home would make good propaganda material. Citing the military Code of Conduct, which specifies that prisoners must be released in the order they were captured, McCain repeatedly refused early release, and was tortured further for his refusal. He was finally released in 1972, the same year that Bush entered the Texas National Guard.

McCain went on to become a senator from Arizona in the Goldwater conservative mold, though with a bent toward contrariness, as when he took on his own party establishment to battle for campaign finance reform, another linchpin of his campaign: "When our government has been taken from us by the special interests, the big-dollar donors, pride is lost to shame," he said in his announcement. Again, he didn't mention Bush by name. He didn't need to. The governor's fundraising prowess was one of the few things most Americans knew about him.

With McCain in the race, Bush's piles of green suddenly took on a sinister tint. Bush was running as an outsider, not as big money incarnate, but now money was an issue, right up there with his fitness to govern. And the issue was being raised by someone else with just as much claim, if not more, to the outsider tag. Just by declaring his candidacy, McCain was calling into question some of the basic premises of the Bush run.

For Rove, who had never displayed any particular talent for separating the personal from the political, the insurgency was particularly galling. McCain's campaign was being run by a Texas A&M grad named John Weaver, with whom Rove had worked years before, first for Bill Clements in 1986 and then on George Bush's presidential run in 1988. Something had happened between them—a dispute over payment, it was said—and the resulting split was deep and bitter.

The brilliant and mercurial Weaver, nine years Rove's junior, had gone on to become the state party's executive director before facing off against Rove in the 1993 special election to fill Lloyd Bentsen's Senate seat when Bentsen was named Secretary of the Treasury. Rove had won that one, but hadn't stopped there, according to the Weaver camp, who accused him of spreading rumors about Weaver that made it harder and harder for him to find work. Rove's adherents rejoined that Weaver just couldn't handle being everyone's second choice.

Whatever had happened, it was apparently time for a grudge match, and grudge was the operative word. "These guys absolutely detest each other," said a Republican consultant who knew both. "It's as much personal—maybe more—as it is professional." Weaver, who shared his employer's short fuse and who was prone to dark moods—McCain's ironic nickname for him was "Sunny"— was open in his disdain for the Bush campaign, audibly snorting with derision when the governor stumbled during debates. The news that Bush was presidential timber was apparently late in getting to the McCain camp.

Bush's huge monetary advantage over McCain meant that the upstart campaign was forced to operate in a very different fashion from Rove's stately march to victory. McCain later admitted that it was less tactical brilliance than sheer necessity that led him to give reporters unprecedented access, but for whatever reasons it quickly became his hallmark. McCain would sit in a red leather swivel chair at the rear of his bus, dubbed the Straight Talk Express, and talk to reporters for hours at a time with a candor previously unheard of in political campaigns.

McCain's irreverence and forthrightness—a typical comment began with the phrase "One of the many reasons I hate the French . . ."—did not disappear when he was in front of voters. Constrained by their relatively limited resources, McCain and Weaver had written off the Iowa caucuses, which would yield no delegates, and devoted their attention to New Hampshire, barnstorming the state in a series of more than a hundred "town meetings," at which McCain would take any question from whoever showed up. It was at such a meeting in Portsmouth that he announced that as president he would consider shutting down the Portsmouth Naval Base, a major local employer. "I told you when I started this campaign that I would tell you things you don't want to hear," he said.

Judging from the polls, most voters seemed to agree with Bob Dole, who remarked about his fellow senator that if you spend five and a half years in a box, you get to say anything you want. Drawn by his tale of personal heroism (his autobiography, *Faith of My Fathers*, was #2 on the *New York Times* bestseller list), crowds stayed to listen to his pleas for campaign finance reform and honest government. The fact that some of them were disaffected Democrats brought little cheer to the Bush campaign.

Given that McCain was not attacking Bush directly, there was little Rove could legitimately do but bide his time and hope for McCain to scuttle his own boat with a temper tantrum or particularly impolitic remark. But a December incident involving Rove led some reporters to believe that not everyone at headquarters was sitting on their hands.

Someone had started floating rumors that McCain was mentally unstable as a result of being tortured in Vietnam, and that the pressure of the presidency might cause him to snap. Wayne Slater, a reporter for the *Dallas Morning News*, wrote a piece ruminating about the origin of the whispering campaign in which he recounted a number of questionable practices that had been attributed to Rove over the years: teaching college Republicans dirty tricks; circulating a mock newspaper that featured a story about Mark White's drinking and driving when he was a college student; spreading stories about Jim Hightower's alleged role in a contribution kickback scheme; and alerting the press to the fact that Lena Guerrero had lied about graduating from college—all of which had been reported or attributed elsewhere. Slater also reported that candidates Gary Bauer and Steve Forbes had fingered the Bushies as the McCain rumormongers.

In early December, Rove—who had not returned Slater's phone calls about the story—confronted the reporter in the New Hampshire airport, poking a finger into his chest and saying, "You broke the rules!" The outburst had an effect that Rove had perhaps not reckoned on. A reporter who was present said that as a result of the incident, "everyone on the campaign charter concluded that Rove was responsible for the rumors about McCain."

But whoever was responsible was no doubt disappointed by the results. On the evening of February 1, the Bush team sank into despondency as they watched McCain's lead assume embarrassing proportions—Bush would eventually trail him by 18 percentage points—while McCain himself seemed unable to register the information until his aide and co-author Mark Slater said "You could be president." Turning to Weaver, McCain barked, "A fine mess you've gotten me into!"

It was a mess that Rove was determined to get him out of. Stung by McCain's win—and by the avalanche of stories on how the Bush juggernaut had sprung a leak—he turned his attention to the next primary, in South Carolina, and what he saw there gave him hope.

The South Carolina primary had a reputation as a Republican "firewall"—a quick slapdown for insurgent candidates who had managed to pick up steam in Iowa and New Hampshire. The firewall concept, like so much of modern political warfare, was originally the handiwork of Rove's mentor Lee Atwater. It was in the 1988 presidential campaign that Atwater had first correctly judged that South Carolina's rigidly conservative political hierarchy would turn out for the Republican establishment's candidate, then as in

2000 named George Bush. After all, this was a state that had continued to send the doddering Strom Thurmond to Washington long past the point when such an exercise made any political sense.

After a life spent elevating national politics to the level of those in South Carolina, on his deathbed Atwater supposedly renounced the type of negative campaign he had made the new gold standard in politics, an admirable gesture that had little or no effect on the 2000 Republican primary.

Coming off a huge poll bounce as a result of New Hampshire, McCain proceeded to make a series of mistakes, at least in the context of South Carolina politics. He made comments that hurt him with Confederate flag supporters, the religious right, and pro-life groups—the last even though his pro-life voting record was impeccable—while Bush and Rove swiped a page from his book and started touting the governor as a "reformer with results." Within days, voters had started identifying Bush, rather than McCain, as the reformer.

Then McCain said something about Bush that was apparently unforgivable, even in the rough-and-tumble of South Carolina politics: He accused him of "twisting the truth like Clinton."

To a South Carolina Republican, this was filth tantamount to impugning someone's mother, and the Bush campaign responded with appropriate outrage. Mark McKinnon was now Bush's media maven, and the speed with which he and Rove got a response on the air was decisive. "That commercial McKinnon and those guys cut was the Godzilla judo flip," says Trey Walker, who was McCain's national field director. "McCain's momentum had already started to evaporate, and that just stopped him dead." The response ad, which featured a stern Bush inveighing against McCain, served two purposes: It answered the first ad, and it cemented in voters' minds the idea that McCain was the one using negative ads, an impression that McCain inadvertently confirmed when, a week before the end of the campaign, he promised to *stop* running negative ads.

Seasoned watchers of South Carolina politics seem to agree that McCain never had a chance, given his own gaffes and the overwhelming support of the state's Republican establishment for Bush. And as Walker points out, the Bush campaign hit their marks this time: "It was pretty simple what they needed to do, and they executed it flawlessly. And that was to make John McCain unacceptable to a large segment of conservative South Carolina voters."

But the question that lingers—as it seems to linger whenever Karl Rove is calling the shots—is why the campaign got as nasty as it did, when by all accounts Bush could have won anyway. Because somehow—although nobody will take responsibility—it got incredibly nasty. "I have worked on hundreds of campaigns in South Carolina," says Michael Graham, a conservative writer and radio host who at the time had a show in Charleston, "and I've never seen anything as ugly as that campaign. It was 100 percent 'John McCain sucks.' Bush never said 'Here's why you should vote for me.'"

This time, instead of one rumor about McCain, there were scores. McCain was gay. McCain had fathered an illegitimate child with a North Vietnamese woman, which was why he had gotten special treatment from the Viet Cong. McCain had a black daughter. (McCain and his wife, Cindy, have an adopted daughter from Bangladesh.) McCain voted for the largest tax increase ever. McCain's wife stole prescription drugs from a charity and abused them while she was supposedly caring for their four children. McCain was pro-abortion. McCain left his crippled first wife. McCain was a liar, a cheat, and a fraud.

These canards were repeated on handbills, in phone calls, in push polls, on the radio, in conversation. "I've seen dirty politics, but I've never seen a rumor campaign like this," said Terry Haskins, the speaker pro tem of the South Carolina House of Representatives and a McCain supporter. "It's a vile attempt to destroy a man's reputation just to win an election, and I know it's organized because none of these rumors existed until the day after New Hampshire." Over a ten-day period, McCain's unfavorability rating went from 4 percent to 18 percent, while Bush's dropped from 26 percent to 20 percent.

On February 12, a week before the election, Bush had been caught by a C-SPAN camera talking to State Senator Mike Fair, though neither man apparently knew they were being watched.

"You haven't even hit his soft spots," said Fair, referring to McCain.

"I know," Bush replied. "I'm going to."

"Well they need to be, somebody does, anyway," Fair said.

"I agree," Bush said, adding, "I'm not going to do it on TV."

PART 3

THE MAN
WITH THE PLAN

A Matter of the Numbers

George W. Bush's relationship with John McCain was damaged forever in South Carolina, and the two men's staffs were doomed to a future of mutual loathing. But if the cost of the victory was high, so were its rewards. The advantages in fundraising, party endorsements and grassroots organizing that Rove and the old Bush family network had assembled had indeed proved to be the "firewall" that Bush needed. The polls closed at 7:00 PM in South Carolina, and a couple of minutes later McCain phoned Bush, who was sitting in his fifth-floor suite in the Columbia Sheraton Hotel, to concede the state. Later, in his concession speech to supporters, McCain would say, apparently referring to the tactics that had been used against him, "I want the presidency in the best way, not the worst way."

In his own hotel room, Karl Rove was already planning a general election campaign. Michigan was only three days away. There, despite Republican governor John Engler's vow to use his political organization to push Bush over the top, McCain was running strong. In fact, McCain would win Michigan as well as his home base of Arizona on February 22. But the nomination was all but over anyway. It was a matter of the numbers, something that would appeal to Bush, a man who loves baseball in part because of the order imposed on the sport by its vast array of statistics. Rove is not a baseball fan, but he could rattle off the stats that made Bush's presidential nomination all but inevitable: As the 2000 primary season began, Bush had more cash on hand than McCain, Gore and Bill Bradley combined. In endorsements, McCain had seven members of the House of Representatives; Bush had 175. In the Senate, where McCain served, only four of the war hero's colleagues had signed onto "The Straight Talk Express." Bush had thirty-seven Republican senators backing him.

A look at the nominating calendar showed why such figures were so significant. From that point on it was truly a national campaign, requiring a national organization. McCain's great asset was the McCain persona itself: he was drawing big, enthusiastic crowds that fed off his energy. Bush's campaign, by contrast, was built on his organization, meaning that the governors, senators, and other prominent Republicans backing him could serve as his surrogates, not only speaking on his behalf, but mobilizing their ground troops to get out the vote. This advantage kicked in almost immediately. The Bush campaign also had enough money to run television spots anywhere—and everywhere. Five days after Michigan came contests in American Samoa, Guam, the Virgin Islands, and Puerto Rico, with twenty-six delegates among them. Three days later, on February 29, some ninety-six delegates were up for grabs in North Dakota, Virginia, and Washington. Super Tuesday, on March 7, entailed competing in eleven states simultaneously, including five in New England, one in the deep South (Georgia), three in the Midwest (Ohio, Missouri, and Minnesota) and the bi-coastal megastates New York and California. A week after that came what amounted to a Southern regional primary, with six primaries the length of Dixie, from Florida to Texas. McCain's campaign was built on his personality, but he couldn't be more than one place at a time to showcase it. Bush's campaign was built on his organization, which in those early days functioned just as well without him, sometimes better.

Bush's public comments indicated that he, as well as Rove, was now looking ahead to a general-election campaign. "South Carolina has spoken—and tonight there are only 263 days more to the end of Clinton-Gore," Bush told a happy crowd in the Sheraton ballroom shortly after 9:00 PM. "My reform agenda stands in stark contrast to the current administration."

To counter McCain, Rove and Karen Hughes had wanted Bush to use the word "reform" everywhere he went in South Carolina. The candidate had mastered his lines so well that he couldn't stop. He mentioned "reform" a half-dozen times in his brief victory speech, at one point even lapsing into using the campaign slogan in the third person, telling his loyalists that the South Carolina election returns constituted "the victory of a message that is conservative and compassionate" and "the victory of a messenger who is a reformer with results." In New Hampshire, the late-deciding voters had almost all broken for McCain. In South Carolina, among a more conservative electorate and aided by McCain's decision to pull all negative spots in the last days of the primary, very nearly the opposite had occurred.

Rove's take was that Bush's breakthrough in South Carolina was due to a return to the strategies they had used in the 1994 governor's race. Complementing the attack ads on McCain was Bush's campaign trail demeanor, which was relentlessly assertive, but not in a way that turned voters off. In fact, exit polls showed that slightly more than half of South Carolina's voters believed McCain had run a more negative campaign than Bush. Moreover, the exit polls showed they had blunted, if not co-opted, McCain's reform message in their ads hammering away at McCain's own fundraising practices. This was possible, Rove declared, because Bush had been specific in detailing the reforms he wanted to make. "Bush won this because of a positive message," Rove said. "We run by uniting the Republican Party."

McCain's camp had a different take on what had happened in South Carolina. "They were able to throw a thousand axes through the air and we were only able to fend off so many," countered John Weaver. "That won't happen again."

Rove and Bush had already made the decision to change tactics, but not because they feared a stronger McCain response. After South Carolina it wasn't primarily about McCain for them. It was about Al Gore—and Bill Clinton. The voters' reaction against McCain for running ads comparing Bush to Clinton had bolstered Team Bush's conviction that Clinton was an asset to them, one that would galvanize conservative voters to vote against Clinton's vice president. At the same time, the exigencies of winning in South Carolina had forced Bush too far to the right—not where he wanted to be during the convention season or the general election campaign. Democrats tracked this development with obvious delight. Speaking of McCain as well as Bush, Gore noted wryly in remarks to the reporters traveling with him, "It's pretty clear that they have done a lot of damage to one another." Out in Los Angeles, Bill Carrick, a Democratic operative advising Gore, assured Democrats that the

George W. Bush on display in South Carolina would not play in California—a state Rove wanted to contest in November. Carrick, a South Carolina native who got started in politics by going up against Lee Atwater, told *Los Angeles Times* political writer Mark Barabak that Rove was running "a situational ethics sort of campaign. The thinking was, do whatever . . . to get out of South Carolina with a victory, then clean up the mess afterward."

For the Bush campaign the first step in that process was to atone with Roman Catholic voters—and Catholic Republican office holders—offended by Bush's February 2 campaign event at Bob Jones University, whose founder forbade inter-racial dating and once characterized Catholicism as "a Satanic cult." Bush had protested that an appearance at the school had generally been considered obligatory for GOP presidential candidates and that, in any event, he'd in no way associated himself with Jones' antediluvian views on matters of race and religion. Bush's protestations were accurate, but they weren't getting him anywhere, which he and Rove soon realized. A series of editorials in large newspapers in the primary states still in play called on Bush to do more. On February 27, he did. In a two-pronged chess move, the campaign released a contrite letter the governor had sent to New York Cardinal John O'Connor while Bush himself held a press conference in Austin to apologize personally. "On reflection, I should have been more clear in disassociating myself from anti-Catholic sentiments and racial prejudice," Bush said in the letter to O'Connor. "It was a missed opportunity, causing needless offense, which I deeply regret."

Bush aides asserted that the letter to O'Connor was initially intended to remain private, but it's clear from the calendar (the New York primary was approaching) and the wording of the letter that it was intended for a wider audience. "I want to erase any doubts about my views and values," Bush wrote. "As a public official, I take seriously my duty to encourage tolerance and respect for the religious views of others. As a Christian, I see Catholics as my brothers and sisters in Christ, sharing the same ancient creed and core beliefs. And, as you know, my own brother and sister-in-law are both Catholics."

The letter also had a tone of being aggrieved as well. "What no American should expect—and what I will not tolerate—is guilt by association," Bush added. "This is why I am offended by any suggestion that I tolerate anti-Catholic bigotry—and resent any attempt to create that impression."

Bush made the same point in Austin. Although he began by saying, "I make no excuses. I had an opportunity and missed it," Bush also went on the offensive. Lyndon Johnson, another Texan, once said, "If you're covering your ass, you're losing your ass," and George W. Bush had no intention of losing his. He expressed resentment that McCain's forces had been exploiting the Bob Jones University speech with Catholics, saying he'd been "slandered" by McCain. Bush went further, essentially calling McCain, who'd denied that his campaign had been using the matter in its phone bank work, a liar.

"I'm very disappointed in the senator," Bush said. "It was clear that he looked you in the press corps in the eye and did not tell the truth."

This time it was not the Bush camp with the credibility problem. After the campaign shifted to Michigan, it soon became evident what Rove nemesis John Weaver had meant by his dark hints that the McCainiacs wouldn't be caught flat-footed again. There was no more Mr. Nice Guy from McCain. Telephone calls to Michigan households from callers who identified themselves as being associated with something called "Catholic Voter Alert," read from a script saying that because of Bush's silence about "Bob Jones' anti-Catholic bigotry many Michigan Catholics now support John McCain for president." McCain initially denied that his campaign had anything to do with the calls when in fact, "Catholic Voter Alert" had been paid for by the McCain campaign. McCain admitted to *The New York Times* that he'd personally approved the script. McCain attempted to explain away his denial by quibbling with the wording of the question in his earlier denial. His performance disillusioned even some of the reporters aboard "Straight Talk Express." Rove and Bush pounced quickly.

"That's not plain talk, that's parsed talk," Bush said on February 27, after his campaign plane landed in Seattle. "This is a man who said, 'I'm going to tell the truth and run a positive campaign.' If the facts are what they are, it sounds like he might have violated both."

On the Sunday talk shows, Rove was even more blunt. In a confrontation with former Senator Warren Rudman, a McCain loyalist, Rove accused McCain of "reprehensible" conduct. "Now, right now, he's running a television ad right now saying: 'I'll always tell you the truth.' I guess the real question is, when is he going to *start* telling us the truth?" Rove said. "He had a sleazy, anonymous smear phone campaign in Michigan that only now is being acknowledged."

McCain ended up winning Michigan, but it was far more costly than Bush's win in South Carolina. Out-organized, out-financed and with little in the way of support from the GOP establishment,

McCain's insurgency was built on his credibility and charisma. One of those was diminished now, and Rove knew that the Republican nomination was Bush's for the taking.

By Super Tuesday, March 7, the Bush campaign's aura of inevitability was restored. *The New York Times'* Melinda Henneberger, who provided some of the most telling insights of Rove, was allowed to follow him through the afternoon of triumph. With perhaps more than the usual pleasure of his competitive juices, Rove called Bush from Austin to share the good news coming from the exit polls and to gloat over the "meltdown" of the McCain candidacy.

"It's not pretty, they say," he told Bush. "It's not pretty how the numbers are being received. [McCain is] going to Arizona, and the scuttlebutt is he's going to his cabin and nobody thinks he can continue. Yeah, recriminations, finger-pointing. . . . No, over there. Oh, big time. It's unbelievable." Rove went on to trash a major McCain adviser, Rick Davis. Davis' consulting firm had once accepted as clients Imelda Marcos and the nation of Nigeria. "Yeah, he is a bad guy," Rove assured the governor. "This guy was a lobbyist for Imelda Marcos and General Abacha of Nigeria! Just the consummate inside-D.C. thug. He needs adult supervision."

Later, Bush campaign staff and volunteers gathered at the posh Four Seasons hotel to celebrate the Super Tuesday results, results that would put them over the top in securing the Republican nomination. According to the *Times*, Karen Hughes burst into the suite as Rove was getting off the phone with the governor. He told her he just wanted to "get New York over with so we can go home."

"Go home?" Hughes yelled. "I want to celebrate."

Later, as Rove walked into the victory celebration, someone called out: "The king has arrived!" A Texas magazine publisher knelt before Rove and pretended to kiss his ring. Rove turned, bent over, and raised his jacket, the message being: Kiss My Ass. The reporter from New York asked Rove if he was enjoying himself. "Boring, man, boring!" he yelled. In his moment of national arrival he seemed edgy and distant.

Darby Rove later explained her husband's behavior: "He knows they can turn on you at any time."

If McCain was no longer a hurdle, some of the tactics and atmospherics Bush had used to make the Arizona senator go away might be a problem. The independents and ticket-splitters who had gone for McCain fit the profile of the kind of voters who determine the outcome of national elections. The challenge ahead for Rove was to reposition Bush in a way that made him palatable to these swing voters—McCain voters—who would decide the election in November.

The overt religiosity of the Republican contest—and of Bush himself—was a potential problem. Voters do not mind a deeply religious president, and Bush certainly needed the evangelicals in his corner, but there was something clumsy about the way Bush discussed his faith that left moderates uneasy. An early example came during a debate among the Republican candidates in Iowa on December 13. The moderator, John Bachman, asked them "what political philosopher or thinker" they most identified with. Even in a field that included Alan Keyes and Gary Bauer, two evangelicals who routinely cited God's will as their guide on domestic political policy, Bush's answer was striking. Steve Forbes mentioned John Locke and Thomas Jefferson. Keyes cited *all* the framers of the Constitution. Orrin Hatch answered Abraham Lincoln and Ronald Reagan; McCain named Theodore Roosevelt. When it was Bush's turn, he blurted out, "Christ, because he changed my heart." When Bachman sought to get him to expound on this answer, Bush struggled. "Well, if they don't know, it's going to be hard to explain," Bush said. "When you turn your heart and your life over to Christ, when you accept Christ as the savior, it changes your heart. It changes your life. And that's what happened to me."

Leaving aside the point that Bush's answer wasn't really responsive to the question, it was unimpressive on two other levels. Given a chance to explain Jesus' importance and the significance of his teachings to world history in a secular way, Bush had not done so. But neither had Bush witnessed for Christ as a follower of the faith. His answer was about as illuminating, and about as inclusive, as a phrase popular at the time, *"It's a black thing, you wouldn't understand."*

Rove, too, has displayed a consistent awkwardness in discussing his own beliefs. During the 2000 campaign, *The New York Times Magazine* revealed that Rove himself was not a particularly religious man. The piece quoted one of Rove's Salt Lake City high school debating partners, Mark Dangerfield, now a Phoenix attorney, who recalled that it bothered Rove that "he was raised in a completely nonreligious home." Asked by the *Times* about his friend's observation, Rove replied, "I'm not sure I've ever found faith. Others here—others in the campaign, including George W.— I know how much their faith sustains them. Some of them have a prayer group. I haven't been good enough yet."

It was such a candid disclosure from the man who went on to become the White House's liaison to the Christian Right and GOP-leaning Catholics that in a 2002 interview Rove was asked about it by Alexis Simendinger, who covers the White House for *National Journal*. Rove sought to dismiss the incongruity, first with a disjointed story about his boyhood friend being confused by Rove's efforts to stave off efforts to convert him to Mormonism, and then, a few moments later with a joke. ("I'm an Episcopalian so I'm not allowed to be fervent in my beliefs," he quipped. "We're restrained.") Finally, Rove claimed not to remember the *Times* story. But it made an impression on others. One prominent conservative, an admirer of Rove, described him, not unsympathetically, as a "a nonbeliever among all those evangelicals."

Such awkwardness can be explained, in part, by the intricate dance every Republican candidate for national office has been forced to learn since the time of Ronald Reagan. On the one hand, the GOP needs evangelical support to compete successfully. On the other hand, Democrats—and the media—are quick to label as extremist any Republican who panders too overtly. The steps of this dance require the Republican to pay homage to religious conservatives such as Jerry Falwell and Pat Robertson, while having to duck when confronted with some of the good preachers' nuttier utterances. A corollary is the soft-shoe Democrats perform around African-American activists like Jesse Jackson and Al Sharpton, courting their followers while pretending not to notice the leaders' more incendiary pronouncements.

But with the battle for the nomination grinding along successfully, the need to keep the conservatives on board while nudging the candidate back toward the center was very much on Rove's agenda as the 2000 Republican National Convention in Philadelphia approached. In the minds of Bush aides, transforming Bush back into a moderate-sounding Republican was an exercise in maintaining quality control over his rhetoric rather than tweaking the candidate's actual policy positions. Rove was convinced that Bush's policy prescriptions, particularly on taxes, would do fine with the electorate, even though they were not popular with the press. But this would hold true only as long as voters didn't think of Bush and the Republican Party as harshly conservative. Such a perception had been fostered in 1992 about Bush's father, when his handlers lost control of the convention, held that year in Houston. Reagan had given a captivating address—his convention swan song, as it happened—but the Gipper had been pushed past prime time by a Patrick Buchanan speech, the message of which was anything but inclusive. Coupled with uncompromising speeches by Pat Robertson, who had also challenged Bush senior in the GOP primaries, and by Marilyn Quayle, of all people, the story line that emerged from the 1992 convention was that the Republicans were angry, small-minded and exclusive. Conservatives complained that this was a case of many reporters seeing what they expected to see—and revealing their own bias in the process. If anything, they said, it was the 1992 Democratic National Convention in New York City that demonstrated intolerance—and did so on the same issue, abortion, if in another direction. Pennsylvania's Democratic governor, Robert Casey, was not allowed to address the Democratic convention because he espoused right-to-life views on abortion.

The Democrats in 1992 had also given a prominent prime-time slot to two speakers—Elizabeth Glaser, the wife of the actor Paul Michael Glaser, and Bob Hattoy, a Sierra Club official—both of whom were HIV-positive. In their speeches, Hattoy and Glaser sought to politicize the issue by issuing harsh denunciations of Republicans. Glaser, who contracted the disease from a blood transfusion in 1981 and passed it along to her children before it even had a name, inexplicably blamed the Reagan administration for her plight. Hattoy's language was even more extreme. "If George Bush wins again we're all at risk," he said. "It's that simple. It's that serious. It's that terrible." (By contrast, the Republican convention in Houston would feature a conciliatory prime-time speech by AIDS sufferer Mary Fisher, who worked in the Ford administration and was the daughter of a wealthy GOP donor. "The AIDS virus is not a political creature," Fisher said. "It does not care whether you are Democrat or Republican. It does not ask whether you are black or white, male or female, gay or straight, young or old.")

Bush family loyalists had never forgotten the Democrats' harsh language. Nor had they forgotten what they perceived as the media's double standard. To Rove and the other Republicans preparing for Philadelphia there were two lessons of 1992. The first was that the reporters, most of whom were liberal, could not be counted on to cover the conventions fairly. The second, flowing directly from the first, was that you couldn't lose control of the gavel for even a moment. "Ours will be a different kind of convention because we have a different kind of Republican running for President," vowed Andrew H. Card Jr., the GOP convention's general co-chairman. In truth what the Republicans had was a new determination to control things tightly, and a heightened appreciation for the purely symbolic nature of modern political conventions. With the media waiting to pounce on the Republicans for any sign

of small-mindedness, intolerance or generally Neanderthal attitudes, the convention speakers had to have perfect pitch. The right
demographics would help, too. And so a convention lineup was
prepared that included not only Colin Powell, Condoleezza Rice,
and Bush's own handsome young Hispanic nephew, George P. Bush,
but also Erik Weihenmayer, a blind mountain climber who led the
convention in the Pledge of Allegiance, California Assemblyman
Abel Malonado, whose father was an immigrant farm worker (and
who addressed the convention in Spanish), and Nancy Goodman
Brinker, founder of the Susan G. Komen Breast Cancer Foundation.
The theme of the first night, "Opportunity with a Purpose: Leave
No Child Behind," gave the convention the feel of a Democratic
convention opening night.

If movement conservatives found the tone of the Philadelphia
convention disconcerting, most kept their own counsel. One of
those who didn't was Pat Robertson, head of the Christian Coalition. "It's prepackaged," he complained. "It's slick. It's homoge-
nized. It's pabulum."

Coming from one of those who the Bush crowd believed had
sabotaged Big George in 1992, this criticism didn't cut much ice.
But Robertson wasn't alone. Conservative author John O'Sullivan
groused about the direction the Bush crowd was taking the Republican Party—he mentioned Rove by name—in an essay in *National
Review*. "Is this a Republican convention or the annual dinner of
the Bilingual Friends of Feminism?" O'Sullivan wrote in the voice
of a perplexed (but mythical) GOP delegate in Philadelphia.
"Frankly, I've had it up to my keister with tostadas and I'm beginning to wonder if the Bush people aren't going overboard with all
this inclusiveness. Since when does being inclusive mean excluding

Republicans? Or conservatives? Or white males? Or all three combined?" Fred Barnes, another prominent conservative writer, writing in another conservative magazine, *The Weekly Standard*, also lamented how the Bush Republicans had tossed some cherished conservative ideas overboard. Barnes homed in on term limits, and also seemed to attribute this apostasy to Rove, who had told him, "Term limits is not our fight." "So term limits simply vanished as a GOP issue," Barnes added, "and with scarcely a peep of dissent."

Rove also dismissed the old GOP ways as an "old paradigm" and a timeworn "Southern strategy" that would never work again. "People are more attracted today by a positive agenda than by wedge issues," he said in the days leading up to the convention. "If you have knocked down the Berlin Wall and the Evil Empire has disappeared, it makes it a little bit difficult to run on a platform of 1956 or 1960." Rove was saying that in the new world of the twenty-first century, the GOP needed to soften its face to continue to compete in national elections. What is interesting about this in hindsight is how little thought even the Bush brain trust gave to George W. Bush as a future wartime leader. Colin Powell, a warrior by training, was offered up to the convention—but not as a soldier. His was the face and the voice of a moderate African-American Republican whose own stated concerns were primarily racial equity, education, and inclusion.

"In pursuing educational reform as well as in all other parts of his agenda for Texas, Governor Bush has reached out to all Texans—white, black, Latino, Asian, Native American," Powell told the convention in his role as the first-night headliner. "He has been successful in bringing more and more minorities into the tent by responding to their deepest needs. Some call it 'compassionate con-

servatism.' To me, it's just caring about people. I believe he can do
the same thing as president. I am convinced he will bring to the
White House that same passion for inclusion. I know that he can
help bridge our racial divides—I know that. Recently Governor
Bush addressed the annual meeting of the NAACP. He spoke to the
delegates about his plans for housing and health and educational
programs to help all Americans. He also spoke the truth to the delegates when he said that the party of Lincoln has not always carried
the mantle of Lincoln. I talked with him again today, and I know
that, with all his heart, Governor Bush welcomes the challenge. He
wants the Republican Party to wear that mantle again."

Two years later, in his book *Bush at War*, Bob Woodward would
expose some of the nerves that Powell touched in the Bush political
team, even with Rove, in the campaign. "After Bush won the 2000
Republican presidential nomination, Powell signed on to help, but
Karl Rove found that the campaign had to move heaven and earth
to get him to appear at an event with Bush. Nearly every other
important Republican fell in line, not Powell," Woodward wrote.
"His people always wanted to know who else would be at an event,
what would be said, who the audience was, what the political purpose. All this seemed designed to determine the political fallout—on
Powell, not Bush. Rove detected a subtle, subversive tendency, as if
Powell were protecting his centrist credentials and his own political
future at Bush's expense." But regardless of Rove's feelings, when
Bush needed him the most—at the 2000 convention—Powell was
there.

McCain, too, came through for Bush—and then some. Putting
aside any lingering bitterness, McCain labored on his speech, tele-
vised in prime time on the second night of the convention, even to

the point of practicing it. In so doing, McCain showed that, like Powell, the military ethos of lining up behind the ranking officer (even if you have private doubts) dies hard. "I say to all Americans, Republican, Democrat or Independent, if you believe America deserves leaders with a purpose more ennobling than expediency and opportunism, then vote for Governor Bush," declared the old Naval officer. "If you believe patriotism is more than a sound-bite and public service should be more than a photo-op, then vote for Governor Bush. . . . He wants to give you back a government that serves all the people, no matter the circumstances of their birth. And he wants to lead a Republican Party that is as big as the country we serve."

In his own acceptance speech, Bush filled out the themes of inclusiveness and decency with a couple more. He promised to bring leadership and bipartisanship to Washington, making it plain that he believed Bill Clinton and Al Gore had provided neither. In so doing, Bush sought to distance himself from both Clinton's tawdry behavior and the punitive partisanship of the Republicans in Congress who tried to make him pay for it.

"I have no stake in the bitter arguments of the last few years," Bush told the nation. "I want to change the tone of Washington to one of civility and respect. This administration had its moment. They had their chance. They have not led. We will."

Bush emerged from the convention ahead in the polls and with the GOP's Reagan-era coalition intact. His selection of Dick Cheney as his running mate was the last piece in the puzzle. This choice, the first most Americans outside of Texas had seen Bush make, was contrasted starkly to his father's pick of Dan Quayle, a too-cute-by-half gambit designed to bridge generation and gender gaps. In choosing Cheney, a former Secretary of Defense, White House chief of staff and Wyoming congressman, George W. Bush was clearly picking someone he thought could help him govern. And although Cheney had compiled a remarkably conservative record in Congress, he was seen in Washington as someone who wasn't overly ideological by nature and whose unpretentiousness bridged all strains of conservatism, even those on the religious right with whom he'd never been particularly close.

And so, as they left Philadelphia, Team Bush had all the elements in place. Rove and Card's success in averting a fight over the GOP abortion plank (it stayed in the Republican platform, but accompanied by vague language about Republicans being a diverse lot) kept religious conservatives happy. Cheney's presence on the ticket, as well as Bush's emphasis on tax cuts, kept economic conservatives happy. McCain had neutralized the independents as best he could, and Powell and Rice and all the diverse faces kept the reporters happy—or as happy as they could be with Republicans. Team Bush was also playing the expectation game right. Mark McKinnon was telling reporters that the race was bound to tighten up and would probably be a dead heat by Labor Day. Rove, who hoped that Bush could sustain his five-to-seven-point lead in the polls right though Election Day, believed McKinnon was using good strategy in lowering expectations, but McKinnon was saying the same thing in private to friends. (McKinnon turned out to be right.)

The Bush camp was also attempting to diminish expectations for Bush's performance in the upcoming debates with Gore. This is Politics 101, but somehow it eluded Gore's advisers, who began early in the year smugly predicting that Gore would wipe the floor with Bush when they debated. This played into the Democrats'

Bush-as-moron theme, but it wasn't very savvy. By the time the debates rolled around, all Bush had to do was avoid drooling on himself and he'd have held his own. Rove, playing it by the book, told reporters in August with a straight face: "Our debate strategy can be summed up in one word—survive. We hope to survive Governor Bush's necessary appearance in debates against the world's most preeminent debater." Rove's sarcasm was detectable, but it wasn't aimed at his own guy—or even at Gore—but instead at the Gore team, which had inexplicably raised expectations of their candidate to unattainable levels. In a larger way, however, Rove was playing it straight. The Bush strategy for winning the presidency did not hinge on the debates. Rove and the others knew Bush could pull his weight—they'd seen him do it against Ann Richards—and they figured the three debates would be a wash. Their real strategy for winning the presidency contemplated waging war on two different fronts, one demographic, the other geographic.

Traditionally, Democrats preferred to wage a purely national campaign, appealing to their core constituencies: organized labor, liberals, blacks, feminists, environmentalists. Republicans believed that relying on such a strategy alone makes winning more difficult because it ignores the pronounced geographical differences among Americans. Support for gun control dooms a Democrat in Montana, for example, while in New York, opposition to gun control is considered bizarre. Presidential campaigns, Rove knew, are fifty separate elections, state-by-state, winner-take-all. In the television age, a candidate can't take one position in Missoula and another in Miami, but he can change his emphasis in those two towns. He can also decide which media markets to spend money in—and which states to spend time campaigning in.

As recently as the 1980s, Democrats paid short shrift to this kind of strategic planning. Walter Mondale's aides openly disdained regionalism and Michael Dukakis and his cabal of Bostonians never got outside their own world enough to know how to implement it. When the Democrats did think about regionalism, they thought about it wrong. Harking back to FDR, they dreamed of a ticket that could carry New York and the Deep South at the same time. In today's America, this is a pipe dream. The way for Democrats to win is to secure the two coasts, starting with New York and California, and then carry enough of the heartland to provide an Electoral College victory. A former Carter White House aide named Les Francis tried to sell his party this theory in the mid–1980s, but it wasn't until after the Dukakis defeat in 1988—a campaign Democrats had expected to win—that geography earned its rightful place in the thinking of Democratic Party strategists. A rumpled Massachusetts Democrat named Paul Tully became a complete convert. After the 1988 loss, he went to work for the Democratic National Committee and on his walls were maps, lots of maps, with various colored pins in them that showed how states and counties voted in the past. Tully convinced party chairman Ron Brown that Democrats couldn't win until they started paying attention to these pins, and in 1991 and 1992 both men found a willing listener in Bill Clinton, who didn't build his coalition in his homestate of Arkansas or in Gore's Tennessee (although he carried them both), but on the West Coast and the East Coast and in selected large states of the Midwest.

The challenge for Rove and his team was to reconstitute the Electoral College map in a way that once again favored the GOP. A realistic look at the map in 2000 conceded New York, New England, and much of the eastern seaboard to Gore. California, too, seemed an uphill fight, although Bush made promises to campaign there. Invincible in Texas and the Mountain West, strong all across Dixie—Jeb can hold Florida, they believed—the Bush forces looked to the Midwest, to Michigan, Illinois, Pennsylvania, Missouri, West Virginia, and Ohio. If they were to win, they'd need some of these states. And to do *that*, Rove explained over breakfast with reporters in Philadelphia, Bush would need to hold his own among three sometimes overlapping groups of swing voters: Catholics, Latinos, and those living in the outer suburbs. This is where geographical politics and demographic politics merged. Rove was already working the demographic groups, and had been for some time. At the outset of the 2000 campaign, for example, Rove had put in a call to Deal Hudson, editor of *Crisis* magazine, a Washington-based Catholic monthly that had published several in-depth articles about Catholic voting patterns. Hudson had sent his material to all the campaigns; only Bush's responded. And on Rove's invitation, Hudson brought small groups of Catholic activists to Austin to meet Bush.

Suburban voters, a category so large it defies easy description, were more amorphous. To the Gore campaign it was an article of faith that suburbanites are susceptible to a pitch for sensible growth and environmental protection. The Bushies didn't dispute this view, but they stressed another issue that would give them traction with suburbanites: high taxes. The nation's editorial writers weren't keen on Bush's tax-cutting proposals, but the salience of this issue to the general public could be seen by the fact that after Bush unveiled his $480 billion, ten-year tax cut proposal, both McCain and Gore offered huge—though not *as* huge—proposed tax cuts of their own.

Everywhere he went, Gore dismissed the Bush plan as a "risky tax scheme." On a campaign swing to Washington state, Bush countered with the point that Gore wanted tax cuts, too, but that they were all "targeted" tax cuts, meaning that you got them only "if you do what government wanted." Bush dubbed this, without embarrassment at his evident cribbing, "an iffy tax scheme."

Rove looked at the polling and the electoral map, and pronounced that Bush had an "embarrassment of opportunities" to pick up states that had been in the Democratic column in 1992 and 1996. There were two ways to do this: the first was to focus the resources of the campaign, mostly TV ads and campaign visits by the candidate, to specific geographic hot spots. The second was to target the three demographic groups Rove had mentioned.

Latino outreach had been a priority during the convention itself. In Philadelphia, a steady stream of Hispanic musicians were heard from the stage; one of the most visually appealing rallies of the week was a Spanish-speaking event sponsored by the "Amigos de Bush" at the Philadelphia Museum of Art. Amid signs of "Viva Bush!" and "Un Nuevo Dia," Bush himself addressed the crowd in Spanish and sung along with Latino singer Jon Secada in a Spanglish version of "America the Beautiful." That was the broad brush; an example of a more targeted stroke came in the last week of the campaign in Wisconsin, a state targeted by both campaigns. The *Spanish Times*, a Milwaukee paper that covers the city's growing Latino community, ran a quarter-page ad with a photograph of Bush and this message: "*Cuando Hay Educacion, Hay Oportunidad.*" ("When There Is Education, There Is Opportunity.") The body of the ad, all in Spanish, explained Bush's support for school vouchers, which were opposed by Gore but popular in Milwaukee's inner city neighborhoods.

This kind of on-the-ground campaigning takes organization and money—lots of money—and in the waning days of October 2000, there wasn't much talk of Rove's highfalutin' theories about how the 2000 election was shaping up like the 1896 election with George W. as the William McKinley of his day. No, this was the kind of hand-to-hand political combat that took nerve and brains and, most of all, deep pockets. "We've got more money than God," boasted Republican Party spokesman Bill Pascoe. The trick was to know where to spend it. "We like fighting on their turf," Rove boasted publicly. But the idea wasn't just to take Democratic ground; it was to hold it through November 7. "It's an old infantry expression," said Governor Tom Ridge of Pennsylvania, a Vietnam War veteran. "Once you take ground, you have to keep it."

Both sides believed this, but throughout the autumn, both sides inevitably made miscalculations in how to go about it. Gore grew complacent in West Virginia when polls showed him up by seventeen points. The Democrats pulled their ads off the air to save the money for other places. Sensing that Gore's environmental activism would hurt him in a traditionally Democratic, but economically hard-pressed state, Rove sent Dick Cheney there to promise miners and steel workers unsympathetic to tight environmental regulation that they'd be back at work if they voted Republican in this election. By the time those in Gore's camp realized that they had a problem in West Virginia, the state was lost. Gore also probably gave up on Ohio too early. He never made a visit to the state after the first week of October, and pulled his ads out as well. And yet Bush—

after expending major resources there—carried it by only four percentage points. Conversely, Bush's last-minute swing through California, and his last-minute flurry of expensive television ads, were a
waste of time and money. Bush lost the Golden State by nearly 1.3
million votes.

In any election as close as this one, there will be this kind of second-guessing, especially for the candidate who comes up short.
Should Gore have made more use of Clinton in Arkansas? Is there
anything he could have done to help him in his home state? Or to
neutralize Ralph Nader, who cost him New Hampshire? As the
election wound down to its final hours, both sides realized how
close it was going to be.

"This election," Rove predicted with two weeks to go, "is going
to be decided in the last precinct, in the last state, in the last hour, on
the last day."

But where would that precinct be? One place where Gore began
a late, almost stealth, effort was Florida. Bush's polls always had
him ahead in the Sunshine State and his brother was the governor,
so at first the Gore push there was seen as a feint. But when grassroots Democratic efforts in such disparate areas as Orlando,
Tampa, and West Palm Beach began paying off, the Gore campaign
got serious, extending its frantic last-minute get-out-the vote efforts
to the Florida Panhandle and other Republican strongholds. Gore's
running mate, Senator Joseph I. Lieberman of Connecticut, was
practically living in Florida. The polls showed the race tightening.
This was no feint after all. This was a gutsy pincer movement by
Gore. Both sides had the color-coded maps that Paul Tully had
made a staple of modern political campaigning, and both sets of
maps showed that if Florida wasn't in Bush's column it would be

hard for him to get to the magic number, 270, in the Electoral College. By the last week in October, Team Bush had spent $8 million to nail down a state they once considered safe. And they hadn't nailed it down at all. Barnstorming through the state the Thursday before the election, Gore sensed this.

"It's come down to Florida," he said simply.

On Sunday, forty-eight hours before the voting started, Rove predicted publicly that Bush would win the Electoral College with about 320 votes while carrying roughly 50 percent of the vote. Rove dismissed questions about whether Bush could win without Florida as a meaningless "hypothetical"—meaning they *were* going to carry the state. Bush's top political aide was so loosey-goosey that in a hotel in Jacksonville, Rove grabbed a silver coffeepot and imitated a waiter, bringing reporters coffee. The candidate himself was feeling a bit cocky. A day earlier, Bush was asked what he was going to give his wife for her birthday. "New Jersey," he quipped. In this case, the candidate and his "boy genius" were overly optimistic; Bush would not come close to 320 electoral votes, nor would New Jersey be in the Republican column in 2000.

Actually, it was Rove's earlier prophecy about the election coming down to the last precinct that turned out to be correct. And Al Gore was prescient in predicting where that precinct would be. Privately, Rove and the rest of Team Bush was starting to worry about Jeb Bush's state. Jeb was dispatched on a last-minute fly-around on Monday, from the western part of the Panhandle to Miami, with pleas that grew increasingly urgent as the day wore on, to inspire local Republicans to get out the vote.

At a senior citizens recreation hall in Miami, Jeb was the headliner at a Spanish-language get-out-the-vote rally. Florida's gover-

nor led the crowd in a chant of "Doble V! Doble V!" On his way
out of the hall, Jeb was mobbed by a group of elderly Cuban-
American women. "I'm having an out-of-body experience," he
exclaimed. "At the end of a campaign, it's like a Fellini movie."

But the campaign wasn't actually going to end the next day. And
the out-of-body sensations experienced by Jeb Bush, Karl Rove and
everyone else associated with Team Bush were about to get a whole
lot weirder.

11

The Last Precinct

On election night all five television networks, based on exit polling from the network polling consortium, Voter News Service, projected Al Gore the winner in Florida. The first to call the race was Fox News, at 7:49 PM. By 8 PM—eleven minutes later—ABC, CBS, NBC, and CNN had followed suit, even though the polling booths in the parts of the Panhandle that operate on Central Standard Time were still open. Rove was stunned and horrified. Stunned because the campaign's own poll watchers had reported back to headquarters that turnout in Florida's Republican areas had been extremely high, a sign things would end well that night. Horrified because Rove knew by then that if his sources were mistaken and the networks' polling consortium was right, the presidency was almost certainly lost.

Rove had had some warning that Election Day 2000 would be a travail. The first wave of exit polls received by the campaign in the early afternoon had shown that Rove's cocky prediction of 320 electoral votes was overly optimistic. If Bush was going to win, it was going to be by the thinnest of margins. More likely, Bush was headed for a loss. Rove felt obligated to share the gloomy early exit polls with the candidate, who was at that moment heading to the gym at the University of Texas with three workout partners.

"I got the smell," Bush later recalled in an interview with Dan Balz of *The Washington Post*. He was talking about the smell of defeat. Rove, Bush told Balz, had been full of "all the cautionary notes" about margins of error and possibilities. But Bush knew right away that what he was hearing "could be trouble." Bush finished exercising, but clammed up on the way back to the mansion. He did not, as was his custom, ask his gym partners to stay for lunch. He prepared his twin daughters, Jenna and Barbara, for the possibility that their dad might be going down to defeat. "The numbers don't look so good now," he told them. "It could be a long night." Later, Bush used the same expression on the way to the Shoreline Grill for dinner with his parents.

In truth, it would be a long thirty-six days. But at Bush campaign headquarters, aides had distributed a schedule for the night's activities, detailed in typical Bush fashion down to the precise time of the governor's victory speech (11:39 PM) and the time celebratory fireworks were to begin (11:51 PM). But as the networks gave Pennsylvania and Michigan—and Florida—to Gore, Bush found himself in no mood to celebrate. Cutting short dinner with his family, he headed back to the mansion.

The networks' predictions galvanized Rove, however, and he rushed to get himself on the air. His message, aimed at Republican-leaning voters in the Panhandle and other swing states, was simple enough: Florida is *not* decided. Get to the polls, quick!

"I would also suggest that Florida has been prematurely called," Rove told the nation in a hookup with NBC anchor Tom Brokaw. "First of all, I thought it was a little bit irresponsible of the networks to call it before the polls closed in the western part of Florida. Florida is split between two time zones, Eastern and Central. You all called it before the polls had closed in the central part of the country. And what is happening is that we're piling up significant numbers of votes in a lot of counties in Florida and the absentee ballots are going to come in very strong for Bush."

In a quick phone call to Bush, Rove was more succinct. "Florida's wrong!" he said flatly. Rove's outrage was genuine. But so was his fear. He suddenly realized that this was going to be *very* close. On the air, trying to retain an outward aura of calm, Rove went through the numbers known so far—174 electoral votes for Bush.

"Tennessee with eleven, West Virginia with five, Arkansas with five, Missouri with eleven, Iowa with seven, Wisconsin with eleven, New Hampshire with four," Rove told Brokaw. "All of these are states in which Governor Bush is doing well. That's fifty-four electoral votes, and then there are a bunch of states in the West: Colorado with eight, Montana with three, Idaho with four, Utah with five, Nevada with four, Arizona with eight. That's another thirty-two electoral votes. That gets you a total of eighty-six. And then we have Oregon with seven. We have Maine with one, Washington state with eleven, and Alaska with three, and we get—we get to 270 plus then some."

But only if Bush carried Florida, an implication Brokaw comprehended immediately.

"Do you think by tomorrow at noon you will have won the state of Florida?" Brokaw asked Rove. "Is that what you're saying?"

It was indeed what Rove was saying, but in truth nobody knew what was going on. He rattled on: "I just got a report from

Broward County where . . . big Democrat stronghold, a third of the vote is in. Democrats need to win that county by an excess of 150,000 in order to carry the state. We're down by only 10,000 in Broward County."

Rove wasn't showing off. He was stalling for time.

"We've worked very hard on getting a record number of absentee ballots," he told Brokaw. "In Florida, they keep track of the absentee ballots in virtually all the major counties by your party registration. There are 130,000 more Republican absentee ballots in the state of Florida than Democratic absentee ballots. Plus, we're going to get a chunk of Democrats and a lot of the 'decline-to-states,'" Rove said, referring to voters who didn't list a party preference on their absentee ballot request.

Rove then ran through some vote totals that showed Bush running better than expected. "Let me just give you one example. Here is a county up near—in between Pensacola and Panama City where the Republicans hope to come out with a 30,000-vote margin. We've come out with a 43,000-vote margin. There's a county south of Jacksonville—Clay County, where the Republicans are—are running 4,000 votes ahead of what we need to do statewide in county after county. Pinellas County, that we're not expected to win a big county in the Tampa-St. Pete area. Governor Bush is winning Pinellas County. So we're going to do well in Florida. And I think the call in Florida was a bit premature."

It was indeed, although in hindsight it is clear that Rove had been misled by one of the same factors that had tainted Voter News Service's data: higher-than-expected turnout across the state. In addition, VNS had data entry errors in Jacksonville and a batch of bad information from Tampa. Their sample had been compromised. The same thing would happen on election night in 2002, but by then VNS knew that the right response in such a case was just to shut down their projects and let the votes be counted. This time, with the presidency hanging in the balance, they tried to fix the problems—with fateful results.

The truth, which would become plain in the days ahead, was that the vote totals in Florida were simply too close to call by the projection method. When they realized this, VNS pollsters retracted their projection moving Florida back into the undecided column. About 10:00 PM, the networks passed this information onto their viewers—and to the campaigns. But then at 2:16 AM Fox News, relying on a VNS calculation that there were not enough votes outstanding for Gore to be able to make up a 58,000-vote Bush lead, called Florida for the second time—this time for Bush. Once again the others followed suit. And once again VNS was premature.

But the campaigns had no reason to know that. Gore called Bush and made a brief private concession. Rove, with seventy-five raucous campaign workers in town, marched up Congress Avenue in Austin, heading for the plaza where Bush had been scheduled to speak. But as the festive crowd gathered in Austin waiting for Bush to claim the mantle of the presidency, up in Nashville Gore was having second thoughts. As his own motorcade made its way to where loyal Democrats were gathered to hear his public concession speech, Bush's cushion in the Florida election returns kept dwindling. By the time Gore arrived downtown and prepared to address his crowd, it was down to a few hundred votes. Gore's brain trust urged him not to give the speech. One of them, campaign chairman William Daley, apologized to Gore for even having allowed him to make the first call to Bush. Now, Gore made a second.

"Circumstances have changed dramatically since I first called you," Gore told Bush, citing the necessity of a mandatory recount under Florida law. "The state of Florida is too close to call."

"Are you saying what I think you're saying?" Bush asked incredulously. "Let me make sure that I understand. You're calling back to retract that concession?"

"Don't get snippy about it!" Gore replied. He added that as he saw it, Florida—and the election—was still in the balance.

Bush replied that his brother, who was there with him, was certain that Gore had lost Florida.

"I don't think this is something your brother can take care of," Gore replied.

"Do what you have to do," Bush said tersely.

The following morning, the top officials in Team Bush—Cheney, Rove, Hughes, campaign manager Joe Allbaugh, campaign chairman Don Evans and Bush himself—convened at 10:00 AM in Austin to form their battle plans. A team of Gore lawyers, recount experts and campaign hands headed by former Secretary of State Warren Christopher had already descended in Tallahassee. Late getting started, the Bush team wanted to make sure it made the right moves. The first move it agreed on was to counter Gore's ex-Secretary of State with one of their own, James A. Baker III, the Texan who had run Bush's father's 1980 campaign, and had served as White House chief of staff and then Secretary of the Treasury under Reagan. When George H. W. Bush ascended to the presidency, Baker was made Secretary of State.

Rove himself recalls being upbeat. Not because he knew anything about recount law—but because he didn't. He assumed it would take a few days, Bush would win, and it would be a footnote in history. Both the Gore and Bush camps realized that there was a legal as well as a public relations battle to be waged. In Baker, Team Bush had someone who could do both, and when he hit the ground in Tallahassee, Baker wasted no time in pressing the public relations aspect of the case. In asking for "recount after recount," Baker said on November 10, the Gore team was willing to "destroy . . . the traditional process for selecting presidents in this country."

However optimistic he was, Rove was not a lawyer, and he and Hughes (and those other aides whose specialty was political communications) were initially unsure of what their role should be. On the Saturday night after the election, the communications staff got together in Austin to strategize. No one could think of anything to do, and the meeting seemed on the verge of petering out when press secretary Mindy Tucker blurted out, "Okay, we're in a battle here, and five senior people are sitting here sucking each other's toes!" With that Tucker and her staff headed to the airport—and on to Florida.

The battle in Florida was primarily a legal one, taking place in local courtrooms across the state, in the office of Florida Secretary of State Katherine Harris, before the State Supreme Court, and in federal court, but Gore and Bush—two non-lawyers—keenly appreciated the public relations front as well. It was not a legal maneuver when Gore went on national television on November 15 and offered to meet with Bush and open up all the counties in the state to a recount, if Bush wanted. Bush rushed from his ranch to Austin to make a speech of his own. The Bush side was unimpressed by Gore's offer, which was standard recount tactics from the side that was behind: stall, ask for more counts, keep the process going while you look for votes. But Bush was impressed by Gore's political maneuverings. "So long as the Florida Supreme Court was rewriting the law and people were divining intent, we had a battle on our hands," Bush said. "And if he [Gore] wasn't willing to address that, then all the rest of it was PR. That's why I rushed back: PR."

Both sides, intent from the outset on winning the election, were loath to acknowledge the obvious: in a state where 6 million votes had been cast, the results were, statistically speaking, a tie. But the tie had to be broken, and however the case ended up being resolved—either in the courts or in the House of Representatives—the final challenge for the winner would be ensuring that the decision was considered legitimate by enough of the country that he could actually govern. Each side knew this, but there were no guidelines on how to accomplish it. Even Rove's beloved historical analogies were of limited value. They were all improvising as they went along.

As the complicated legal cases grinded through the courts on issues that ranged from the farcical (the difference between a "dimpled" and a "pregnant" chad) and the peculiar (the number of elderly Jewish voters in Palm Beach County who misread their "butterfly" ballots and voted for Patrick Buchanan by mistake) to the truly fundamental (whether Florida's politicized state Supreme Court had violated the due process rights of the voters), the stakes in the public relations battle kept ratcheting upward. One man, Gore or Bush, was going to be a loser. How he conducted himself in this period would help determine whether he would ever be a viable national candidate again. Likewise, one of them would be a winner. His ability to govern effectively after taking the oath of office hinged on acting presidential—before he even knew if he'd ever get to be president. That's why Gore's demeanor on television—out-wardly respectful of Bush—was so effective. In addition, the mantra of the Gore team ("Count every vote!") seemed to put the vice pres-ident on the high ground. Suddenly, however, an issue arose that shifted the terrain. That issue was the question of late or otherwise technically flawed overseas absentee ballots from American service-men. Mark Herron, a Democratic lawyer, wrote a memo for the Gore team about how to get these ballots, most of which were pre-sumed to be for Bush, tossed out. If they lacked a postmark, Herron wrote, challenge them.

Here was the kind of issue Rove and the political team had been waiting for. When Gore campaign chairman William Daley had pro-nounced the "butterfly" ballots indefensible, Rove had already embarrassed the Gore forces by producing a similar butterfly ballot from Cook County, Illinois, Daley's home. But that was a cute, one-news-cycle stunt. The issue of military ballots was more serious, espe-cially to military families, and it subtly undermined Gore's "count all the ballots" theme. Whatever the legitimacy of the Democratic lawyers' position, it seemed to many Americans—including some prominent Democrats—unseemly on its face to advocate the discard-ing of votes cast by servicemen and women stationed overseas.

Team Bush swung into action. The campaign got in touch with retired Army General H. Norman Schwarzkopf, a Tampa resident and prominent Bush backer, and asked him to weigh in. Schwarzkopf was only too happy to oblige. Calling it "a very sad day in our coun-try" when members of the armed forces had their votes discarded "because of some technicality out of their control, the Desert Storm commander explained that the military's postal system, not the sol-diers and sailors, was to blame for the lack of postmarks on some of the ballots. "These men and women do not have the luxury of getting in their cars and going to the post office to mail their ballots," Schwarzkopf explained in a widely quoted statement. "They must depend upon a system that takes their ballots directly from their front-line positions on a circuitous route to the ballot box."

In Austin, Montana Governor Marc Racicot, in town to give Bush some moral support, made his debut as a Bush surrogate—and upped the ante higher. "The vice president's lawyers have gone to war, in my judgment, against the men and women who serve in our armed forces," he said at Bush headquarters. "The man who would be their commander in chief is fighting to take away the votes from the people he could command."

This story line, one of the few in the recount saga that could easily be understood by an increasingly perplexed and impatient public, caught on. The Bush forces on the ground in Florida located the wife of one military man whose ballot had been rejected—and talked her into going on *Good Morning America*. The issue was scheduled to be Topic One on the talk shows on Sunday, November 19, and Gore's team wanted to make it go away. Joe Lieberman was chosen to quell the firestorm. Lieberman did so, but in a way that complicated the legal effort and may have helped put Bush in the White House. Asked about the matter by Tim Russert on *Meet the Press*, Lieberman answered, "If I was there, I would give the benefit of the doubt to ballots coming in from military personnel generally." Lieberman urged Florida's exhausted election officials to "go back and take another look," adding, "Because, again, Al Gore and I don't want to ever be part of anything that would put an extra burden on the military personnel abroad who want to vote."

This was the right political answer, at least in the long run, and

Florida's other leading Democrats immediately sought to distance themselves from the Gore effort to stand on a technicality concerning military absentee ballots. But in real time, it might not have been the right legal answer—and this case was being decided in a legal forum. The reason was that on November 21, in a decision seemingly tailored to help Gore, the all-Democratic Florida Supreme Court had ruled in another context—the context of the "under-voters" that ballots should not be discarded because of the "hyper-technicalities" of Florida election law. Armed with this language and with Lieberman's own admonishment, Republican lawyers applied it to the military absentee ballots, and quickly succeeded in convincing canvassing boards in twelve Florida counties to reopen some of the discarded military ballots. This resulted in a net gain to Bush of some 176 votes. In its book on the Florida recount, *Deadlock: The Inside Story of America's Closest Election,* *The Washington Post* noted that at one point Bush's lead in the recount over Gore was to shrink to 154 votes. Without those sketchy military absentee ballots, Gore might have pulled ahead, forever altering the PR mojo of the great Florida recount.

But raising hell about absentee ballots and some of the irregularities in the vote counting was about the extent of the contribution Rove and the rest of the political and speechwriting team could make during the five incredible weeks of the Florida recount. Allbaugh and Evans had kept a political presence in Tallahassee; Rove and Hughes had held down the fort in Austin. But the case was won in the courts by platoons of lawyers—Florida lawyer Barry Richard and his team that handled the state court litigation in the state courts, Theodore Olson and George Terwilliger before the U.S. Supreme Court, with Jim Baker overseeing the whole effort. But at

10:00 PM on December 12, 2000, the high court, on a 5–4 vote in which five Republican-appointed justices lined up behind Bush, ended the recounting once and for all, giving Bush his victory.

The following day, Rove and Hughes were back in business. Hughes called Bush that morning to discuss his speech. A week earlier, Hughes and Bush had agreed that if the time came to claim victory, the governor should do it from the chamber of the Texas House of Representatives and that he should be introduced by the Democratic Speaker of the House, as a way of signaling that after the rancor of the Florida recount Bush still intended to be the "unifier, not the divider" he had promised to be during the long campaign. Earlier, chief speechwriter Mark Gerson had written a draft of the speech, one that had been extensively reworked by Hughes and Bush, with contributions from Mark McKinnon. But there was something missing. Cognizant now of the unique historic circumstance of Bush's acceptance speech, Hughes turned to Rove, the staff history buff, for some further help.

"This cries out for historic reference," she told him.

"Look at the election of 1800," he replied.

Rove lent Hughes a book on the first bitterly contested presidential election in the nation's history, which was thrown into the House of Representatives after Thomas Jefferson and Aaron Burr had come up tied in the Electoral College. Ultimately, after six days of acrimonious debate, Jefferson was chosen as the nation's third president on the thirty-sixth ballot. "The steady character of our countrymen is a rock to which we may safely moor," Jefferson wrote in a subsequent letter. "Unequivocal in principle, reasonable in manner, we shall be able, I hope to do a great deal of good to the cause of freedom and harmony."

Hughes loved those lines, and incorporated them into Bush's

speech. That night, Bush continued: "Two hundred years have only strengthened the steady character of America. And so, as we begin the work of healing our nation, tonight I call upon that character, respect for each other, respect for our differences, generosity of spirit, and a willingness to work hard and work together to solve any problem." Bush's speech also employed a memorable phrase Abraham Lincoln had used in the context of the Civil War. "Our nation," Bush said that night, "must rise above a house divided."

The Florida recount process revealed a great deal about elective democracy, not all of it reassuring, and one of the most fascinating to students of history is that the traditional concession speech is more than an exercise in good form. It is part of the election process itself; it tells a losing side's supporters when it is time to stand down. It is actually what brings elections to a close. For that reason, as well as media reports that persisted all day long that Gore would "withdraw," but not actually "concede," Team Bush had been keenly interested in Gore's speech, which was scheduled immediately before Bush's. Gore did truly concede, of course, and he did so with class and eloquence. He made a point of referring to Bush as "President-elect Bush," and deliberately chose phrases and cadences that were also evocative of Lincoln—specifically, Lincoln's second inaugural address. "Neither he nor I anticipated this long and difficult road," Gore said of his rival. "Certainly, neither of us wanted it to happen. Yet it came. And now it has ended, resolved as it must be resolved—through the time-honored institutions of our democracy."

Bush, clearly moved by Gore's grace, lauded the vice president at the outset of his speech, and returned to him near the end. "I have something else to ask," Bush said. "I ask you to pray for Vice President Gore and his family."

Rove had sat one row behind Gore's daughter Karenna during

the oral arguments before the Supreme Court on December 11, and it had brought home for him how desperately hard this ordeal was getting to be on the families involved. He certainly knew how badly he had wanted to win himself. Twice, during the crucible of the Florida recount, Rove had taken incremental judicial or bureaucratic decisions in Bush's favor to mean victory. Once, eleven days into it, he'd given high-fives to everyone at headquarters. Another time, Rove had actually given Bush a cigar. But he'd been premature both times, just as he'd jumped the gun with his predictions the weekend for Election Day. But now it was real. They had finally prevailed. Moments before Bush entered the hall in the Texas statehouse, Rove and Hughes spotted each other waiting for the President-elect's arrival. The two loyal aides hugged spontaneously. Later, thinking back to the days after South Carolina, Rove allowed himself a brief moment to crow about what they had accomplished. "March through June, we began the general election while Gore was still figuring out where he was or what he'd begun," Rove recalled.

Years before, when a George W. Bush presidency was a figment of Rove's imagination, and hardly anyone else's, the governor had signed a picture of himself and given it to Rove. "To Karl," read the inscription, "the man with the plan." Now the man and his plan, not to mention his victorious candidate, were heading to the White House.

12

The Crucible of Power

The campaign had been interminable, but when it was finally over, George W. Bush had managed to attain the Oval Office without making many specific promises. This was a good thing, because presidents are expected to keep their pledges. "Politicians are the same all over," Soviet Premier Nikita Khrushchev once said. "They promise to build a bridge, even where there is no river." That may be true in Russia, and it may be true for every other elective office in the United States, but as Rove was aware, it is decidedly not true for the American presidency. In a study of the five presidents elected and party platforms from 1960 to 1984, American University government professor Jeff Fishel charted how, on average, two-thirds of the promises made during the campaign were later kept. Rutgers University professor Gerald Pomper found much the same thing in looking at presidents and party platforms from Harry Truman to Gerald Ford. And in Bill Clinton's first term, Knight-Ridder Newspapers tallied his promises and discovered he was right in the middle of the historic norm—at about 66 percent. Former Clinton aide George Stephanopoulos is remembered, and not fondly, for blurting out to Larry King that his boss "kept the promises he meant to keep." More indicative than Stephanopoulos' unfortunate quote—or Khrushchev's trenchant observation—was the attitude of Clinton domestic policy adviser William Galston, who came to the White House in 1993 and promptly posted on his wall a list of Clinton campaign promises. "I looked at it every morning to make sure I remembered what the President said we ought to be doing there," he said.

Rove wanted to help his boss succeed in office as well, but he wasn't in need of a written bill of particulars to keep track of Bush's campaign promises. There weren't that many of them. It wasn't much of an exaggeration to say that the man with the plan's actual plan wasn't much longer than Rove's White House title, "senior adviser to the president for strategic initiatives." In all those months of disciplined campaigning—of remaining "on-message"—Bush ran primarily on three issues, or more precisely, two major issues and a theme. He promised to cut taxes. He emphasized the need for the federal government to do more to bolster elementary and secondary education. And he said he'd try to restore civility to the political discourse in Washington and, in the process, bring back the art of compromise to the nation's capital. To be sure, he mentioned other issues, including his support for "faith-based" programs to tackle social ills, school vouchers, and the establishment of private investment accounts as part of Social Security.

Still, Rove's agenda for Bush's first year in office was a minimalist one, especially coming after the activism and policy wonk-ism of the Clinton era. Neither Rove nor Bush expressed any grand ideas for "reinventing government," which had been in Vice President Gore's portfolio, or for building bridges to future centuries, or for defining a new world order. During the campaign Bush sounded scarcely interested in foreign policy, and he did not spend the

Christmas holidays following his election to the presidency (as Clinton had) in Hilton Head at the pretentiously named Renaissance Weekend, listening to panelists hash out the fine points of "Global Population Pressures" and "The 21st Century Superpower Sweepstakes." He spent it at his ranch in Crawford.

This is not to say Team Bush was uninterested in governing. Rove immersed himself in the briefing books prepared for him about the beginning of every presidency since John F. Kennedy's. "It's important to strike the right starting note," Rove explained to those around him. "Time is precious."

This was one of the lessons in Rove's briefing books. Another was that glitches arise when presidents try to keep promises they never should have made in the first place, or when they don't prioritize their campaign pledges well. An example of the first mistake is when presidents—and this is a perennial pitfall—vow to cut the federal bureaucracy or, even worse, the White House staff itself. This is nearly always a mistake. They end up either breaking their word, getting rid of essential personnel, or sending the wrong symbolic message. (Andrew Card, the new chief of staff, nearly fell into this trap by suggesting in an interview in the early days of George W. Bush's presidency that he was going to decimate the White House office on AIDS. Card quickly backed down in the face of hostile publicity.) An example of the second danger, putting the president's priorities in the wrong order, had come eight years earlier when President-elect Clinton, a full two months before he was even inaugurated, blurted out that he was planning to open the U.S. military to gays and lesbians. There was nothing inherently wrong with this proposal, which many Americans consider long overdue, and Clinton had first floated the idea during the 1992 campaign. But by making it his first order of business, Clinton undermined his assurances that he would govern as "a new kind of Democrat." Moreover, gays in the military hardly seemed the most urgent problem facing the nation. What Clinton should have done, his aides later conceded, was tackle welfare reform or revamping the nation's campaign finance laws first.

As it was, however, Clinton's first real legislative fight as president was over the federal budget and taxes, just as Ronald Reagan's was—and just as George W. Bush's would be. On March 8, less than seven weeks after Bush took the oath of office, his budget plan passed the Republican-controlled House on a virtual party-line vote of 230–198. The package was estimated to cost the U.S. Treasury some $1.6 trillion over ten years, but such figures are always guesswork. The bill would cut income tax rates in all brackets until they were fully phased in by 2006. The top rate would drop from 39.6 percent to 33 percent. The lowest rate was cut from 15 percent to 10 percent. The bill also repealed the estate tax, expanded deductions for charitable contributions, and increased the tax deduction for married couples. Predictably, Democrats claimed that a huge proportion of the tax cuts—43 percent by one estimate—would flow to the richest 1 or 2 percent of taxpayers. The White House countered that argument with charts showing that another way of looking at it was that it was lowest-income taxpayers who would see their tax bills reduced by the largest percentages. Both sides were right, and the measure was headed to the Senate, divided 50–50 between Republicans and Democrats and with Vice President Dick Cheney poised to break a tie, if need be—as Gore had done eight years earlier on Clinton's budget bill that raised the rates on the highest earners.

It never came to that. On April 6, the Senate passed a compromise $1.25 trillion tax cut, sending the bill into a House-Senate conference committee to forge a compromise. On May 26, that compromise was ironed out—$1.35 billion over ten years. The top rate would fall not to 33 percent, which Bush wanted, but 35 percent. The lowest rate would max out at 12 percent instead of the 10 percent Bush had called for. Nonetheless, it included rebate checks of $300 for a single taxpayer and $600 for a couple, checks that were mailed out starting in late summer. On June 7, a beaming Bush signed the bill in the East Room. It was only the third across-the-board income tax reduction in the past fifty years. The first was proposed by John F. Kennedy, the second by Ronald Reagan. Bush, clearly believing he was in good historic company, invoked Kennedy's and Reagan's names and said, "And now it's happening for the third time—and it's about time!"

It was an undeniable legislative achievement for Bush, although it was hard to tell that from the news coverage. At first, the mainstream media lambasted Bush for ramming his tax cut through the House on a party-line vote. (A failure of the "bipartisanship" Bush had promised, complained the *Los Angeles Times*.) Then, when the bill passed the Senate, the press reversed field, saying that Bush had compromised too much. ("Is this a stinging setback?" asked CBS News. For the answer, the network quoted Senate Democratic Leader Thomas A. Daschle: "If this is a victory for them, then we want more victories just like it.")

Rove and his colleagues in the White House were irritated by the tone of the news coverage. When Gore had broken a tie on the budget deal eight years earlier, the media hadn't accused the White House of committing any grave offenses against bipartisanship.

Besides, fifteen Democratic Senators had voted for Bush's tax cut—wasn't that a sign of compromise? As for the second line of attack, that Bush had been outmaneuvered into giving up too much, on this point Daschle was clearly talking out of his hat. The plain facts were that Bush got his tax cut faster than Reagan (or JFK, for that matter) and that whatever the Democrats might be telling CBS, Bush's tax reduction was three times larger than the one Al Gore had proposed.

What the Bush team didn't realize is that they had stepped on congressional prerogatives. Not by rounding up mostly Republican votes, but by pushing to call the roll so fast, before the entire budget was prepared. Daschle and House Democratic Leader Richard A. Gephardt had warned the White House that such a move would be considered strong-arming Congress. Fellow Texan Charles W. Stenholm, a conservative Democrat, had beamed proudly when Bush gave his well-received address to the Joint Session of Congress on February 27. But that pride had turned to dismay days later when the White House held tightly to its fast track tax-cut strategy. "It just cut the heart out of me," Rep. Stenholm said. "I think the honeymoon is effectively over," added Rep. Robert T. Matsui, a respected California. "They're going to be very right-wing and very partisan." Democrats unfamiliar with Rove's collection of past presidents' First 100 Days briefing books couldn't for the life them figure out what Bush's hurry was. But they knew how little they themselves thought of being stampeded. "I think what happened in the House . . . will be interpreted by many Democrats in the Senate as almost an insult, a slap in the face to a real democratic process," Senator John F. Kerry of Massachusetts said on ABC's *This Week*.

It also didn't help Bush's cause that he had given three separate explanations for why he thought a tax cut was desirable. During the campaign, when federal budget surpluses were projected, Bush said it was matter of simple common sense. It was the people's money, not the government's, and if government was collecting too much it ought to be repatriated back to the taxpayers quickly before Washington figured out how to spend it. After the surpluses disappeared, Bush switched gears, saying tax cuts could spur spending, helping to jump-start the flagging economy. At other times, Bush spoke about tax rates as though moral principles were involved. Paying more than one-third of your income to the federal government, Bush opined, was just plain wrong.

Political observers were also reluctant to give Bush his due on the tax cuts because by the time he signed that bill in the East Room, Republican control of the Senate had vanished with the defection of Vermont Senator James M. Jeffords, who expressed displeasure with the Bush spending priorities. Because Rove's portfolio was politics, among other things, Jeffords' desertion was seen as a failure on his watch. Worse, he hadn't even seen it coming. Nevertheless, Rove was gradually assuming the kind of power in the White House that made him a logical scapegoat when almost anything went wrong. And it wasn't just politics. It was policy, too. Cabinet appointments were vetted through him, judicial nominations crossed his desk, as did the details of a proposed energy bill, administration policy on stem-cell research, steel tariffs, and health care policy. Nearly every speech was shown to Rove before it was delivered. He often suggested changes. The question of who should head the RNC was his bailiwick, as was the ever-constant challenge of mollifying the conservative wing of the Republican Party. When Bush wanted to reward Montana Governor Marc Racicot, a longtime personal friend, for his loyalty and effectiveness during the Florida recount, with the job he wanted—Attorney General—it was Rove to whom the conservatives appealed. Racicot was squishy on abortion and other social issues, they said. John Ashcroft got the job instead. The line separating politics from policy is never clearly delineated in any White House. Rove made no pretense that there was a line. Asked in early 2002 if there was any domestic issue he *didn't* have his hands on, Rove quipped, "Anything involving baseball."

By this time, Rove was well along in remaking his own image. A long time removed from the direct mail specialist whose most obvious talent lay in conceiving of a devastating negative attack, Rove was increasingly seen in Washington as the well-read history buff whose counsel was eagerly sought by the president on almost everything. He was asked in April 2002 in a ninety-minute interview with *National Journal* if he considered himself primarily a policy adviser.

"Well, look, part of my job is to look after the politics of things, but the fact of the matter is, if you make an electoral calculation about everything, it will blow up in your face," he replied. "The best politics is sound policy. The question is: 'Is this in conformity with the President's principles, and will it seek to achieve a goal that he laid out during the campaign?'"

But whatever one called what Rove was doing, it seemed to be working. In Bush's first summer in office, his job approval rating, as measured in the Gallup Poll, hovered in the mid–50s, which is acceptable, but not great. To keep it there—or, better yet, to increase it—Rove needed to keep the legislative victories coming. But just as Team Bush had been blindsided by Jim Jeffords' defection, they also underestimated how much the change of one vote in the Senate would interfere with The Plan. With Senator Daschle, a liberal with presidential fancies of his own, now in charge of the legislative calendar, Bush could suddenly not even get his pet bills, such as his faith-based initiative, to the Senate floor for a vote. Meanwhile, new Judiciary Committee Chairman Patrick Leahy of Vermont was using his control to stall Bush's judicial nominees—and sometimes to publicly eviscerate the reputations of those deemed too conservative.

But even as conservatives were carping that the White House was letting judicial nominees hang out to dry, Rove concluded that fighting too hard on these messy appointment battles was not how he wanted to spend Bush's precious, limited, political capital. Answering Democrats in kind was a trap. They had learned in Austin that keeping the tone of political debate on a civil plane wasn't just good government—it was good politics. In 1994, Ann Richards had derisively referred to Bush as "Shrub," while the challenger always called her "governor."

Once, in his debate with Richards, she made some kind remarks about volunteers who had responded to a natural disaster in Texas. Bush didn't try to one-up her.

"Well spoken, governor," was all he replied.

His civility, however calculated, struck voters as reflective of good manners. And although their private comments about the Democrats could be quite pointed, Rove and Bush resisted being goaded into a public pissing match with Daschle or Leahy.

In fact, while Daschle was first sniping at the tax bill, Bush responded by posing for pictures with Daschle while in South Dakota. "Sometimes we'll agree, sometimes we won't agree, but one thing that Senator Daschle and I have agreed on is to respect each other," Bush said on March 9 while standing beside the Democratic Leader at a community health center in Sioux Falls. "People want civility. We're going to give them civility."

This charm offensive was swell, but with the Democrats running the Senate and Bush's momentum stalled, Rove longed to replicate his successes in Austin, where the typical prescription had been to have Bush push hard rhetorically on an initiative, then let the legislative process work its way. After compromise was reached, Bush could take the credit at a festive bill signing ceremony, often sitting under a big campaign-style banner with some slogan on it reading something like, "Leave No Child Behind."

In Washington, they'd done this on taxes, but now they needed another victory. They needed an education bill.

The "No Child Left Behind Act of 2001"—that was actually its name—passed the House in late May on a vote of 384 to 45, a landslide that included 197 Democrats. This bill, despite its Orwellian title, was a scheduled reauthorization of the 1965 Elementary and Secondary Education Act. The text of the bill was long and complicated, but the gist was that the Bush administration agreed to spend more money in return for more accountability from states and local school boards. What the administration demanded, ultimately, was annual testing of each school in the country—and a series of sanctions for schools that didn't get better. The vote tally was so lopsided because each side had given something. Bush had thrown in the towel on vouchers before the negotiating even got serious, a gesture that showed good faith. His reward was the defeat of a liberal amendment to kill the testing requirements. This compromise had the blessing of Democratic Representative George Miller, a hulking

California liberal with a big laugh, big ideas about what government could accomplish—and a desire to get things done. One of the House's four remaining "Watergate babies" from the huge Democratic class of 1974, Miller had campaigned in 2000 for Bill Bradley, not Gore, because he was tired of "incrementalism" in Washington. Miller's passion has become education policy—and he's willing to buck even the teacher's union to get more federal money into schools and some genuine education standards. Bush promptly dubbed Miller "Big George," the same name the Bush family employed to delineate Bush's father from George W. Bush, who as a boy, was called "Georgie." More to the point, Bush had found in George Miller someone he could work with. The bill they ultimately fashioned—and the process that produced it—satisfied the White House and impressed liberals. "There have been extensive bipartisan negotiations on the education bill, there's no doubt about that, and they have been real," proclaimed Ralph Neas, president of People for the American Way. But if the rapport between "Georgie" and "Big George" was impressive, it was nothing compared to the unusual alliance the president formed with Senator Edward M. Kennedy.

Republican candidates—and Republican political operatives such as Karl Rove—spend so much of their time bashing Ted Kennedy on their way up the ladder that they are invariably and pleasantly surprised when they finally meet the man. He is personable and earthy; he has the Kennedy charisma and is disarmingly candid and straightforward in his closed-door legislative negotiations. Bush laid the groundwork even before his inauguration by calling Kennedy. And in his first week in office, he invited Kennedy and much of his clan to the White House for a screening of the movie *Thirteen Days*. (The invitees included Representative Patrick Kennedy, who had said during the 2000 South Carolina primary that the visit to Bob Jones University proved Bush was a "wing nut." About his invitation to eat hot dogs and hamburgers in the White House theater, Patrick Kennedy remarked, "I thought it was very gracious of him to invite me.") After Kennedy and Bush found common ground on the education bill, Bush literally traveled around the country singing Kennedy's praises. "I told the folks at the coffee shop in Crawford, Texas, that Ted Kennedy was all right," Bush said at one joint appearance. "They nearly fell out. But he is. I've come to admire him. He's a smart, capable senator. You want him on your side, I can tell you that."

If this was vaguely patronizing—certainly not everyone in Crawford considers Kennedy a pariah—the senator went along. In the scheme of things, the relationship with Bush helped him, too: Beneath the banter was the tacit implication that even for a Republican president, liberal Ted Kennedy remains the go-to guy in the Senate's Democratic caucus. Kennedy walked the walk as well. He personally talked liberal senators out of their misgivings, pointing out to them all they'd gotten from the White House by way of compromise. On June 14, with Kennedy personally sheep-dogging it, the No Child Left Behind Act passed the Senate ninety-one to eight.

"I think the president deserves credit," Daschle said after the vote. "He has been resolute in his effort to find that middle ground on this bill, and I want to compliment him for his willingness to do that. . . . I think this is good for schools."

There was the little matter of spending levels for the educational provisions in the bill, never fully resolved. The White House was envisioning that the new school plan would cost about $19 billion in the coming year. The House version called for $24 billion. The Kennedy version was a lot more—$41.8 billion—but back then everybody told themselves: that's what House-Senate conferences were for. Eventually, this disagreement over funding levels would become bitter and would undo much of the goodwill formed between the White House and the liberals on Capitol Hill. But as Bush's first summer as president was coming to a close, Karl Rove's plan for the first year was proceeding apace. The tax bill was law, the education bill was in conference, and Bush's civility campaign was attaining tangible results.

Rove was pleased as pie, although there is always an Eeyore or two in the crowd. Bush had inherited an under-performing economy, and it wasn't getting any better. In peacetime, a president's job approval rating typically rises and falls with the state of the economy. On August 31, 2001, the unemployment figures released by the government showed the jobless rate had risen to 4.9 percent. The following Tuesday, September 4, at the Metropolitan Club in Washington, about a dozen Republican eminences had met for a private dinner with Rove, White House budget director Mitchell E. Daniels Jr. and Nicholas Calio, the White House's liaison to Capitol Hill. These Republicans, who included former White House chief of staff Kenneth M. Duberstein, GOP pollster Linda DiVall, conservative activist David Keene, and a former party chairman Haley Barbour, had no specific agenda. But as the dinner progressed, several of them voiced concern that the administration wasn't acting decisively enough on the economy. They wanted Bush to do something— exactly what was not a matter of consensus—and suggested that Republican candidates in 2002 would be at peril if the economy were still sluggish and Bush was perceived as being passive about it.

Rove mostly listened at that dinner. A few of these Republicans were his friends or allies from past campaigns, but he thought they were being a little panicky. "A lot of people in Washington are trying to dismiss the success of this president by raising the bar higher on the next thing down the pike," he complained a few days later. Besides, Rove already had big plans. He was planning on getting active himself in speaking at GOP fundraisers. And he was devising ways to get more out of Laura Bush, who as a campaigner and a public speaker was proving to be a huge, and popular, draw. Several such appearances, mostly for female GOP candidates, had already been scheduled for later in the month. Rove also had mapped out ways to keep the focus on the education bill, which seemed stuck in that House-Senate conference committee

The following Tuesday, Laura Bush was scheduled to testify on Capitol Hill on early childhood development. As it happens, she was to appear before Kennedy's Senate committee. Rove himself was heading to Florida for a couple of days with the president, who was scheduled to begin a week of education-related speeches and media events focusing on reading. The first school on the list was Justina Road Elementary School in Jacksonville on Monday, September 10. The second, the following morning, was Emma E. Booker Elementary in Sarasota. And that's where they were when the planes hit.

During the Florida recount, the lawyers had realized that spin and political strategizing might help, but that the real work had to be done by the experts. Rove and Karen Hughes had abided by that judgment; they had done what they could, but it was precious little.

On the surface, war might seem a similar set of circumstances. The war would be won by the generals and the soldiers and the civilians with martial backgrounds, be they Secretary of Defense Donald H. Rumsfeld or "Gary," the CIA station chief who choppered into Afghanistan with $3 million in cash for inducing fickle warlords to side with the United States instead of the Taliban. But it became apparent within hours on September 11, 2001, that communicating with the public is as important a mission as an American commander in chief has during wartime.

The morning of the attacks, Bush and his entourage (which included Rove; Andy Card; Dan Bartlett, who was Hughes' deputy; White House press secretary Ari Fleischer; another press aide named Gordon Johndroe; education adviser Sandy Kress and Representative Dan Miller of Florida) followed the advice of their Secret Service detail instead of their gut instincts. This was a public relations mistake, one of the last Bush would make for months. Air Force One didn't head north toward the White House, but west to Barksdale Air Force Base, in northwestern Louisiana. There, Bush taped a statement, relayed fuzzily by the networks because of technical difficulties. The president's plane took off again, this time for Offutt Air Force Base near Omaha, Nebraska. Once there, the president made the decision to return to Washington. His plane landed at Andrews Air Force Base at 6:34 PM, and he rode in the presidential helicopter, Marine One, back to the White House. At 8:30 PM he addressed the nation from the Oval Office in a five-minute statement that started incongruously. "Good evening," Bush said on a night that was anything but good. But the president picked up steam as he read his remarks from a TelePrompTer. He began to find his stride, which would sustain him for the months ahead. In that brief speech, he touched on all the themes that would animate him in the coming year: He expressed sorrow for the victims and their families, especially the children left without parents; he denounced the perpetrators of the attack as "evil," a word he would employ again and again; he vowed to bring the perpetrators to justice, and, more ominously, vowed to make no distinction between the terrorists "and those who harbor them"; he alluded to his faith by quoting the 23rd Psalm ("Even though I walk through the valley of the shadow of death I fear no evil—for You are with me"); finally, Bush said that the nation had been attacked before, and had always prevailed.

"America has stood down enemies before, and we will do so this time," he said that night. "None of us will ever forget this day. Yet, we go forward to defend freedom and all that is good and just in our world."

Bush deliberately avoided using the phrase "act of war" that night, which he thought the country might not be ready for in those uncertain hours. But he did use it the following day, in a grim-faced comment to the White House "pool" of reporters gathered for photographs as Bush sat down with his national security team. His remarks included the following passage:

The American people need to know that we're facing a different enemy than we have ever faced. This enemy hides in shadows, and has no regard for human life. This is an enemy who preys on innocent and unsuspecting people, then runs for cover. But it won't be able to run for cover forever. This is an enemy that tries to hide. But it won't be able to hide forever. This is an enemy that thinks its harbors are safe. But they won't be safe forever.

This enemy attacked not just our people, but all freedom-loving people everywhere in the world. The United States of America will use all our resources to conquer this enemy. We will rally the world. We will be patient, we will be focused, and we will be steadfast in our determination.

This battle will take time and resolve. But make no mistake about it: we will win.

For well over a year after the attacks, Rove and other White House advisers insisted that, contrary to what anyone said, Bush did not "grow" in office. They maintained that he was always the steely, substantive fellow on display on September 12. It is unclear why they do this: The evidence is all in the other direction, and it is hardly unflattering to Bush that he rose to the occasion and did so almost immediately. Nor that he had help in doing so, not only from Rumsfeld and Colin Powell, but from Rove, Hughes, Gerson, Bartlett, and others in the White House communications shop.

Long before September 11, Bush had shown he knew how to hire speechwriters, and that he could deliver a written speech. It was a good thing—because Bush Unplugged could certainly be something to behold. During the campaign he had mesmerized the press with such Quayle-like rhetorical flights of fancy as "We won't raise trade terriers," and "We ought to make the pie higher." He once allowed as how "more and more of our imports come from overseas," and riffed that, "Families is where our nation finds shape, where wings take dream." As president he dazzled audiences with made up words such as the redundant, but catchy "misunderestimate" or the descriptive "embetterment," apparently inspired by the co-mingling of "empowerment" and "betterment."

On occasion, the unscripted Bush would just leave his listeners wondering exactly what was taking place inside his head. Consider this exchange with the White House pool on July 2, 2001, at the Jefferson Memorial.

Q. What's the occasion, Mr. President?

BUSH. Wanted to come over. We're looking right out our window every day at the Jefferson. It's a beautiful day. Wanted to come over and begin the beginning of the Fourth of July celebration here at the Jefferson Memorial; it's an opportunity to say hello to some of our fellow Americans.

Q. What does the Fourth mean to you, Mr. President?

BUSH. Well, it's an unimaginable honor to be the President during the Fourth of July of this country. It means what these words say, for starters. The great inalienable rights of our country. We're blessed with such values in America. And I—it's—I'm a proud man to be the nation based upon such wonderful values. I can't tell you what it's like to be in Europe, for example, to be talking about the greatness of America. But the true greatness of America are the people. And it's another reason we're here, is to be able to say hello to some of our fellow Americans who are here to celebrate.

Just eight weeks later, this man would be a wartime commander in chief to a hard-hit nation—and that level of communication wasn't going to cut it. This is where Rove, Bartlett, Gerson, and Hughes really earned their stripes. As the war took shape, Rove slipped from the news; to those who asked, he would say self-effacingly, "I don't do intelligence." It was true, but only as far as it went. Bush's communications team had never been more invaluable. They were not making policy in Afghanistan, but they were helping the president craft every formal utterance he made on the war—as the whole world looked on. After Bush's powerful remarks to the pool on Wednesday, the staff prepared for what all thought would be their toughest challenge. On Friday, September 14, Bush was to give a speech at Washington National Cathedral and then travel to New York, to Ground Zero, to visit with some of the families of the missing.

It started well enough. The speech at National Cathedral was a triumph. "We are here in the middle hour of our grief," the president began with simple eloquence, to an audience that included his father, his predecessor, and the man who nearly beat him in Florida. "So many have suffered so great a loss, and today we express our nation's sorrow. We come before God to pray for the missing and the dead, and for those who love them."

But the National Cathedral speech was much more than a prayer service. Although the setting was a church, it was a martial address intended to rally a nation, and serve notice to the world. "This conflict was begun on the timing and terms of others," Bush said in words that, like the December 2000 victory speech at the Texas statehouse, were inspired by the phrasings of Lincoln. "It will end in a way and at an hour of our choosing. Our purpose as a nation is firm."

The very eloquence of such words presented a potential problem for Bush. If the gap between those speeches and the unscripted Bush were too great—if the rhetorical bumbler of the Jefferson Memorial were to reappear—it would be jarring to the American people. Just hours after he left National Cathedral, Bush was put to the test.

This time Rove couldn't help his onetime pupil. Neither could

Gerson the great wordsmith nor Hughes, who was so close to Bush that she once said that she didn't know where he started and she left off. Bush was on his own. The scene was the World Trade Center pile.

Bush had gone there to look, and make a show of support to the rescue workers at the site. As he passed through the area they shouted to him, "Whatever it takes!" and "Don't let me down!" A familiar chant went up, "USA! USA! USA!" Rove and the other White House aides got goose bumps. It dawned on them that Bush needed to say something back.

"They want to hear him," Nina Bishop, a member of the White House advance staff yelled in the din. She was trying to make herself heard to Rove, who was walking near the president.

"They want to hear their president!"

No provision had been made for Bush to speak. There was no sound system, no stage, nowhere he could even be seen by the rescue crews, let alone heard.

"Can you find a bullhorn?" Rove asked Bishop.

The president climbed atop a burned-out fire truck where he joined a retired New York fireman named Bob Beckwith, one of the volunteers who'd responded to the attack. Beckwith tried to get down, but Bush put his arm around him, motioning him to stay. A bullhorn somehow appeared out of the crowd and was handed up to Bush. The chant of "USA!" began anew.

"Thank you all," Bush began. "I want you all to know . . . "

"CAN'T HEAR YOU!" one of the workers shouted from the crowd.

"I can't go any louder," Bush protested before starting again. "America today is on bended knee in prayer for the people whose lives were lost here . . . "

"I CAN'T HEAR YOU," came another voice from the crowd.

Bush looked briefly taken aback. But then, his arm still around the aging fireman's shoulder, he shouted back through his bullhorn in a scene aired around the world. "I can hear *you*! The rest of the world hears you. And the people who knocked these buildings down will hear all of us soon!"

When asked about Bush's popularity, Bush's success after September 11, Karl Rove himself would invariably point to this moment at Ground Zero, to a moment when Bush, without polls, talking points, any four-point plans, or even so much as a scribbled note, had indeed answered the call in such an evocative, natural way.

Who knew Bush had this in him?

We all did, Rove insisted.

Maybe that's right. If so, then perhaps the true nature of Rove's "genius" was simply this: Way back in their Texas days, he saw it first.

13

The End of Democratic America?

Two months after the terrorist attacks, Americans went to the polls for the first time in the era of the George W. Bush presidency. On that day, November 6, 2001, U.S. troops were in the process of collapsing the Taliban and scattering Al Qaeda to the four winds. With Americans rallying to the flag and their commander in chief, Bush's job approval rating hit 90 percent in the Gallup Poll, a historic high previously reached only by one other president—Bush's father—since Gallup began asking the question in the time of Franklin Delano Roosevelt.

And yet the first test of Bush's coattails in such an environment was a fiasco for the GOP. Three big races were held that day: the governor's races in Virginia and New Jersey and the mayoral race in New York City. Democrats captured the statehouses in Virginia and New Jersey. In New York Michael Bloomberg won while running as a Republican, but Bloomberg had been a registered Democrat who admired Bill Clinton and contributed to Democratic candidates; running as a Republican was a ruse to assure him a place on the general election ballot. Even then, Bloomberg only won because of disarray and racial politicking on the Democratic side and because outgoing, term-limited Mayor Rudolph W. Giuliani had campaigned for him.

Rove was peeved at the performance of the Republican Party apparatus he was supposed to be overseeing. Perhaps New Jersey couldn't be saved—the state had gone for Gore in 2000—but Virginia was another matter. Virginia's governorship had been open because it, alone among the fifty states, allows its governor only one four-year term. But Rove believed he'd taken steps to hold Virginia, which has become a Republican-leaning state in the past two decades, and that others had dropped the ball: namely the state's outgoing governor, James S. Gilmore III. The loss of the Richmond statehouse set in motion changes that would prove significant in 2002.

At the time of the 2001 election, Gilmore was chairman of the Republican National Committee. He had been installed there by Bush, who had befriended the Virginian when both were southern governors. Gilmore was a Bush kind of Republican. He made it his mission to court minority voters and union leaders, and he stressed education as his number one issue. In fact, Gilmore's 1997 campaign slogan, "Education First, Then Cut Taxes," was a kind of precursor to "compassionate conservatism." In his tenure as governor, Gilmore had approached his goal of securing Republican control in the Legislature with a tenacity and a shrewdness that belied his reputation as a technocrat. He appointed seven conservative Democrats to posts in his administration—and then campaigned for Republicans in the special elections to fill their vacant seats in the Legislature. These districts had, over time, become more conservative and Republican candidates won them all. As part of this effort, the decidedly uncharismatic Gilmore imported Republicans with more sizzle to be the headliners at GOP fundraisers. One of them was George W. Bush, who appeared at two events. Bush's wife spoke at a third Virginia fundraiser, his father at a fourth. And even though Bush was simpatico with Gilmore, all this help didn't come without strings. With Rove as the go-between, the governor agreed to move Virginia's 2000 primary to February 29, as a kind of second "firewall" in case South Carolina didn't pan out. Thus was Jim Gilmore introduced to the fact that doing business with Rove generally carried a price tag.

In the wake of the 2001 election, the relationship between the two men became stressed past the point where it probably could be fixed. The White House had counted on Gilmore to keep Virginia in Republican hands, but he hadn't done it. And in Rove's mind Gilmore had all but sabotaged that effort by picking a fight over the budget with the Republican-controlled Legislature in the summer of 2001, thus giving the Democratic candidate, Mark Warner, an opening to run as someone who would get things done—a "reformer with results," you could say. Gilmore believed he had no choice but to fight the good fight on the budget. But in Rove's shop, the consensus was that Gilmore hadn't kept his eye on the big picture, which was another way of saying he hadn't paid sufficient deference to what was good for the White House. Gilmore's real transgression was that he actually thought he was in charge at the RNC. The negotiations over his titles and duties had taken place between Rove and Gilmore's chief of staff, Boyd Marcus. Originally, Rove offered Gilmore the more ceremonial title of "general chairman," but Marcus insisted that Gilmore not be a ceremonial head. Eventually, Gilmore was given the title of chairman, but Rove installed his own man, Jack Oliver, as deputy chairman. Oliver, a longtime Bush family loyalist from Missouri, was the finance chairman of the Bush 2000 presidential campaign, and essentially reported to Rove. This didn't sit well with Gilmore, who ordered Oliver not to convene any senior-level RNC meetings unless Gilmore was present.

But after the 2001 election debacle, Gilmore's sensibilities became moot, at least at the White House. He was eased out of the RNC post in favor of Marc Racicot, the man Bush and Rove had originally wanted as Attorney General. Another former governor, and one who was much closer to Bush personally, Racicot had proved his mettle during the Florida recount. His political acumen was respected at the White House; more importantly, his loyalty to Bush was above question.

The installation of Racicot at the RNC meant that the 2002 Republican political team was in place. At the White House, Rove had as his deputies Chris Henick, a fifth-generation Mississippian from Yazoo City whom Rove had imported to the Austin staff in 1994, and Rove's protégé, White House political director Kenneth B. Mehlman, a thirty-four-year-old Baltimore native with a degree from Harvard Law School. Mehlman was known for working fourteen-hour days, broken up only by his penchant for seven-mile runs, which he often undertook with his cell phone plastered to his ear. Both men are intensely loyal to Rove.

Despite the coup at the RNC, Rove still had to share power with two congressional Republicans. They were Representative Thomas M. Davis III, another Virginian, and Senator Bill Frist of Tennessee. Davis headed the Republican Congressional Campaign Committee; Frist chaired the Republican Senatorial Campaign Committee. Davis and Frist are strong-minded men, but the friction between

them and Rove was kept to a minimum by the fact that at the top of
this political pyramid was a president who enjoyed the near-total
loyalty of Republicans on Capitol Hill and a level of fealty among
grassroots Republicans that was almost unheard of. As 2002
dawned, Bush's job approval rating remained around 84 percent.
Among self-identified Republicans it was 99 percent. These were
the kinds of numbers that left pollsters at Gallup searching in their
archives for something to compare it to. Liberal pundits were
forced to take solace in gallows humor. (In one *New Yorker* cartoon, a generic politician is being given a presentation on the polls
by his handlers; the numbers show his approval ratings have literally gone off the charts, going well past 100 percent. The handlers
look smugly satisfied, while the skeptical candidate asks if it isn't
likely that "the voters are toying with us." It was becoming that
kind of year.)

Democrats didn't expect Bush's gravity-defying approval rating
to last forever. Neither did Rove, who instructed Ari Fleischer, the
White House press secretary, to start lowering expectations. Fleischer did so, telling reporters that the president realized his numbers
would inevitably drop by the time the 2002 midterm elections
rolled around. What nobody knew for sure was how much they
would decline.

And so as the 2002 midterm season began, the RNC was march-
ing in lockstep with the White House, where Rove was in opera-
tional control of all things political—and of a number of policy
matters perceived to have political ramifications. It was Rove, for
instance, who helped steer the administration into implementing
steel tariffs aimed at Europe and Japan. Those countries squawked,
as did ideologically pure economic conservatives, who complained

that the policy seemed mostly motivated to help Bush in key battle-ground states of Pennsylvania, Ohio, and West Virginia. Rove ignored the criticism. He concentrated his attention on pleasing his sole client, the president of the United States. Rove argued to Bush that on the merits, the steel tariffs were the right policy, and that the Japanese and Europeans subsidized their steel producers in ways that disadvantaged Americans. Rove also weighed in on a long-standing controversy seemingly far out of his area of expertise: the Navy's use of Vieques Island in Puerto Rico as a bombing range. The Navy and pro-military members of Congress defended the use of the site, saying that there simply was nowhere else on the planet that was as suitable for this purpose. But the issue had become toxic in New York. As a way of appealing for support among Puerto Rican activists, liberal Democrats from New York City had taken to going down to Puerto Rico and getting "arrested" in sit-ins over the bombing runs. New York's Republican governor, George Pataki, who had gotten almost 25 percent of the Latino vote in 1998—and who wanted to do even better in 2002—lobbied Rove half a dozen times to make this problem go away. A few days after the last such meeting, the White House announced that use of the base for target practice was to be phased out in 2003, effectively neutralizing it as an issue. Pataki thanked Rove publicly.

But one man cannot have this much influence without ginning up critics. As early as the summer of 2001, *The Washington Post* had published an article raising the propriety of Rove's role in policy making. It suggested that polling, of all things, played a role in Rove's calculations. Even worse, the story questioned whether the Bush White House was all that different from the Clinton White House in this regard. To Republicans, this was an unspeakable comparison. But some of the complaints about Rove came from Republican office-holders. Senator James Inhofe of Oklahoma, incensed over the Vieques decision, angrily predicted that it would "cost American lives." Generally, such critics made it a point to lash out at Rove, not at Bush. "As much as I love George W. Bush, he was ill-advised by political advisers who thought this was a way to win some votes," Inhofe said.

Rove, with similar motivations, also waded into the issue of a proposed new round of amnesty for Mexican immigrants residing in the United States illegally. Bush all but promised Mexican President Vicente Fox that he would take this step. Again, it was Bush's top political adviser who was singled out for criticism by agitated conservatives. In March 2002, Representative Tom Tancredo, a Colorado Republican, lambasted Rove by name. "There are people in the White House—specifically, I think, Karl Rove— . . . who say, 'Look, I don't want to stay up all night, or maybe for a couple of months, after the next election counting ballots, so let's go out and get the Hispanic vote.'"

But making the Republican Party seem hospitable to Latinos and other minorities was clearly part of Rove's brief. Where he was more vulnerable, especially after September 11, was on the question of whether he had his fingerprints on policies over which he had no expertise—and no real business being involved. National security, for example. And international affairs.

Reporters traveling with Bush to Russia, Germany, France, and Italy in late May 2002 were a bit surprised to find Rove along on the manifest. The White House explained that he was there for the Rome portion of the trip. This made some sense. An American President's visit to the Vatican is not a foreign policy meeting in any real sense of the word. It is, practically speaking, a political gesture—

aimed at American Catholics. At the time of Bush's European trip, the Catholic Church in the United States was engulfed by a burgeoning scandal involving sex abuse by priests. Before the president left for Europe, National Security Adviser Condoleezza Rice was asked if Bush would raise this issue in his scheduled meeting with Pope John Paul II. She indicated he would not. "The president's view, of course, is that this is a matter for the Catholic Church, the clergy, Catholics worldwide to resolve," Rice said. It was the answer one would expect from a diplomat. A similar one would have been given in the foreign ministry of a hundred foreign capitals. Except that it was decidedly the wrong answer. Normally, showing this kind of deference to the pope would have made sense. But in the spring of 2002 a sea change in Catholic opinion had taken place in America, and it had happened over the issue of priests and sexual abuse. To avoid mentioning the scandal would have sent the wrong political message, Rove knew. It would have put Bush on the side of the church heirarchy instead of the Catholic laity in a power struggle in which abusive priests and the bishops who protected them were on one side and children and victims' families were on the other. Bush had to bring it up—but delicately—and Rove was there to make sure he did just that.

The pitch was carefully choreographed. Before Bush went to see the pope, with Rove in tow, the president addressed the traveling White House press pool: "I will tell him that I am concerned about the Catholic Church in America, I'm concerned about its standing. And I say that because the Catholic Church is an incredibly important institution in our country." Bush added that he would also tell the pope that he appreciated his "leadership in trying to strengthen the Catholic Church in America."

Apparently, the meeting went well. When the press was allowed in to see the two leaders for a photo opportunity after their meeting, the two men engaged in an easy banter. John Paul asked Bush if he consulted with his father and as the meeting ended, the pope said, "God bless America." As Bush rose to leave, the pope added in words beamed back to the United States, "I hope to be able to meet you again."

In two years, Bush and Rove had come a long way from having to fend off calls from Catholic Voter Alert. But Rove's expansive White House role was attracting increased scrutiny. Just before the European trip, in fact, a warning shot was fired across Rove's bow. It came in the form of a lengthy page-one article in *The New York Times* on May 13. The piece, written by David E. Sanger and Richard L. Berke, related an anecdote in which one of Powell's longtime friends ran into him and said, "Who runs foreign policy, you or Rove?"

It wasn't clear if the exchange was related by Powell himself or by someone loyal to Powell—or even whether it came from inside the administration. But the context of this reference was clear: Rove had given a speech at the RNC winter meeting in Austin on January 18 in which he seemed to be telling GOP candidates how to exploit Bush's handling of the war in Afghanistan to partisan advantage. "We can go to the country on this issue because they trust the Republican Party to do a better job of protecting and strengthening America's military might and thereby protecting America," Rove said.

The Democrats, who had been looking for a chink in the White House armor, were quick to respond. "Nothing short of despicable," said Terence R. McAuliffe, the chairman of the Democratic National Committee. "For Karl Rove to politicize the issue is an affront to the integrity of the entire United States military," he added. House Minority Leader Dick Gephardt chimed in, too. He denounced Rove's comments as "shameful," and called on Bush to repudiate them. "I hope the president will set the record straight," Gephardt said. "This is not a partisan issue."

To be sure, there was some posturing in the Democrats' claims that they were shocked, shocked that politics was taking place inside the White House. But both Bush and Rove had invited just this sort of scrutiny. Less than two weeks before Rove's remarks, Bush had made an appeal to the patriotic, bipartisan instincts of lawmakers. In a January 4 town hall meeting in Ontario, California, that was devoted mostly to Hispanic outreach, the president said, "It's time to take the spirit of unity that has been prevalent when it comes to fighting the war and bring it to Washington, D.C." And Rove himself had asserted in an interview with *The Washington Post* that Bush had told his staff in the aftermath of September 11: "Politics has no role in this. Don't talk to me about politics for awhile."

But Bush did not repudiate Karl Rove. Racicot tried to soften the tone of the Austin speech, saying that in the speech he heard, Rove wasn't saying that the war would help Republicans. Racicot said that what Rove had really meant was that "an unfortunate circumstance" had revealed qualities of Bush's that were already there. For his part, Rove was unrepentant. "I'm not talking about *them*," he said of the Democrats. "Our job is to describe who we are."

Thus by January 2002, a pattern was emerging: Rove and other Republican operatives and office-holders would proceed, as though 2002 was, indeed, an election year, while Bush himself would stay above the partisan fray—a strategy reminiscent of Bush's days as governor of Texas and the run-up to the 2000 Republican primaries. The idea was that the GOP would reap the best of both worlds. Bush's operatives would be working on the ground, just as they would have had the nation been at peace. Bush himself would talk as the leader of a united nation—and talk mostly about the war. In the aftermath of September 11, Americans old enough to remember said the only thing that had ever happened like it was Pearl Harbor. While Rove didn't have personal memories of December 7, 1941, he did go back into his beloved history books to look up the State of the Union Address Franklin D. Roosevelt had delivered a few weeks after America had entered World War II. Some of FDR's most powerful phrasing made it into Bush's State of the Union address on January 29.

Just as Roosevelt had spoken of an "Axis"—fascist Germany, Japan, and Italy—that was "evil," Bush singled out three nations he said constituted an "axis of evil" in our own time: Iran, Iraq, and North Korea. European liberals and a handful of American intellectuals had the bad form to point out that Bush's unholy trio was an unlikely "axis" of anything. Iran and Iraq were mortal enemies, while North Korea's help in building up its nuclear arsenal had come primarily from Pakistan, America's new ally in the war on terrorism, and from China. But if the Bush-Rove historical analogy was inexact, the echoes in the speech of the voices of American presidents were palpable. And it struck a chord with its listeners. Liberal commentator Mark Shields, among the 94 percent of Americans with a positive reaction to the address, called it a "noble speech." Historian Doris Kearns Goodwin said that Bush's "galvanizing words" brought to mind Roosevelt himself. There were other powerful echoes as well. In one passage, Bush evoked Lincoln, Kennedy and his own father, one right after the other.

"After America was attacked, it was as if our entire country looked into a mirror and saw our better selves," Bush said. "We were reminded that we are citizens, with obligations to each other, to our country, and to history. We began to think less of the goods we can accumulate, and more about the good we can do."

The "mirror" imagery recalled Lincoln's 1861 inaugural phrase, "the better angels of our nature." Bush's words about obligations to country paralleled JFK's "Ask not what your country can do for you" from his 1961 inaugural address. Thinking beyond material possessions evoked his own father's challenge to be a point of light, and extended his own theme of "compassionate conservatism." For emotion, Bush turned to the old master, Ronald Reagan. Bush singled out the widow of slain CIA operative Michael Spann in the audience, quoting the conclusion of her eulogy to her fallen husband: "*Semper fi*, my love." Mrs. Spann stood, nodded at Bush and mouthed the words, "Thank you." Reagan, who popularized this device, would have been proud.

Bush did not go so far as to pretend there wasn't a campaign looming over the horizon. He just acted as though it wasn't going to change a thing he said or did—even as the issues he raised were designed to ripen in November. "I'm a proud party man," Bush said on a campaign-style trip to Oregon in January. "But I'm American first, and that's what we ought to be dealing with when it comes to legislation. There are troubling signs that some in the nation's capital want to go back to the old ways. And I don't think we ought to let them do that." He didn't mention scuttled judicial appointments, a stalled homeland security bill, or Democratic efforts to repeal his tax cut. That would come later in the year, when Bush and Cheney took to the road, campaigning for Republicans on themes crafted by Rove.

Cheney was especially active on the hustings. He spoke on behalf of ninety-six candidates, including fifty-seven House members, in races coast to coast. The conservative magazine *National Review* asked, tongue-in-cheek, "Who's representing the U.S. at foreign funerals these days? Cheney has been far too busy boosting Republicans."

The stock speech given by both the president and the vice president rarely varied. Vote for Candidate X, they would proclaim, because he's a good man (or, occasionally, a good woman) who will help Bush cut taxes, pass the administration's energy policy, promote free trade, restrain the deficit, and appoint judges "who respect the Constitution and understand the limits of judicial power." That was the first half of The Speech. The second half was a seamless segue into national security, the status of the war on terrorism and the need to disarm Iraq. Cheney soon had it boiled down nicely into two short sentences: "The President and I look forward to welcoming Adam to the nation's capital come January," Cheney said at an appearance in Kansas City for House candidate Adam Taff. "He'll be vital in helping us meet the key priorities for the nation—in terms of winning the war on terror, strengthening the economy, and defending our homeland."

There is nothing new about a president campaigning on foreign as well as on domestic policy, or about a president incorporating his official duties as chief executive into his campaign duties as the titular head of his political party. In fact, the Rove-led effort was only too willing to borrow pages out of a book of a president they claimed to have contempt for, but whose political instincts they admired enough to imitate. Upon his election in 1992, Bill Clinton promptly held a two-day economic conference in Little Rock with some 329 invitees. In August 2002, Rove put together a similar forum at Baylor University. (The differences reflected the two president's personalities: Clinton's conference went for two days; Bush's for one, a five-hour session mostly devoted to having people give testimonials in favor of Bush's approach.) The message of the conference was then grafted onto Bush's addresses in an ever-escalating campaign and fundraising schedule. At a September 27 event in Denver for a House candidate named Bob Beauprez, Bush explained what he'd gleaned of the economy.

> Here's the page of the textbook which we read: It says, if you have more money in your pocket, it means you're more likely to demand a good or a service. And if you demand a good or a service, in the American system somebody is going to produce the good or a service. And when somebody produces the good or a service, somebody is more likely to find work.
>
> The tax cuts came at the right time in American history. The tax cuts stimulate economic growth. The tax cuts are good for small business creation. Small businesses create 70 percent of the new jobs in America. Most small businesses are not incorporated. Most small businesses are sole proprietorships or limited partnerships, and therefore pay income taxes at the individual rates. And so when you drop the rates, you're encouraging capital creation in the small business sector of America. Those who oppose tax cuts do not understand job creation and what the small business community does for job creation.

Bush emulated Clinton in another area, as well—fundraising. Rove and other White House aides were quick to point out that this president didn't hold fundraising "coffees" in the White House the way Clinton and Gore had done. Nor did they rent out the Lincoln bedroom to the highest bidder. Moreover, the Republicans noted, when he left office Clinton had bequeathed his chief fundraiser, Terry McAuliffe, the chairmanship of the DNC. This was all true enough; in the midterm election cycle, Federal Elections Commission records showed that the Democrats raised some $199.6 million in the soon-to-be banned "soft money" so detested by John McCain. But during the same midterm election cycle, the Republicans, with Bush as their most prolific fundraiser, brought in even more soft money—nearly $221.7 million. Such dollar amounts had been unheard of in non-presidential years. One reason for the upward spike was that McCain had finally gotten his campaign finance bill through the Congress and onto Bush's desk, where Bush signed it, albeit reluctantly. This made the 2002 election cycle the last chance to raise money in huge amounts. A second reason was that both sides knew the stakes to be high. "President Bush needs the Senate, and Democrats see it as the last line of defense," observed Larry Makinson, a senior fellow with the Center for Responsive Politics. "It's an Armageddon scenario whether you're a Democrat or a Republican."

To wage war for this decisive battle, the GOP amassed a lead over Democrats in "hard money"—individual donations of $1,000 or less—that was even greater. Here, too, George W. Bush was the prime drawing card. And in the waning days of the campaign, this money didn't always go to political activities consistent with Bush's theme of being a "uniter, not a divider." The most egregious example may have been in Georgia, where Republican senatorial candidate C. Saxby Chambliss ran television ads against incumbent Democratic Senator Max Cleland that criticized Cleland's lack of support for the administration's version of the homeland security bill. Chambliss' ad ran pictures of Osama bin Laden and Saddam Hussein before fading into a picture of Cleland. Many top Georgia Democrats, led by former President Jimmy Carter, reacted angrily, treating the spot as though it were an attack on Cleland's patriotism, especially given the fact that Cleland had lost both legs and an arm while serving in Vietnam. (Chambliss had avoided service because of a trick knee.) The best that could be said about the spot was that it was unseemly. Chambliss was shamed into withdrawing the likenesses of Arab war criminals from his TV spot, but he kept the rest of it on the air.

It was clear by autumn, the homestretch of the campaign, that Rove, Bush, and the Republican candidates believed that going after the Democratic senators who'd sided with Daschle in slowing up passage of the homeland security bill was a legitimate issue—and it was working. By October it had become a stock part of Bush's campaign speech in swing states. Usually, Bush was more careful than Chambliss, but on one memorable occasion, he wasn't. Bush typically criticized Senate Democrats for being too beholden to special interests to act expeditiously on homeland security legislation. But at a September 23 event in New Jersey, Bush skipped the niceties and said flatly, "The House responded, but the Senate is more interested in special interests in Washington and not interested in the security of the American people."

This remark caused a huge flap in Washington—it was discussed on the floor of the Senate for the better part of a day—in a contretemps made all the more confusing to voters because *The Washington Post* had erroneously reported the remarks as being in the context of Iraq. This was a small break for the Bush team because it muddied the issue and meant that Daschle's original comments of outrage had to be recalibrated slightly. When the dust-up sorted itself out, the White House remained unbowed and unapologetic. In fact, in the waning hours of the campaign, while stumping in Iowa, Bush employed similar language to that he'd used in New Jersey. "But the Senate has a lousy version," the president said of the homeland security legislation. "They're more interested in special interests, which dominate the dialogue in Washington, D.C., than they are in protecting the American people."

These then, were the dual themes worked out by Rove and the rest of the GOP political team. They talked about the economy and they talked about the war, always in the same speech, and if it struck Democrats that they were being hit high and hit low, they had problems of their own, not the least of which is that they were on both sides of Bush's tax cut issue, and they were openly conflicted on Iraq. At the same time, polls showed that a majority of Americans assigned a great deal of credibility to Bush and were thus inclined to give him lots of leeway.

In addition to shaping the president's grand rhetorical themes throughout the year, Rove and his political operatives were also laboring in the political trenches, doing the less glamorous, but essential, work of party politics. These duties included talking some people into running and talking others out of running. It meant deciding some races were winnable—and cutting other people loose. It meant figuring out where the campaign's not-so-secret weapon, Bush himself, could best be used on the campaign trail—and exactly whom he should meet and what he should say when he got there.

Almost nothing was left to chance. By October, Bush's stock speech always covered the same ground: On foreign policy, he stressed his determination to fight the war on terror no matter how long it took and why he believed Saddam Hussein must be disarmed. On domestic policy, he boasted about the education bill, advocated his desire to make the tax cut permanent, and called for bipartisanship in Washington. On this last point, Bush would stress, almost reluctantly, how that translated at this moment in the need to send a few more Republicans to Congress, especially in the Senate where his homeland security bill and his judges were bottled up by Democrats beholden to their party's special interest groups. Bush didn't generally say that these judicial appointments were some of the most conservative jurists ever appointed to the federal bench. And in Maine, where he campaigned beside Senator Susan Collins, a pro-choice moderate, on October 22, Bush simply omitted the riff about judges entirely.

After Minnesota Senator Paul Wellstone, the most liberal Democrat in the Senate, died in a plane crash ten days before the election, Rove argued that Bush still had to visit the state, despite the skittishness of some Republicans. Rove argued that Wellstone's death was not a reason to abandon Republican senatorial candidate Norm Coleman. Rove won that argument, and he then played a role in crafting a speech prefaced by a gracious tribute to Wellstone. Long before that time, however, Rove had help set up the Republicans' eventual win in the Minnesota race by helping to get Coleman into it in the first place. Polling paid for by the Republican Senate Campaign Committee suggested that a centrist Republican could give Wellstone a real run for his seat. The most logical Republican was the moderate Coleman, the mayor of St. Paul and a former Democrat. It fell to Bill Frist to buttonhole Coleman one cold night in Washington outside the Ronald Reagan Building. For an hour, under the light of a street lamp, Frist explained to a skeptical Coleman what the data showed—and how much the national Republican Party would help him. If Frist, a former heart surgeon who many Republicans see as a potential national candidate himself, was the good cop, Rove was the bad cop who had to help clear the GOP field of other ambitious Minnesota Republicans who fancied themselves senatorial material. Rove called these Republicans and encouraged them not to run. When Tom Pawlenty, another strong contender, balked at taking orders from Karl Rove, Pawlenty got a call from Dick Cheney, who urged him to run for governor instead. (He did so, and both Coleman and Pawlenty won on November 5.)

There was plenty of that kind of manipulation out of the top-down Bush-era Republican Party. When Georgia's Republican House delegation seemed to be taking too long to come to a consensus on who would challenge Democratic Senator Max Cleland, whom Rove believed was vulnerable, Frist helped them make up their minds by throwing the RSCC money behind Saxby Chambliss. Frist also interjected himself in the Louisiana senatorial primary, running ads for Suzanne Haik Terrell, a little-known GOP Louisiana officeholder who happens to be friends with the president, even though a sitting Republican congressman was in the race. Frist also joined Rove in making overtures to Elizabeth Dole about entering the North Carolina Senate race. And in the search for a candidate to challenge first-term Senator Jean Carnahan in the all-important state of Missouri, Rove himself put the arm on former Missouri Representative James M. Talent. Moreover, how these candidates conducted themselves was not left to chance. In many cases their ads were written by the Republican Senatorial Campaign Committee. Rove himself was in contact with the campaigns' key operatives, including former Christian Coalition lobbyist Ralph

Reed, a political consultant who advised several southern campaigns. Moreover, he helped steer Scott Howell, a little-known Dallas-based political consultant who'd rarely ventured out of Texas, into the role of producing TV ads for several key senatorial races, including Coleman's, Chambliss's, and Talent's.

There were missteps, of course, the most obvious being when Rove and Bush recruited Los Angeles Mayor Richard Riordan to run against California Governor Gray Davis. Republican polling showed Riordan to be the strongest general election candidate against Davis, an incumbent made vulnerable by his frosty personality and questions about whether he'd crossed ethical lines in his political fundraising. But Rove and Bush were embarrassed by Riordan, an unmanageable and undisciplined candidate who inexplicably ran as a far-left liberal in the Republican primary and finished third. Davis, with his prodigious $68 million war chest, was unimpressed by any of the Republicans, including primary victor Bill Simon Jr. In one of the most candid self-assessments ever uttered in recent American politics, Davis observed wryly that he didn't need Californians to do "cartwheels" of joy on their way to the voting booth. They just had to pull the lever beside his name. They ended up doing just that on November 5 when Davis was re-elected.

There was also a minor discomfiture in early June when a backup computer disc containing a Power Point presentation on the campaign prepared by Rove and Mehlman and delivered to GOP donors was dropped in Lafayette Park by a White House intern. It was discovered by a Democratic aide on Capitol Hill who had no compunction about making it public. Democratic Party officials, still smarting over Rove's red-meat speech to Republicans in Austin, tried to portray the material in a way that made Rove and Mehlman seem sinister: The two operatives boasted of having tens of millions more than Democrats to spend, and listed several Republican candidates as vulnerable whom they were publicly claiming were safe. In truth, most of the stuff in the presentation, delivered to GOP donors at the posh Hay Adams Hotel, was boilerplate political fare. Still, it *was* embarrassing to misplace your own campaign materials. Hardly the stuff of genius.

In private, Democrats were starting to get frustrated that they couldn't lay more of a glove on Rove. In 2001, they'd tried to make an issue of his delay in putting his stock holdings in a blind trust—at a time when he was advising Bush on a host of domestic policies that had an impact on various companies in which Rove was invested. Rove's explanation turned out to be that he offered to sell off his portfolio, then worth some $1.6 million, when he joined the administration, but was told by the White House counsel's office to hold off until they provided him with a formal "certificate of divestiture," a document the overburdened counsel's office didn't produce until June 6. Rove's answer under-whelmed the Democratic members of Congress investigating the matter, but when it was revealed that the delay had *cost* Rove $138,000—his entire first year's salary as a government employee—in a declining stock market, the imbroglio lost its steam.

Democrats were starting to appreciate the kind of adversary they had in Rove. Political consultant Mark McKinnon was now doing business weekly in Washington. He still had a lot of Democratic friends, and over beers in watering holes such as Fran O'Brien's Steakhouse, McKinnon would tell them what they were up against. "He kicked my ass many times," McKinnon liked to say. "I quit politics before joining up with Bush, but I never had any trouble remembering Karl because I've got his license plate number stamped on my forehead because of all the times he steamrolled me in campaigns."

Rove enjoyed hearing that kind of talk, but he also knew he wasn't in Texas anymore, and it could all go south on him with one adverse election cycle. Rove recalled that going into the last week of the 2000 election, he'd been confident enough to horse around with the reporters on the campaign plane and to make predictions about an easy victory. This time, he took the opposite tack. Asked for his predictions, the boy genius expounded the same nerdy, political-junkie answer half a dozen times, from April until November. Something has to give, historically speaking, he'd insist. "I don't know what's going to happen," he said. "Somebody's going to make history, one way or another. It's very rare that a party in power that holds the White House makes gains in this election; on the other hand, it's very rare that a party gains seats in the U.S. House of Representatives four elections in a row, which is the task the Democrats face."

But if Rove was cautious in his public statements, his strategy was daring. At a time when Washington's political wise guys were questioning the wisdom of putting Bush's prestige on the line for marginal candidates such as Norm Coleman and Saxby Chambliss, Rove was pushing the president to be ever bolder. In the last days of the campaign, Bush visited Georgia twice as part of a 10,000-mile, fifteen-state, five-day marathon that seemed out of character for Bush, a notorious homebody. The president went to all the swing states in which Frist and Rove had handpicked Senate challengers: Minnesota, Missouri, North Carolina, Tennessee, South Dakota,

and New Hampshire, where the White House had thrown its support behind John E. Sununu as early as the Republican primary.

Finally, election night arrived. Bush and Rove had been in training for this since 1993. Bush had defeated Ann Richards in 1994,
capturing 53.5 percent of the vote in an election in which he was the
underdog. Two years later, with Rove making strategic decisions
and Bush campaigning hard, Bob Dole carried Texas against Bill
Clinton while Republican candidates swept to victory in one house
of the Legislature while extending their control of the other. That's
what Rove had in mind for 2002. That was part of The Plan. Rove
could look back on all he'd done: taking the spears for inoculating
Bush and the Republican Party on such touchy policy issues as
Vieques and stem-cell research; bruising feelings to take control of
the RNC; haggling with Tom Davis and Bill Frist—and a hundred
state and local officials—to find the best GOP candidates coast to
coast; helping the party raise record sums of money; crafting the
messages that kept the president at stratospheric levels in the polls;
finally, risking the president's political capital by cajoling him to
take to the road in an election in which Bush's name would never
appear on the ballot.

Election night fell on George and Laura Bush's silver wedding
anniversary. Hoping for the best, the president invited Marc Racicot, Tom Davis, Bill Frist, House Speaker Dennis Hastert, Senate
Republican Leader Trent Lott, and their wives for a celebratory dinner in the West Sitting Hall. A television was set up there, and the
crowd eventually included several members of the senior White
House staff. The president himself was in frequent phone contact
with Rove, who had set up a command center in a West Wing office.

Unlike election night two years earlier, the news from the start was positive. Many of the elections were terribly close, but the trends were all in the same direction. By the end of the night, the Republicans had held their own in the gubernatorial races, expanded their margin in the House, and retaken the Senate. Among the winners were Chambliss (who gave all the credit to Bush), Sununu, Talent, Dole, Coleman and Lamar Alexander in Tennessee, a man who'd once served in Bush's father's cabinet. These were the candidates who'd given Bush and Rove the victory that they, and everyone sitting there, craved so much. Lott would be Senate Majority Leader again and would have control over the legislative agenda, Bush's agenda, once again. Hastert would have a larger margin to work in the House. All the men in that room—and one man who wasn't—could take satisfaction in a job well done.

Bush, who had voted in a Crawford, Texas firehouse that morning and then flown to Washington, put in some thirty calls to winning candidates, beginning with his brother Jeb, who was victorious in his Florida gubernatorial reelection campaign. The president was tired. He'd done a lot in the last two weeks of the campaign. But before calling it a night, he walked his dogs, Spot and Barney, on the White House grounds.

It was about 11:45 PM. Then Bush made one more congratulatory call, his last of the night. It was to Karl Christian Rove.

PART 4

THE PLAN COMES TOGETHER

14

The 101st Senator

A month after the Republican Party victories in the November midterm elections, a flap arose that presaged the future direction of American politics, even as it tested the clout of Karl Rove and his boss. The event that foretold the future began harmlessly enough—it was a flattering tribute to a politician at his birthday party.

This was no ordinary birthday celebration—it was outgoing South Carolina Senator Strom Thurmond's 100th birthday—and the toast in question, delivered by Mississippi Senator Trent Lott, was no ordinary compliment. On December 5, 2002, as Lott was set to resume his role as majority leader when the new Senate convened in January, he mused aloud at Thurmond's party that the world might have been oh-so-much better if the South Carolinian had been elected president of the United States when he ran as a third-party candidate back in 1948. Lott further noted proudly that his home state of Mississippi, in its infinite wisdom, tried to do just that—choosing Thurmond's States' Rights Party over the Democratic ticket headed by Harry Truman or Republican candidate Thomas Dewey.

"I want to say this about my state: When Strom Thurmond ran

for president we voted for him," Lott said. "We're proud of it. And if the rest of the country [had] followed our lead we wouldn't have had all these problems over all these years, either."

This kind of remark might once have been acceptable blarney within the Washington establishment—Lott was merely flattering the old man—but times were changing, and fast. Even Democrats didn't comprehend this at first. None other than Tom Daschle, about to relinquish the post of Senate majority leader after the Democrats' losses in November, initially brushed aside assertions that Lott had been inappropriate. "There are a lot of times when he and I go to the microphone and would like to say things we meant to say differently," Daschle said. "And I'm sure this is one of those cases for him as well." Al Gore weighed in, and though tougher than Daschle, he basically called on Lott to be censured unless he apologized. But Lott had already apologized by the time Gore piped up, and Lott would apologize three more times, including during a deferential performance on Black Entertainment Television in which he expressed fealty to affirmative action, a doctrine Lott had never supported before. None of this professed chagrin was enough. Politics was changing and becoming more egalitarian in the process. But that did not mean the political arena was becoming friendlier or more forgiving.

A decade earlier, as president-elect Bill Clinton was assembling his cabinet, his transition team had been blindsided by the power of conservative talk radio hosts who had drummed up tremendous grassroots opposition to his first choice for attorney general, Zoe Baird. Until Clinton was forced to withdraw her name from consideration for the top Justice Department job, the nature of the controversy—she had fudged records relating to her nanny's resident status—was the kind of blemish that Washington veterans had assured Clinton would blow over.

Trent Lott was the recipient of similar attention from a new-found medium that did not bedevil Clinton: individual Internet web logs (blogs). Some liberals were hoping that bloggers could be their version of talk radio, and, at least in the Lott case, they were not disappointed. The event was aired by C-SPAN, and Mark Halperin, producer of the online political-insider report "The Note" for ABC News, gave it a mention. The first to draw broader implications about Lott's peculiar remarks about Thurmond were two liberal blogs: one called Talking Points Memo, produced by influential liberal commentator Joshua Micah Marshall; the other called Tapped, the online tout sheet of the liberal magazine *The American Prospect.*

Marshall pointed out that Strom Thurmond had run for president as a segregationist, having walked out of the Democratic National Convention after Hubert Humphrey's stirring call for integration. Before heading the "Dixiecrats" that year, Thurmond had never been much of a race-monger, and he eventually switched to the Republican Party and largely overcame his racist past. But in his choice of language at Thurmond's centenary party, the tin-eared Lott expressed nostalgia for the lowest point of Thurmond's career. "Maybe he was just trying to be nice to Strom on his birthday," Marshall wrote on his website. "But perhaps at a minimum he'd like to apologize or just take it back?"

Lott clearly wanted to take it back, but the play-for-keeps mores of the blogosphere make that difficult. Nor were all his critics Democrats. Libertarian writer Andrew Sullivan posted scathing comments on his website about Lott's remarks, as did prominent conservative David Frum, fresh off a stint as a speechwriter in Bush's White House. All of this commentary came between December 5 and December 10, the first time the major media covered the story. In the meantime, Lott's predicament had drawn the attention of Rove and Bush, and for a reason that Marshall hit upon in his first posting. "Just another example," he said in summing up Lott's statements, "of the hubris now reigning among Capitol Hill Republicans."

Marshall wasn't alone in extrapolating the Lott comment onto the Republican Party as a whole—and the Bush White House by implication. "Republicans are going to have to deal with the impression that there's a strain of racism in the party," independent analyst Stuart Rothenberg wrote in the nonpartisan *Rothenberg Political Report*.

This unwelcome assessment was very nearly the opposite of the story line Karl Rove was pushing. Lott's aptitude as a Senate leader had never been highly esteemed by Team Bush, and now his faux pas over Strom Thurmond had made him expendable. But how to ease Lott out? The answer: very delicately.

And so, as Rove began working the phones, chief White House speechwriter Michael Gerson went to work on a draft of presidential remarks.

Among GOP insiders, the two senators who quickly emerged as the most likely Lott replacements were Don Nickles of Oklahoma and Tennessee's Bill Frist, Rove's ally in recapturing the Senate for the Republicans. Nickles, believing he had the support of a cadre of conservative senators, telephoned Rove asking for his blessing. Rove was noncommittal about whom the White House would support, but he offered tacit support for Nickles's idea of appearing on the Sunday network news shows and calling for a leadership election.

Bush himself had no special affection for Lott—or particular loyalty to him. When Bush was governor of Texas, Lott had high-hatted the Republican Governors Association, rejecting the group's requests for frequent meetings with congressional leaders. Bush was present at a 1998 meeting between Lott and then-Governor Bill Janklow of South Dakota that turned hostile. Janklow finally turned to Bush, his friend, and said, "I've had enough of this bullshit," before getting up and walking out in a huff. Lott had crossed the Bush clan even earlier than that, Rove knew: In 1988, when Bush's father ran for president, Lott endorsed Jack Kemp instead of Bush, even to the point of introducing Kemp at his presidential announcement ceremony.

Kemp, however, had his own ties to some members of Team Bush—Gerson had once written speeches for him—as well as a long record of racial sensitivity. Kemp's eloquent address on the House floor explaining his change of heart on a bill creating a holiday for Martin Luther King Jr. smoothed the way for passage of that legislation. A call was made to Kemp; he had no problem saying publicly what he thought of Lott's comments. They were, Kemp said publicly, "inexplicable, indefensible, and inexcusable."

By December 12, when Bush flew on *Air Force One* to Philadelphia for a speech on his faith-based programs to a largely black audience, calls were mounting for the president to take a stand. So far, White House spokesman Ari Fleischer had been content to term it a Senate matter. But on that flight, Bush showed Pennsylvania Senator Rick Santorum, a conservative Republican, the draft response Gerson had prepared.

"Recent comments by Senator Lott do not reflect the spirit of our country," it said. "He has apologized, and rightly so. Every day our nation was segregated was a day that America was unfaithful to our founding ideals. And the founding ideals of our nation and, in fact, the founding ideals of the political party I represent was, and remains today, the equal dignity and equal rights of every American."

Bush delivered it just that way, and it was the lead item on the network news that night. After the speech, Fleischer reiterated what he had been cleared to say—that the president did not necessarily believe Lott needed to resign. Rove made sure Lott knew of the president's comments before they were delivered, but Bush's speech quickly raised the bar. Lott, not quite understanding the dynamics inside the White House, authorized a statement in response to Bush's speech: "Senator Lott agrees with President Bush that his words were wrong, and he is sorry," the statement said. "He repudiates segregation because it is immoral."

Arizona's John McCain urged Lott to go further and hold a press conference. But Lott and his allies figured, probably correctly, that he had apologized so many times by then that another mea culpa would not help. Senator Mitch McConnell, a Kentuckian with a good-sized following in the Republican caucus, put aside his own ambitions and began making calls to his colleagues to shore up support for Lott. By then it was too late. Bush and Rove now had a candidate: They wanted Frist.

Senator George Allen, a Republican from Virginia, had come to the same conclusion on his own: Lott must go, and Frist was the best option to replace him. Allen told journalists that a letter from a fellow Virginia Republican "who happens to be an African-American" had convinced him of the need for change. The writer said that Lott's comments "made it very hard for him to be in the Republican Party."

By the time Nickles pulled the rug out from under Lott on the Sunday talk shows, the ground was shifting under Nickles as well. Frist's name had surfaced. It was not leaked directly by White House officials, who were careful not to be seen as usurping Senate prerogative, but it was leaked by those like George Allen who had been in touch with Rove. On Monday, December 16, White House officials revealed that Rove was "monitoring" the situation. On Tuesday, Jeb Bush suggested that Lott would have to leave—and sooner rather than later. "It doesn't help to have this swirling controversy that Senator Lott, in spite of his enormous political skills, doesn't seem to be able to handle well," Governor Bush told *The Miami Herald*. "Something's going to have to change. This can't be the topic of conversation over the next week."

On Wednesday, Secretary of State Colin Powell, the highest-ranking African-American official in government (or in the history of the United States, for that matter) took aim. Lott had asked Powell to defend him, an overture the secretary had spurned. Instead, Powell issued a chilly public rebuke: Powell "deplored the sentiment" behind Lott's December 5 remarks, he said, adding that nothing about the Dixiecrat platform "should have been acceptable in any way to any American at that time—or any American now."

The previous week, Lott had received support from Oklahoma congressman J. C. Watts, the only black Republican in Congress and a Lott ally. Watts had dismissed Lott's comments as being "as serious as the venue in which they were delivered—a birthday party." But after Powell spoke, the pressure began to snowball. As

demands mounted among Democrats for Lott to step down, Watts
echoed this call, although he was speaking out of solicitude for his
friend's feelings. "Do you want to put your family and your grand-
kids through this, and the party? Do you want that?" Watts said.
"If it was me, I just would not put my family through it."

The same day, Senator Lincoln Chafee, a liberal Republican
from Rhode Island, became the first GOP lawmaker to call publicly
for Lott to step down. And he did so in a way that made it clear that
the anti-Lott Republicans were looking to Rove and the president
for a solution. "The only way to have a change, in my opinion, is
for the White House to come in here and say to majority leader
Trent Lott, 'It's time for change,'" Chafee said.

The White House team had tried assiduously to stay in the background as events played out, but Chafee had now blurted out what
everyone knew to be true—the impetus had been seized by Bush
and Rove. On Thursday, December 19, Lott acknowledged as much
as he mounted his last line of defense. Despite repeated calls by Lott
to the White House seeking the president's backing, Bush had said
nothing publicly since his Philadelphia speech. This was tantamount to a refusal to support Lott, which the Mississippian was
beginning to sense would be fatal to his chances of surviving as Senate majority leader. White House officials were, to use imagery from
another administration, letting Lott twist slowly in the wind. On
Thursday, a bitter Lott complained in a television interview that
anonymous leaks from the White House were undermining his ability to mount an effective defense. "I've spoken to White House officials this very morning, and they assure me that they understand
that this has become a very unfair thing," Lott said. But it was only
going to end when Lott threw in the towel, which he did the fol-

lowing day, Friday, December 20, 2002, in a terse written statement
after some thirty Republican senators had lined up behind Frist.

Because Lott's anguish was so public, the unpleasant affair
seemed to drag on. In truth, fewer than fifteen days elapsed from
the birthday party to Frist's ascension as the all-but-certain new
Senate leader. The episode had demonstrated the power of the Internet political sites—and how unforgiving real-time politics could be.
But there was a third lesson as well: George W. Bush, and those who
advised him on political matters, were now in uncontested control
of the Republican Party. This influence was so pervasive, it need not
be flaunted. Bush had spoken only once publicly about the matter;
Rove not at all. Their actions were laundered through others, hidden from public view, but unmistakable all the same. It was, James
Carville said admiringly, "a clean extraction."

In the aftermath, Washington's punditry turned, as it often does,
away from the rabbit and to those who had set the rabbit traps. *The
Washington Post* lauded Frist's ascension in an editorial even as it
affected a scolding tone. "Mr. Frist's close ties to the White House
need not be an impediment to getting things done," the *Post*
observed. "They could, in fact, be an asset, provided the new
majority leader avoids becoming a rubber stamp in the hands of
President Bush and Karl Rove."

ABC White House correspondent Terry Moran, in his handoff
from Peter Jennings the night the story broke, was even more blunt.
"Well, Peter," Moran said in his White House stand-upper that
night, "it's clear that Karl Rove and the president preferred someone other than Trent Lott." Senior correspondent Juan Williams of
National Public Radio informed his listeners about "resentment-
filled zingers" on Capitol Hill aimed at Rove—the most pointed of

which was when members or their staffs would say to each other sarcastically, "What does the 101st senator think?"

Senator Santorum, asked if Rove had been pulling the strings on Capitol Hill, momentarily forgot about Senate prerogative and treated the question as though it were one about Bush's influence in his own White House. Santorum related the story of how Bush had shown him the text of his speech criticizing Lott while on *Air Force One* en route to Philadelphia. "He did so with his jaw set and with a lot of passion in his voice," Santorum said. "This is a man who really believes he has . . . an opportunity to present a new agenda and a new way of uniting people."

And so Bush and Rove helped install a Senate leader they believed better fit their "compassionate conservative" narrative. If Rove was walking around Washington with a target on his back, that was the price of his success. "No one should doubt for a moment the political sagacity of Karl Rove, the extraordinary White House political counselor whose fingerprints are all over the strategy that dethroned Trent Lott from his coveted Senate leadership post," wrote Scripps-Howard columnist Dan K. Thomasson. "Is Machiavellian a proper description of his approach?" Thomasson thought so, and compared Rove directly to "the Medieval Italian political genius." This was not necessarily a compliment, judging by the adjectives the columnist assigned to the old Italian spin doctor, words such as "duplicitous" and "deceitful."

To be sure, the man critics saw as the master manipulator did not win every battle. As soon as Republican Senator Peter G. Fitzgerald of Illinois announced he was not seeking a second term, Rove was on the phone to former Illinois Governor Jim Edgar, a friend of Bush's from their gubernatorial days, beseeching him to run. But Edgar declined—even after Bush himself made the same pitch to his old friend in a phone call from the White House. Rove was surprised but not discouraged. With Edgar out of it, Rove gave his public blessing to Jack Ryan, a handsome financier, who had left investment banking after making his fortune to teach Catholic school in an inner-city Chicago neighborhood. Ryan proved to be too good to be true, although what did him in was unexpected: Ryan's ex-wife Jeri Ryan, who played the curvy Seven of Nine on *Star Trek: Voyager,* represented an unsung archetype—the prudish Hollywood sex symbol. Jeri Ryan asserted in her divorce papers that after Ryan attempted to have conjugal relations with her inside a swingers' club, she became sick to her stomach, cried in shame—and fell out of love with her husband. When this account made the Chicago newspapers, Ryan withdrew from the race. Eventually, far-right Republican gadfly Alan Keyes maneuvered his way into the senatorial nomination, setting in motion a huge GOP calamity that not even Karl Rove could prevent. Both Keyes and his opponent, Democratic state senator Barack Obama, are African-American, but the similarity between them ended there: Keyes, not even an Illinois resident, managed only 27 percent of the vote against Obama, an emerging political star whom Rove may find himself opposing in a future national campaign.

As 2002 gave way to 2003, Rove's attention turned to how the president could press his advantage. Bush's job approval rating, which had been stratospheric following the September 11 attacks, was now steadily declining. There were several reasons for this, not the least of which was political gravity. "Polls go up," former White House press secretary Marlin Fitzwater once said. "Polls go down." Another reason was the rough-edged rhetoric on both sides during the partisan fight for control of Congress. Perhaps the biggest factor was public apprehension over the looming war in Iraq.

Nevertheless, neither Rove nor his boss was inclined to go slow. That January, Rove began telling allies and a few journalists he knew well that the opening session of the 108th Congress constituted "the second hundred days." Rove's goals were even more ambitious. As one GOP operative told political writer Joe Klein of *Time* magazine, "The strategy is total domination: Don't let the Congress up for air."

It didn't take long for this attitude to manifest itself.

In January, Iowa Republican Senator Charles Grassley told reporters that Bush's tax bill would have to be modified to pass Congress. Less than a month later, Grassley emerged from a White House meeting with the president and reversed himself in the presence of reporters, hinting only indirectly at the heat that had come his way. "And I think I should have kept my mouth shut back in January," Grassley told the reporters assembled on the White House grounds. Grassley's staff denied that the senator had been Roved, but it is a matter of public record that Rove was present at that February 11 meeting Bush held with the congressional delegation.

These were not idle threats Rove was issuing, as Florida congressman Mark Foley learned when he bucked the administration on a free-trade vote despite heavy lobbying from the White House. Afterward, Foley fretted publicly that he might be in for the "Pawlenty treatment," a reference to when Rove pressured Tom Pawlenty, the Republican leader in Minnesota's state legislature, to bow out of the U.S. Senate race to make way for Rove's handpicked candidate, Norm Coleman.

"People have come to realize that it is better to be seen helping the administration than pulling down parts of his plan," Foley said ruefully. His premonitions were correct. At Rove's urging, Housing and Urban Development Secretary Mel R. Martinez subsequently left the Bush cabinet to run for the Senate from Florida—the seat Foley was eyeing.

And Congress wasn't the only target over which the White House was exerting its authority. At the winter meetings of the National Governors Association, its executive committee issued a call for more money to the states for homeland security and other emergency-related functions. This was pretty standard fare from the governors, but the president had already warned the group that as he prepared for war with Iraq, no more money was likely to be forthcoming; now Bush and GOP governors loyal to him treated the NGA resolution as a partisan hit job. Governors Bill Owens of Colorado, George Pataki of New York, and Jeb Bush of Florida led an attempt to rescind the NGA resolution. Rove allies Grover Norquist and Stephen Moore, movement conservatives who head antitax groups, weighed in as well, calling on conservative governors to withhold their dues to the NGA unless it purged certain liberal staff members.

Loyalty to this White House *most* of the time wasn't good enough, either: Later, regarding other issues, both Moore and Norquist found themselves on the receiving end of Rove tirades.

"If I bitch, guess what?" Norquist told *The Washington Post*. "I get coal in my socks."

Moore got the full Rove treatment after his organization, Club for Growth, made public a letter of protest it had sent Bush objecting to White House support in GOP primaries for "liberal-leaning

Republicans" such as Senator Arlen Specter of Pennsylvania.

Rove also called Moore's boss, Richard Gilder, chairman of Club for Growth, to complain about ads the organization was running attacking two Republican senators—Olympia Snowe of Maine and George Voinovich of Ohio—for resisting the latest Bush tax cut. The ad compared them to French President Jacques Chirac, a low blow that Rove publicly denounced as "stupid" and "counterproductive."

Moore was unfazed. "I think this monomaniacal call for loyalty is unhealthy," he said publicly. "It's dangerous to declare anybody who crosses you an enemy for life. It's shortsighted."

After 9/11, Bush had famously warned world leaders that they were either with Americans in the fight on terror—or against them. At home, Rove was applying the same logic to political leaders, even those of his own party. Karl Rove was now, clearly, the most respected, feared, and influential political operative in the country. Nonetheless, the issue that appeared as though it might define the presidency of George W. Bush—and jeopardize his reelection—was out of Rove's bailiwick.

That issue was the impending war in Iraq.

At that time, there was little daylight between Bush and the top-tier Democrats on the war. In October 2002, all the Democrats considered by Rove to be legitimate presidential contenders had supported Bush on Iraq. John Kerry, John Edwards, Joe Lieberman, Tom Daschle, Dick Gephardt—even Hillary Clinton—had voted aye on the resolution granting the president explicit authority to go to war; Lieberman and Gephardt had followed up their votes with strong statements in support of Bush.

This left an opening for an antiwar Democrat, and it appeared briefly that this role would be filled by the man Bush had run against in 2000: On September 23, 2002, Al Gore delivered a fiery speech to a California audience warning that an Iraq invasion might undermine the effort against the terrorists who attacked America on 9/11. But Gore revealed his own ambivalence about running for president again by all but disappearing from public view in October while Congress debated—and passed—the war resolution. Doves in the progressive wing of the Democratic Party seemed to have no obvious candidate, even as the 2004 Democratic presidential field was rounding itself out.

That began to change in January 2003 as liberals, many of them quite young, coalesced around an outside-the-Beltway candidate with no readily visible geographic—or even ideological—base of support. This candidate had passion, a confrontational speaking style, an unseen but highly effective online fundraising network, and his voice tended to rise in indignation whenever he mentioned George W. Bush.

His name was Howard Dean.

15

Master of the House

In the spring of 2003, as U.S. armed forces marched into Iraq, George W. Bush's job approval rating was in the low to mid–60s, significantly lower than the 80-plus percent he attained after 9/11—and sustained through most of 2002—but solid enough to give Rove confidence as he began reconstituting Bush's reelection campaign team.

For their part, the Democrats were unworried as well. The success of Bill Clinton had taught them that poll ratings taken twenty-two months before Election Day meant nothing. Clinton had set his campaign in motion in 1991 at a time the first President Bush was near 90 percent approval in the public opinion surveys; on Clinton's inauguration day, the Democrats who had been cowed by Bush's hugely popular prosecution of the Persian Gulf War—Mario Cuomo, Dick Gephardt, even Al Gore—could only wonder at what might have been. With this case study as their model, there was no shortage of would-be challengers to George W. Bush in the 2003–2004 presidential election cycle.

Even after U.S. troops raced into Baghdad and Bush appeared on the deck of the USS *Lincoln* in his flight suit, the crop of Democratic presidential challengers reminded themselves that Bush's father had been beaten—and the son could be, too. By 2004, the image of the jaunty Bush speaking beneath a "Mission Accomplished" banner would be used by Democrats as an example of Bush's obliviousness to the difficulties of pacifying Iraq. But at the time of the Bush photo-op aboard the aircraft carrier, the Democrats had a different complaint: They accused Karl Rove of politicizing the war.

Yet the Democrats who learned so clearly the lessons of 1992 made new miscalculations. If George Santayana was correct that those who do not remember the past are condemned to repeat it, a corollary in modern American politics might be that those focused only on avoiding the mistakes of past elections are doomed to make new errors in future campaigns. One reason Gephardt did not run for president in 1992, for example, is that many of his supporters told him his 1991 vote against the Gulf War resolution would make it difficult for any Democrat. In 2002, Gephardt voted differently— supporting another president named Bush in yet another resolution to go to war against Saddam Hussein.

In announcing his support of George W. Bush in 2002, Gephardt said his vote eleven years earlier "was not the correct decision," but he bristled at the notion that his change of heart was motivated by political considerations. "It is unfair and wrong to infuse political motives into everything that everybody is deciding. It is immoral to play games with this. We are talking about people's lives," he told reporters on Capitol Hill. "I wanted to do the right thing (in 1991). But I didn't know everything that I now know. I didn't see what Saddam Hussein did in the last 11 years. And so now I come to a different conclusion."

So did John Kerry, and his change of heart was more surprising than Gephardt's. Unlike Gephardt, Kerry had spent months criticizing Bush's foreign policy, and he had done so largely on the basis of a lack of support elsewhere in the world for a U.S. invasion. In a pattern that was to dog him for the next two years, Kerry delivered caveats to his support for an Iraq invasion before, during, and after the debate on the Iraq war resolution—even as he cast a vote in support of it.

"I will be voting to give the president of the United States the authority to use force—if necessary—to disarm Saddam Hussein because I believe that a deadly arsenal of weapons of mass destruction in his hands is a real and grave threat to our security," Kerry said in a speech on the Senate floor the day before the debate. He added that he would support a multinational effort to remove Saddam "by force, if we have exhausted all other options. But I cannot—and will not—support a unilateral U.S. war against Iraq unless the threat is imminent and no multilateral effort is possible."

It was statements like this that left such a large opening for Howard Dean, although his message was not entirely clear at first, either. As late as October 2002, Dean said in a CBS interview, "Why do we have to do everything in a unilateral way?"—before adding, only two sentences later, "We clearly have to defend the United States, and if we must do so unilaterally, we will."

But Dean soon realized that when he just let it rip, he connected with his audiences, and the money flowed into his campaign website. At a January 21, 2003, cattle call sponsored by the National Abortion and Reproductive Rights Action League, Dean served notice that he might shake up the field. That night, Dean gave a fiery, utterly unequivocal rap in support of abortion rights—but so did most of the other Democrats at this mandatory event. Dean went further, saying flatly he would have voted against both Bush's tax cuts and the Iraq war resolution. Influential *Newsweek* political writer Howard Fineman came away from that dinner predicting that Dean would be a player in the Democratic nominating process. Rove had come to the same conclusion, and eventually developed a morbid fascination with the former Vermont governor that would lead him to believe Dean was going to be the Democrats' nominee long after most others had given up on him. Of course, by early 2003, Rove had begun gathering potentially useful string on all the likely Democratic presidential challengers.

One White House correspondent familiar with Rove visited him in the White House and found he was already dissecting John Edwards's legal career. After ignoring the presidential announcement speeches of other Democratic candidates, the Rove-controlled Republican National Committee greeted the North Carolina attorney's announcement with a spate of press releases pointing to Edwards's career as a wealthy trial lawyer. White House press secretary Ari Fleischer even referred to Edwards as an "ambulance-chaser." In the guarded environment of the Bush White House, where Rove would rarely give an on-the-record interview, this reaction was seen as evidence that Edwards was the candidate most feared by Team Bush. This was most likely a feint; privately, Rove told friends that, lawyer aspersions aside, he just did not believe Americans would vote during wartime for a presidential candidate as inexperienced as John Edwards.

The presidential primaries were still six months off, however. In the meantime, Rove had other Democratic dragons to slay—including some of the most venerable Democrats in President Bush's home state congressional delegation. In fact, Rove and House Majority Leader Tom DeLay targeted virtually every white Democrat in the Texas congressional delegation. This group included several congressmen who often supported Bush on legislation, such as Charles Stenholm and Chet Edwards. But Rove and DeLay wanted more than part-time support for the president in Congress—and felt entitled to it because of the makeup of the Texas electorate.

The Texas redistricting progressed from contentiousness to farce when eleven Democratic state legislators fled Austin for Oklahoma as a way of stalling redistricting by denying proponents a quorum. To the Democrats, the question was simple: Historically, redistricting is done once every ten years, after the results of the U.S. census are completed; the Republicans, led by Tom DeLay and Karl Rove, were trampling this tradition by trying to pull off a second redistricting—one that targeted Texas's white Democrats in the House.

This was not how Karl Rove viewed the matter. For him, the story started earlier, back in 1991. George W. Bush was not even involved much in Texas politics then, but Rove was; and he could do nothing as Texas Democrats produced one of the most baldly partisan gerrymanders in decades. When it was finished, the Democrats in the Texas Legislature had protected every incumbent Democrat in the delegation, while bringing such inventiveness to drawing boundaries that Democrats won all three seats in newly created districts. This feat was accomplished with ingenious mapmaking that carved up Midland County into parts of three different congressional districts, drew up various suburban districts that looked like long narrow snakes, and carefully apportioned Latinos, blacks and rural whites in ways designed to keep them from going Republican.

When the 1992 results were in, Democrats had managed to capture twenty-one of Texas's thirty House seats, even though they carried the popular vote for the House by only 50 percent to 48 percent. But Texas was going Republican so fast that in 1994 the Democrats lost two of the seats anyway. Texas Republicans were hardly mollified: They thought they should have more to show for a stunning 56–42 percent popular vote victory in all the House races combined.

The census of 2000 gave Texas another two seats. Republicans understandably wanted those, but that wasn't all they coveted. They also wanted to undo the gains of the Democrats' shrewd 1991 gerrymander, which had ultimately given Texas Democrats a seventeen-to-thirteen advantage in the House. Finally, Republicans wanted Martin Frost's head itself. Frost, active in the Democratic leadership and an implacable Bush foe, had been instrumental in bringing off the successful gerrymander.

Austin Democrats dug in their heels. The statehouse was occupied by Bush successor Rick Perry, a Republican, but with only a narrow GOP lead in the state Senate, and a slight Democratic majority in the lower house in Austin, the grand Republican plans to produce a spectacular GOP gerrymander were stalled by the Democrats. The whole tangled skein ended up in the courts, where a three-judge panel of federal jurists accepted boundary lines that gave Republicans the two new seats but left the map much the way Democrats had drawn it up ten years earlier. That would have been the end of it—except for the massive Republican victories at the ballot box in 2002.

That year, with Bush flying high, the GOP won all twenty-seven statewide races, including the governor's mansion; upped its advantage in the state Senate; and captured the lower house of the legislature by the whopping margin of eighty-eight to sixty-two. With this kind of power, Republicans felt entitled to more than fifteen of the state's thirty-two seats in Congress.

The intramural war in Austin over redistricting was suddenly on again, and the early signal that the Republicans were not interested in bipartisanship—or even common courtesy—came in their treatment of Democrat Pete Laney, Speaker of the Texas House. In 2000, when the U.S. Supreme Court ended the Florida presidential recount, George W. Bush had claimed the presidency from the House chamber in Austin. Governor Bush had asked Laney to introduce him, and Laney had obliged. The president-elect, in a speech written for him by future White House chief speechwriter Mike Gerson and edited by Karen Hughes and Karl Rove, drew attention to this symbolism during his address:

> Tonight I chose to speak from the chamber of the Texas House of Representatives because it has been a home to bipartisan cooperation. Here in a place where Democrats have the majority, Republicans and Democrats have worked together to do what is right for the people we represent. We've had spirited disagreements. And in the end, we found constructive consensus. It is an experience I will always carry with me, an example I will always follow. I want to thank my friend, House Speaker Pete Laney, a Democrat, who introduced me today. I want to thank the legislators from both political parties with whom I've worked.

But that was then, and this was now.

With Rove plotting the overall strategy and DeLay raising the money and twisting the arms, Pete Laney not only was deposed as

House Speaker—that was inevitable—but was not even given committee assignments. In a predawn vote on May 7, 2003, a legislative committee in Austin approved a redistricting plan produced by a political action committee founded by DeLay. Congressman Nick Lampson of Beaumont took one look at it and dubbed the scheme the "Texas Chainsaw Massacre." He wasn't far off.

Lampson was one of seven or eight senior Democrats in the Texas congressional delegation, all white, targeted by the proposed Republican gerrymander. For most of these Democrats, their sin did not lay in their voting records—some of them supported Republican presidents going back to Ronald Reagan—but rather in their vulnerability. Six were Democratic congressmen representing districts that typically voted Republican in presidential years. DeLay's and Rove's reasoning was clear-cut: With a bit of tweaking in the makeup of the electorate, these districts could go Republican on the down-ticket races as well. Besides Lampson, the others in this category were Chet Edwards of Waco, Max Sandlin of East Texas, Charles W. Stenholm of West Texas, Jim Turner of Crockett, and Ralph Hall of Rockwall.

The seventh target was Martin Frost of Arlington. Rove knew Frost would be the loudest protester of the GOP proposal, although for old Texas Republicans like Rove, Frost's grousing was especially rich: The 1991 gerrymander was the brainchild of Democrat Party professional Bob Mansker, who was at that time employed as an aide in Frost's congressional office. Aside from that, as well as Frost's opposition to Bush on nearly all other fronts, the Republicans targeted Frost's suburban Dallas district for the most basic of reasons—because they could.

If enacted, the new congressional boundaries would almost

certainly bring about the massacre Lampson alluded to, but these maps were not carved with a chainsaw. They were drawn, with scalpel-like effect, by a computer. The African-American wards in Galveston County were taken away from Lampson and put in DeLay's twenty-second district, a wealthy suburban enclave of Fort Bend County outside Houston. Martin Frost found that he no longer lived in his district at all. To separate Chet Edwards from black voters loyal to the Democratic Party, his Waco was divided at the Brazos River, which runs right through the city. Fort Hood, to the west of the city, was taken from him as well.

And so it went.

Stenholm's hometown of Abilene was stuck in the conservative district represented in Congress by freshman Republican Randy Neugebauer of Lubbock. This district took on an unusual jigsaw shape that included parts of twenty-seven counties in West Texas and up through the Panhandle—covering some 29,000 square miles.

Jim Turner and Max Sandlin were essentially put in the same East Texas district—one suddenly turned so conservative it seemed neither man could win it. Turner didn't even try, withdrawing before the primary. Representative Chris Bell of Houston watched as his district was reconstructed into one that only an African-American candidate could probably win. Indeed, that is what happened. In the Democratic primary, Al Green, a local NAACP official, bested Bell.

Ralph Hall's Red River Valley district was nipped and tucked in ways that would have made even this conservative "Blue Dog" Democrat a sure loser. Anticipating defeat, Hall abruptly switched party registrations, thus giving the Republicans a gain of one seat before the campaign even began.

"Tommymandering," the normally staid *Dallas Morning News* called all this partisan mapmaking. The flavor of these newly created districts was so Republican that Charlie Stenholm was the lone targeted Texas Democrat seeking reelection who had the mettle even to attend the Democratic National Convention in Boston that nominated John Kerry. This fact underscored that there was a national component to all this maneuvering—and a political intelligence at work more acute than Tom DeLay's.

"Sheila Jackson-Lee will be the spokesman for the [Texas] Democratic Party, and ought to be," chortled Karl Rove confidant Grover Norquist publicly, in a reference to the gregarious and outspokenly liberal congresswoman from Houston. "She accurately reflects what the Democratic Party is all about."

It must be said that the Texas Democrats did not go down without a fight. Facing certain defeat that May, fifty-five Democratic members of the lower house in the Texas legislature sneaked out of Austin one night and holed up at the Holiday Inn in Ardmore, Oklahoma, while the clock ran out on the legislative session. Governor Perry circumvented the Democrats' gambit by calling a special session of the legislature that summer. But eleven state senators fled Texas during that session, setting up camp in Albuquerque, New Mexico. The objective was to deny Republicans the quorum they needed to vote on a new plan. The theater on both sides was imaginative and entertaining. Governor Perry, at some point, dispatched the Texas Rangers to bring back the reluctant Democratic solons—and the Republicans in the state Senate cut off their state cars, expense accounts, and cell phones. A member of DeLay's staff instructed the Federal Aviation Administration to track down Pete Laney's airplane. A DeLay aide also sought a Justice Department advisory on whether the FBI could forcibly repatriate the missing Democrats to Texas.

During a second special session, the Democrats went on the lam again, this time to New Mexico, where a Democratic governor had offered them a safe haven. When one of their number defected—his return to Texas gave the Republicans the numbers they needed to introduce a new redistricting bill—the Democrats launched one last public relations effort: It consisted of publicly blaming DeLay and Rove—and appealing to George W. Bush's better instincts.

Some of them came to Washington.

"Under the direction of Karl Rove and Tom DeLay . . . our democracy is in peril," said San Antonio–based state Senator Leticia Van de Putte." This is not just about Texas. There is only one person who can stop it—he could stop it with a phone call—and that's President Bush."

The renegade Democrats, after partnering with liberal advocacy group Move On, began running ads and holding press conferences denouncing the Republicans' power grab, which they linked with Bill Clinton's impeachment, the Florida recount, and the California recall of Governor Gray Davis. "We are here to sound the alarm," said state Senator Eliot Shapleigh, D–El Paso. "If a majority can change the rules to win anytime they want, then democracy loses."

"What's happening here is people in the Republican Party are trying to overturn the results of elections," Texas congressman Martin Frost, chimed in at the same press conference. "They are trying to overturn the results of elections in Texas two years ago. They are trying to overturn the results of the election in California. They are trying to overturn results of the election in Colorado."

Colorado's Republicans had also attempted to redistrict for a second time in the decade (although the courts there overturned the effort), and the state's Democrats were convinced Rove was behind the effort. Colorado Republicans denied this vehemently, but evidence that Rove was involved in state politics came from a Texas Republican legislator named Bill Ratliff who was uncomfortable with the gerrymander and whose support DeLay's side needed. Ratliff admitted he had discussed the matter with Rove who told him that his vote "could be important to the president." Later that summer, Texas Lieutenant Governor David Dewhurst conceded that he, too, had discussed the Texas redistricting with Rove.

That Rove had an interest in redistricting was no mystery in Austin. In the early 1980s, Governor Bill Clements had assigned that decade's redistricting to his deputy chief of staff. His name? Karl C. Rove. "I handled redistricting," he told *National Journal* in 2002. "And, you know, political stuff for Governor Clements," he added in classic understatement.

The Democrats were convinced that what occurred in Colorado and Texas was a stark and illegitimate power grab, and they had held together steadfastly. Howard Dean had even visited New Mexico in a show of solidarity. They had put together well-done ads tying the Bush White House to the affair, and the national media gave them fairly respectful coverage. Even with all these successes, they had still lost the fight. Some discouraged Democrats chalked up their loss to the pervasive, almost mystical power wielded by Karl Rove. The truth was probably somewhat more mundane. The great Democrat Tip O'Neill could have explained it to them. (So could Rove, if he had so desired.) All politics was local, and the national headlines could not help the Texas "Bandits" for the simple reason that absconding to New Mexico did not sit that well with Texans, who by poll margins of two to one disapproved of their flight tactic.

"This is the state of the Alamo," noted Wayne Slater, a Texas political writer with the *Dallas Morning News*—and the coauthor of another book on Karl Rove. "You don't run. You fight."

That was precisely Rove's game, and as the summer of 2003 slipped into autumn, he was putting the finishing touches on the machine he would use to fight his next great battle. Nothing fancy about the name: Bush/Cheney '04. The headquarters was even more nondescript, a plain brick-and-glass building in the Courthouse neighborhood of Arlington, Virginia, without so much as a sign out front. The mission of those who staffed it was nothing less than the election—the reelection—of the president of the United States.

In 2000, Rove had predicted a significant-sized Bush victory right up until the polls closed on Election Day. Instead, those results were so close—with Bush even losing the popular vote—that the jury had been out on Rove until November 6, 2002. He knew it, too, and he also knew enough to rein in his natural cockiness. "If we win, it'll be because of the president and the quality of our candidates and campaigns," Rove told *National Journal* before the 2002 elections. "If we lose, it'll be because of me."

But the Republicans didn't lose, and in the days that followed the midterm results, even the skeptical *New York Times* lauded Rove as the "mastermind" of a huge victory in which Rove himself had "emerged as one of the biggest winners." Writing in *The Washington Post*, eminent political commentator David S. Broder went even further. He detailed the similarities in Bush's rise in Texas and his ascension to the national stage: the narrow victory the first time, achieved without coattails, followed by a whopping midterm election triumph two years later. In Texas, what followed was a one-sided gubernatorial reelection victory that helped reshape the landscape in a way quite favorable to Republicans. Broder wondered: Could Bush and Rove be in the process of replicating that model on a national scale? "History does not automatically repeat itself," he wrote. "But it would be foolish for anyone, including the Democrats, to ignore its lessons."

The top-of-the-ticket races in 2002 in Texas confirmed that Karl Rove's legacy there would be writ in stone—perhaps a headstone for the party that had dominated the state since the Civil War ended. The Democrats believed they had assembled a "Dream Team." For governor, they ran a wealthy Latino; for lieutenant governor, a veteran centrist who had served as state comptroller and in both chambers of the Legislature; for the U.S. Senate, a telegenic African-American who had been the downtown business establishment's mayor of Dallas; and for attorney general, a talented trial lawyer who had served as mayor of Austin.

This slate was the old-Texas Democratic Party model, recalling an era when Senator Lloyd Bentsen spent so much money at the top of the Democratic ticket that he pulled candidates like Ann Richards and Jim Hightower along behind him. Yet the $60 million that Laredo banker Tony Sánchez spent on his gubernatorial campaign was not enough to propel him to Austin; nor did the money he poured into the race salvage a single statewide candidate for the Democrats. The party was moribund, and for the moment, no amount of money would bring it back to life: 2002 was an enduring and absolute victory that Rove could savor in Washington while Republicans celebrated in Austin.

The Texas state house races DeLay and Rove believed would

help lock in the "permanent Republican majority" in Congress might not prove so enduring, however. Redrawing the state's congressional districts required winning the lower house of the state legislature, which had been in control of the Democrats for 130 years. For ten years, the Republicans had been gradually moving toward a majority. But in 2000 that elusive grail still required them to pick up six more seats—a goal that was perhaps ten years away. DeLay couldn't wait that long. In the spring of 2001, he and his D.C. political aide Jim Ellis set up a Texas political action committee (TRM-PAC) that would function much as DeLay's hugely successful national PAC (ARMPAC) did: recruiting candidates, funding their races, and providing them with political consulting and support that ensured the money was well-spent. DeLay's Texans for a Republican Majority raised approximately $1.5 million and spent it on twenty-two House races in 2002. (It helped that the Texas Association of Business had raised an equal amount and spent it on the same races.) They won seventeen, providing the Republican Party with the House majority it would need to pass DeLay's reapportionment plan.

Unlike Rove's long and carefully calculated plan to remake Texas, DeLay's impatient battle plans had a central flaw: Half the $1.5 million raised was corporate money, a source of funding explicitly prohibited under state law for use in Texas elections. In September 2004, almost two years after the election that delivered DeLay the statehouse majority he needed to redraw the congressional districts, his three TRMPAC fundraisers were indicted in Austin, along with eight corporations that had contributed to the political action committee. If Lyndon Johnson had stolen one big Texas race, his celebrated Senate victory over Cooke Stevenson in

1948, DeLay was now accused of orchestrating the theft of seventeen campaigns. "You can't steal an election in Texas and brag about it," said Travis County district attorney Ronnie Earle.

DeLay cried foul, claiming he was the victim of a partisan witch hunt. But the Austin district attorney—a Democrat who had prosecuted twelve Democrats and three Republicans in his twenty-seven years in office—was confident he had both the law and the facts on his side. And in November 2004, the U.S. Supreme Court ordered the three-judge panel that approved the new congressional districts to take a second look at the partisan nature of the process that produced them. The Republican House Conference in Washington responded by caucusing behind closed doors to rescind a rule that required any member of the leadership who was indicted to step down until exonerated. The 2002 elections that were such a clear victory for Rove remained under a cloud in Texas. If David Broder was advising Democrats to learn some lessons from the recent history of Republican success in Texas, Rove had learned some history lessons of his own, one being that everything was riding on the upcoming race: the fate of the conservative policies enacted by his handpicked members of Congress, his own reputation as a wizard, his preeminent place in the Republican Party, and his dreams of long-term political realignment. Also on the line in the 2004 presidential election was Rove's relationship with the man in the Oval Office, the man who dubbed him "Boy Genius," but who had been known to employ another, less flattering moniker, "Turd Blossom," when he wanted to take Rove down a peg.

George Stephanopoulos, a top aide to Bill Clinton, put it this way in a Little Rock interview: "Getting reelected is the currency in

deciding whether someone is a successful president. If you don't—
no matter what your accomplishments are—all that is remembered
is that you lost. You're a loser."

In one conversation, Rove concurred with this assessment,
though he would never phrase it this way in front of Bush, whose
father lost his reelection campaign. But that was not the only lesson
Rove had absorbed in Washington. He had learned that the United
States really was evenly divided—and that landslide victories of the
kind he had engineered for Bush in 1998 were unlikely.

On May 7, 2003, Rove made a rare public appearance—a day of
appearances, really—in New Hampshire. Guests waited over an hour
for his arrival at the Bedford Village Inn to speak to some 300 civic
leaders at a forum known as "Politics and Eggs." Seven television
news crews recorded his every word at a speech to students at St.
Anselm College outside Manchester. His visit overshadowed contem-
poraneous trips of various Democratic candidates, including Howard
Dean, but Rove revealed no secrets, made no real news, and stayed
relentlessly on message. He corrected one student who referred to the
"war in Iraq," saying that it was the "battle of Iraq, not the war"—
and that Iraq was part of the larger war on terrorism. He also said he
had no doubt that weapons of mass destruction would be found
there. But later, addressing a topic on which he is more expert, Rove
suggested that the spirited Democratic primary season already taking
shape in New Hampshire would not hurt the Democrats' chances at
all—but instead would serve to energize the opposition party.

"Four times out of five, the process of selecting the presidential
candidates strengthens the candidate," Rove said. "This will be a
close election."

16

The Architect

For the reelection effort, Rove would remain the brains of the Bush-Cheney campaign, but he no longer would be its field general.

The job had grown too big, even for a man Karen Hughes once described as someone "who makes the Energizer Bunny seem lethargic." Rove could send e-mail and make cell-phone calls and use his BlackBerry all night long; he could sing songs until 3 AM in the campaign vans and have his fingers in a hundred political and issue-related pies; and he could preside over the "Office of Strategery"—an embracing of the *Saturday Night Live* spoof of Bush's elocution. But being the primary big-picture guy for a national campaign and the preeminent tactical expert for a fifty-state multimedia effort while simultaneously weighing in on every significant presidential domestic policy initiative as a White House aide would be too much even for the Energizer Bunny. And Rove had no intention of trading his prestigious West Wing digs for a bland office in the obscure brick-and-glass campaign headquarters in Arlington, Virginia.

So Rove divided and cloned himself—twice: One alter ego was the hyperorganized Kenneth B. Mehlman, whom Rove had initially made White House political director. Mehlman became the official campaign manager, in charge of the day-to-day running of Bush-Cheney '04. The big-picture side of Karl Rove would be represented on the campaign staff by the cerebral Matthew Dowd. Rove had originally hired Dowd in 2000 to massage polling for the campaign, but Dowd swiftly proved himself a highly adept strategic thinker. He was tapped to be the campaign's high-altitude planner.

Rove and White House chief of staff Andrew Card trekked across the Potomac once or twice a week for meetings at campaign headquarters, but Rove spent the bulk of the election year either traveling with the presidential entourage or ensconced in his rustic office on the second floor of the White House. Rove liked that office. It had belonged to Hillary Clinton during the previous administration, and Rove delighted in showing visitors the full-length mirror discreetly tucked along an inside wall.

One evening in 2003, as an off-the-record session with a journalist wound down, Rove abruptly jumped out of his seat and began shaving with an electric razor in front of that mirror.

"I'll bet Hillary never did *this*," he quipped.

"Or this," he added, putting on his necktie.

"Who are you primping for?" the reporter asked. "Has the president complained about your appearance?"

"My wife is coming downtown for dinner," Rove replied. "I will not be late. So you're going to have to beat it, pal."

The tough-guy act notwithstanding, when he alluded to Darby Rove his tone softened noticeably. It was at times like this that Rove was his most appealing. In 2000 journalist Melinda Henneberger told Rove how much she liked Darby, who had endured a long struggle with breast cancer, and Rove's eyes filled with tears. "She is one of the most courageous people I know," he told her.

Unlike Karen Hughes, who left the White House in 2002 because her husband and teenage son had been unhappy away from their Austin life, Rove and his small family had flourished in Washington, D.C. Karl and Darby found a house they liked and imported a carpenter from Texas to build floor-to-ceiling bookcases on all three floors to accommodate those 148 boxes of books. Even better, the couple found a school that seemed a perfect fit for their teenage son Andrew—better, actually, than the one he had attended in Austin. In a town grown accustomed to roguish personal conduct, Rove was positively boring. Like his boss, he doesn't drink. He plays gin rummy instead of poker (and yells, incongruously, "Feed the monkey!" when it is his turn to pick up a card). His version of gambling is to wager a hamburger on the outcome of a political race, and his idea of a big night on the town is a quiet Friday night dinner with Darby and Andrew at the Austin Grill on Wisconsin Avenue. Rove is a self-described "nerd," who likes to putter around in the kitchen. He is an incurable gossip, can sound petty and insecure, and he even let something as trivial as money ruin his friendship with his old Texas running buddy—and John McCain political adviser—John Weaver. But Rove also melts around children, is obsessive about sending thank-you notes, and does not hesitate to reach out emotionally when someone he knows is sick or in need.

When Mark McKinnon's wife Annie was stricken with breast cancer, Rove was one of the first to call. "It's gonna be tough for Annie, it's gonna be tough for the kids and you've got to be there for them, but it's gonna be tough for you, Mark," Rove told him. "There are things you need to know and things you need to do."

Rove proceeded to tell McKinnon what he had learned during

Darby's battle with cancer—and, in the process, solidified the relationship between the two men. McKinnon, as people do in such situations, remembered who called, who visited, who sent cards—and who, because they didn't know what to say, simply stayed away.

Those who work in the West Wing say there are a surprising number of stories like this about Rove. When David Kuo, deputy of the White House Office of Faith-Based Initiatives, had a seizure that required surgery, it was Rove who saw to it that his family, huddled at the hospital in an all-night vigil, got something to eat. At Rove's direction, the Kuo family received a catered meal delivered to them right there at the hospital.

One day, a "Flat Stanley" showed up in Rove's office. It was sent by Marcy Ring, a third-grade teacher at a Chicago inner-city school, to her friend Susan Ralston, who happens to be Rove's executive assistant. Flat Stanley is a kids' book about a little boy who is flattened by a bulletin board but who takes advantage of his disability by mailing himself around the country. The book has become a huge hit in elementary schools as a teaching tool: Kids mail a postcard version of Flat Stanley to friends in far-off places, and then Flat Stanley is photographed in exotic locations, with famous people, and in front of recognizable landmarks—like the White House. Rove's face lit up when he saw this particular Flat Stanley, who ended up being pictured at the White House senior staff meeting, in Condoleezza Rice's desk, and with the president in the Oval Office. Rove snapped pictures of Flat Stanley for three days, took the film home, prepared a twenty-five-picture booklet, got Bush to autograph it—and sent it back to Henry Suder School in Chicago.

Those who work in the West Wing say Rove is particularly kind to the children of White House staffers. When Lawrence B. Lindsey was forced out as director of the National Economic Council, Rove wrote a letter to Lindsey's kids, telling them they were too young to understand now, but when they got older they should know that their father had served the president well in a demanding job—and that they could be very proud of him for a job well done.

Children have reciprocal fondness for Rove.

One night when Peter H. Wehner, deputy assistant to the president in Rove's Office of Strategic Initiatives, was tucking in his three-year-old daughter Christine, the child got it in her head that she wanted to talk to "Mr. Karl." Wehner used his cell phone to dial Rove's number from the girl's bedroom, figuring voice mail would pick up and she could leave a message. Instead, Susan Ralston answered, and Wehner stammered out what he was doing, along with an admonition not to bother Rove. But Rove discovered what was going on, got on the phone, and had a "delightful" conversation with her, according to young Christine. In August 2003, when Bush toured Ice Harbor Dam in Washington state, Ralston arranged for Wehner's family to attend the event. Wehner's brother, a local police officer, ended up working security at Pasco Airport where *Air Force One* landed. During the event, while Bush spoke, Rove went over to Wehner's parents and sister-in-law and her children, chatting with them and praising Wehner.

"He spoke far more highly of me than I deserve," Wehner recalled. "But he knew it would mean a great deal to my parents— and it did." Rove arranged for the president to meet them and have pictures taken, and followed that up with personal notes to Wehner's parents and his brother. When Wehner's youngest child David was born, Rove sent flowers to his wife Cindy, along with a warm note of congratulations.

"That is the kind of fellow Karl is—and the kind of stories people never hear about," Wehner relates. "I knew about how 'brilliant' Karl was before I came to work for him. What I could not have known is how personally kind and gracious he is. It may not fit the stereotype of him but, as Henry Kissinger once said, it has the virtue of being true."

McKinnon makes the same point. "Right in the middle of helping run the free world, he was there for me," he told a friend after his wife's health improved. "I'll never forget him for it. That's the side of Karl Rove that people rarely see."

Karen Hughes saw it, too. Although the two were often on different pages in terms of shaping the Bush message, when Hughes abruptly announced in April 2002 that she was moving her family back to Texas, she phoned Rove at home the night before the announcement.

"I was devastated," Rove told *National Journal* at the time. "Her position will not be filled. It can't be. The kind of standing she has [with Bush] has to be earned, man, you don't just hand it to someone. And she earned it the past six or eight years—being there for him."

In his phone conversation with Hughes, Rove told her this and more: that he himself would miss her, that she was doing the right thing for her son Robert, that her counsel was invaluable to Bush—and for that reason she needed to find a way, even from Austin, to remain in the loop. Hughes, who is more sensitive about her image than might be inferred from her no-nonsense public manner, told at least one friend that Rove's call meant a great deal to her.

Bush's nickname for Hughes is the complimentary-sounding "High Prophet," which plays off both her height (five feet, nine inches) and her maiden name (Profitt), but her brusqueness toward the media while being overprotective of Bush earned Hughes the less complimentary moniker among the press corps of "Nurse Ratched," Ken Kesey's famous mental-hospital dictator in *One Flew over the Cuckoo's Nest*. Hughes found the description hurtful. She is a former Texas television reporter and devout Presbyterian who prides herself on treating people fairly, even journalists, and most Texas correspondents knew that she took her cues on how to manage the Bush press from Bush himself. In addition, Hughes is a large woman, and sensitive about it. Hughes reveals in her book, *Ten Minutes from Normal*, how she taught Bush that women her size prefer to be called "tall," not "big." In that memoir she also fingered the journalist who coined the Nurse Ratched line—Howard Fineman of *Newsweek*.

Despite his good moments, toiling alongside Karl Rove is taxing, and Hughes could only laugh aloud after her White House stint when a West Texan named Les Virgil asked her at a public speaking forum in Austin, "How difficult is it for you to work with Karl Rove?"

At least Hughes was on equal footing with Rove. Others were not so blessed. "Family-friendly" White House or not, Rove is wired to hundreds of fellow Bushies by laptop, cell phone, and the BlackBerry he wears on his belt. He doesn't hesitate to use those gadgets regardless of the hour—he sometimes sends text messages while in bed—nor does he tend to ask first what the person on the other end of the line is doing before launching into the purpose of his call.

These "Rove-grams" can be made to adversaries as well as to colleagues and friends. They can communicate pleasantries, matter-of-fact instructions, expressions of glee ("It's Miller Time!" is a favorite)—or they can convey threats, especially to Republicans who have strayed from the path. Stephen Moore, of the conservative, probusiness Club for Growth, recalls wandering around the garage at Reagan Washington National Airport searching for his car one evening, cell phone to his ear, disoriented by the sound of Rove screaming at him in a telephonic tirade. "Stupid" was one of the milder insults Rove hurled at Moore.

"He's perpetually angry at me," Moore explained later, with a shrug. "I've done so many things to piss him off."

In this instance, Rove was incensed by Moore's efforts to rally fiscally conservative Republicans in Congress to vote against a Medicare prescription-drug benefit being pushed by the White House.

"You're going to screw everything up!" Rove hollered at Moore. "We're going to get the Democrats' bill if you're not careful!"

Rove continues to dismiss environmentalists as "green beans," and would say that Democrats or liberal reporters who accused Rove of dirty tricks were "sniffing swamp gas." Intimidation also remained part of Rove's repertoire—just as it was back in Texas. Freelance journalist Ron Suskind recalls sitting outside Rove's White House office awaiting an interview for an *Esquire* magazine piece when he heard Rove shouting, either at an aide or someone on the phone: "We will fuck him! Do you hear me? We will fuck him. We will ruin him—like no one has ever fucked him!"

White House officials rejoined that Suskind, who has produced numerous pieces critical of Bush, has "a hyperactive imagination." But no one tried to assert that Rove does not talk this way. Besides, Rove's colleagues understand his motivations: In the parlance of the

Bush circle, people like Steve Moore—and the person Rove was yelling about screwing over—are not "team players." And the Bushies are nothing if not team players. It is not just a compliment in the Bush White House; it is a requirement. If this makes them seem clannish, or insular, and resistant to outside ideas, the Bushies' attitude is, so be it. It is one of the costs of the kind of absolute loyalty demanded by Bush, and, in turn, by Karl Rove.

In terms of effective governance, this style of management has clear drawbacks. Chief among them is that this kind of insularity discourages dissent, even on issues that are critical to the peace and well-being of the nation. One example was the apparent pressure felt by government officials to refrain from expressing doubt that Saddam Hussein still had a workable arsenal of weapons of mass destruction—even though the evidence was elusive. Another example was how the Pentagon brass lined up lock-step behind a battle plan for the invasion of Iraq that called for troop levels about one-third as high as those envisioned by Army chief of staff Eric K. Shinseki. General Shinseki had already been pushed into early retirement before he told Congress that he believed the invasion and occupation of Iraq would require "several hundred thousand soldiers," but the lesson of what happened when you disagreed with administration policy lingered on.

In terms of running a campaign, however, the Bush/Rove method of operation has definite virtues. After the 2004 race was over, with Team Bush victorious yet again, the extensive postmortems of the race done by *Newsweek, Time,* and other news outlets contrasted the fractious nature of John Kerry's campaign staff with the bloodless efficiency of the top-down Bush operation. Some of this analysis is to be expected: Winning campaigns usually are

portrayed after the fact as having been brilliantly run, just as commentators feel obliged to find ineptitude and discord in losers'
efforts. But conventional wisdom can be correct.

John Kerry and George W. Bush, as candidates, had good days
and bad days in their eighteen-month campaign against each other.
But whereas the Kerry campaign was rife with turf battles, back-bit-
ing, second-guessing, top-level firings, and waves of new staffers
overlaid on top of old ones, the Bush campaign was a nearly seamless operation. Its internal machinations were as hush-hush as those
at the Mossad, Israel's supersecret secret police. Its cheerful, on-
message efficiency was reminiscent of the Amway Corporation, an
entity from which it actually borrowed concepts about how to
mobilize foot soldiers.

To be sure, there were disagreements among the staff about tactics, strategy, message, even the nature of the electorate. But these
disputes were philosophical, not personal, and the staff was united
by its cultlike devotion to George W. Bush himself. Devotees of this
cult of personality never would knowingly do anything to undermine Bush, which ruled out public bickering and back-stabbing. In
early 2004 when *Ten Minutes from Normal* was published, Hughes
quipped on her book tour about Washington political types who
open her book and hurriedly scan the index for entries reading
"Rove, Karl—author's disagreements with."

Ironically, there is just such an entry—and it is instructive. It
concerns Bush's signing of the McCain-Feingold campaign finance
reform law on March 27, 2002. Bush hated this legislation, as did
the Republican leadership on Capitol Hill. But it had been voted
through in both houses of Congress, and Bush had promised to sign
it (while hoping privately it would never pass). The question was

how to handle the signing ceremony. Rove, who had wanted Bush to veto the thing, argued that if the president had to sign it, he should do so quietly with little or no ritual.

Hughes, traveling in Mexico, argued on the phone for a signing ceremony at the White House. Hughes thought this strategy would send a message to Congress that the heated debate over the measure could be put aside, and would simultaneously make an overture to McCain. Rove, anticipating Hughes's pitch, had his ducks lined up. He had talked to the Republican leadership, including Senator Mitch McConnell, the Kentucky Republican who led the opposition to the bill. And he had Nick Calio, the White House liaison with Congress on the line during the conference call.

"This would be the biggest mistake we ever made," Rove said simply in reply to Hughes's suggestion. Calio agreed with Rove. So did House Speaker Dennis Hastert, whom Bush subsequently called. In the end, Bush signed the bill early one morning, announcing it only after the fact. No White House photographer was present to record the event, which is standard, and McCain was notified by telephone in a call from a low-level White House aide. A member of McCain's staff, asked for the Arizona senator's reaction, replied in two words: "How chickenshit."

This McCainiac was right, of course—although in hindsight Bush probably should have followed Rove's instincts and vetoed this flawed legislation. But Hughes did not include this episode in her book to make that point—or to even a score with Rove. Instead, she aimed to show how well Bush senior staffers complement one other. "Purely in terms of public perception, I believe I was right to advocate a signing ceremony," Hughes said. "In terms of our ability to work with members of Congress whose support we needed to enact the president's proposals, Karl and Nick were absolutely right."

Karl Rove was no Amway salesman. But he served as the man at the top of the organizational pyramid, and he formulated the broad themes that Team Bush executed. When it was over, President Bush himself would proclaim Rove to be "the architect" of his victory. If that is true, the most important work Rove did came in 2003, when he put the team together. Dana Milbank, White House correspondent for *The Washington Post*, began his June 1, 2003, article on the assembling of the Bush-Cheney campaign with a succinct one-liner: "All roads lead to Rove."

One of those back for an encore was Mark McKinnon, the guitar-playing former Austin songwriter who had turned his creative back on politics until sitting down with Bush in 1997 in the governor's mansion—at Rove's suggestion. McKinnon was the most colorful and laid-back of the top-tier Bushies. He was also, at least until he met Bush, a lifelong Democrat, having worked as a press secretary and media ad creator for a litany of well-known Democrats, including Lloyd Doggett, the Michael Dukakis–Lloyd Bentsen presidential ticket, and former Texas Governor Ann Richards. McKinnon admits to having voted for Richards in 1994 when she ran against Bush—after all, he was still a Democrat—but by 1996 McKinnon had sworn off politics altogether.

One of the few Bushies who prefers journalists to politicians, McKinnon remained with Public Strategies Inc., the Austin power-house political consultancy launched by former Bentsen aide Jack Martin in the late 1980s, but he was doing corporate, not political, work. McKinnon explained his disillusionment in a celebrated 1996 *Texas Monthly* piece announcing that he was through with "candidates asking me what their firmly held convictions should be."

But McKinnon was not through, and when Bush and Rove persuaded him to join them, he found himself opposing many of his old Texas friends in the Democratic Party. "I tease him that it's a midlife crisis," quipped one of those friends, Paul Begala, his colleague on the 1984 Doggett campaign. "Cheaper than a red convertible, and more honorable than an affair."

McKinnon sees it more as a midlife course correction, not a crisis, but he is a passionate man and a free spirit as well. After another notable maverick, Phoenix Cardinals' safety Pat Tillman, was killed in Afghanistan, McKinnon had Tillman's number tattooed on his shoulder. (Tillman had responded to the September 11, 2001, attacks by walking away from a $1 million annual contract to play pro football to join the United States Army).

In the 2000 campaign, McKinnon had been the primary creative force behind the Bush television and radio advertisements, and he spent the four years of Bush's first term commuting between his Austin home and an apartment on Sixteenth Street in northwest Washington, two blocks from the White House, where he could be within easy reach of Rove and Bush.

"I didn't make the assumption I'd be on the 2004 campaign in the exact same role, but I wanted to be a part it," McKinnon recalled later. "One day, Karl called and said, 'You're the guy. We really want you to do this again—and to bring in the best people you know to help.'"

McKinnon ran with those instructions: By the end of 2003, he was overseeing a twelve-person creative team that included New

York ad-men Stuart Stevens and Russ Schriefer, both veterans of the 2000 campaign; Californian Fred Davis, called "Hollywood" by the other team members; Alex Castellanos of Alexandria, Virginia, and Chris Mottola, who worked together on Bob Dole's 1996 campaign; Frank Guerra of San Antonio, whose client list included Jeb Bush; Rove protégé Scott Howell of Dallas; and two Madison Avenue types, Harold Kaplan and Vada Hill.

Another reenlistee with Team Bush was McKinnon's friend and Austin business partner Matt Dowd, an even-tempered political strategist whose route to Bush's door was even more circuitous. The son of Michigan Republicans, Dowd's first political hero was Ronald Reagan. At Cardinal Newman College, a small Catholic school in St. Louis, Dowd fell under the sway of a more liberal crowd. He landed an internship in the office of Dick Gephardt, a local hero in St. Louis Democratic circles. When the internship was over, aides in Gephardt's office hooked Dowd up with Texas Democratic congressman J. J. Pickle—and Dowd was off to Austin.

In time, Dowd became the political director of the Texas Democratic Party and was tapped in 1988 to help manage Lloyd Bentsen's simultaneous vice presidential run and Senate reelection campaign. That election did not hurt Dowd's reputation, as Bentsen running by himself fared far better with Texas voters than he did as Dukakis's running mate. After it was over, Dowd teamed up with Jack Martin to launch Public Strategies.

One of the firm's clients was conservative Democrat Bob Bullock, who handily won election as lieutenant governor in 1994 and 1998, even as the Republican at the top of the ticket—George W.

Bush—was also victorious. Once both candidates were in office, Bullock worked closely with Bush, even endorsing him when Bush ran for reelection in 1998. In 2000, Rove and McKinnon persuaded Dowd to take the same emotional plunge Bullock had taken—helping a Republican. Dowd kept a low profile in 2000 and was mentioned in press accounts of that campaign only infrequently. Inside the campaign, however, Dowd's insight and candor were highly esteemed, as was his calm demeanor. "He is not a guy who dances in the end zone," says McKinnon.

In 2004, Dowd was given more responsibility and visibility. He would also brief reporters, usually on background, and earned their respect by not overselling things. To those who commented on his sober attitude and minimalist predictions of glory, Dowd would quip that he was part Irish and thus genetically preconditioned to expect things to fall apart at any moment. This dreary perspective was imprinted, literally, on the wall of Dowd's office in the form of a quotation from William Butler Yeats: *Being Irish, he had an abiding sense of tragedy which sustained him through temporary periods of joy.*

Journalists take pleasure in this kind of "color," particularly those who cover the inaccessible, always-on-message Bush crowd. But one journalist, Ken Herman of the *Austin American-Statesman*, delved deeper and discovered that Dowd's sense of fatalism was genuine and personal—and not rooted in the musings of any poet. On September 12, 2002, Dowd's wife gave birth to twin girls, Nicole and Josephine, born prematurely at twenty-three weeks and weighing one pound each. Only Josephine made it home from the hospital. Little Nicole died sixty-three days after her birth.

"It was horrible," Dowd told Herman. "It was really the toughest thing I've ever been through in my life. They were identical twins. Your one daughter dies in your arms in the hospital . . . and you don't have time to grieve because you have a daughter that's on life support."

Unspoken in this interview was the obvious thought: Losing an election is not the worst thing that can happen. Not by any means. It sounds counterintuitive, but this kind of perspective can help. Campaigns are notoriously oriented toward the short-term, immediate news cycle. Having Matt Dowd aboard meant, at the very least, that one top Bush aide was always able to take the long view.

In mid-2002, in fact, Dowd was dispatched by Rove on a confidential fact-finding tour—into the past. Searching for clues as to how best to serve an incumbent seeking reelection, Dowd visited the presidential libraries of the past three Republican presidents. There, amid stacks of documents and mementos belonging to Gerald Ford, Ronald Reagan, and George Bush the father, Dowd perused old memos, polling data, organizational charts, and internal staff memos. Mehlman and Dowd had already debriefed many of the aides who produced those documents. On his research mission, Dowd discovered what presidential scholars know well: Memories play tricks on participants in and witnesses to historic events, and pertinent documents often tell a different story.

"The papers reflect more fully what people were thinking about," Mehlman told Bill Adair of the *St. Petersburg Times*, who learned of Dowd's trip down memory lane. At the same time, Dowd told Adair, the documents "give you the human dimension . . . of the presidents."

Some of those dimensions—and the quandaries they present for campaigns—are timeless: Dowd was particularly struck by a frank and unsigned 1976 campaign memo from a staffer who fretted that voters were beginning to wonder if Ford was "smart enough" for the job of chief executive of the United States.

Karen Hughes was back for the new campaign as well. Bush had never run for office successfully without her, and he made it clear he did not want to try now. If Rove was the aide Bush listened to the most, Hughes was the one he was closest to personally. In *The Right Man*, a 2003 book by former Bush speechwriter David Frum, Hughes was contrasted directly with Rove—and she did not fare well in the comparison. Rove was a "risk-taker and an intellectual," Frum proclaimed, whereas Hughes "loathed risk and abhorred ideas."

"Rove was a reader and a questioner—a curious man, always eager to learn," Frum added. "Hughes rarely read books and distrusted people who did—anything she did not already know she saw no point in knowing."

Frum, who himself is an intellectual, fleshed out this perception by describing Rove as seeing the electorate as a rich demographic mosaic that he wanted to conquer one voting bloc at a time. In contrast, Hughes cheerily viewed Americans as being essentially alike, and therefore "easily manipulated by the same story line."

In terms of how to position the president rhetorically, these seemingly disparate perceptions do not necessarily conflict, as Frum himself has acknowledged. Moreover, there is something about Hughes's simple faith in the broad appeal of American "exceptionalism" that appeals to Bush—even if neither of them would use that phrase. This is one reason Hughes is able to offer the kind of constructive criticisms of the paranormal phenomenon known as a George W. Bush speech that no one else, except Laura Bush, can get away with. This candor has been a facet of the Hughes-Bush relationship from the beginning.

In the first week of his first campaign for governor, Bush had a line in his speech so clunky that it stopped audiences in their tracks. "I am a capitalist!" Bush would proclaim, apropos of nothing. It was a line he, and he alone, clearly liked. Hughes realized she would have to tackle it directly.

"You know in your speech when you declare, 'I am a capitalist'—it doesn't come across right," she told him on the campaign plane one day. "Why do you do that?"

"Because I am a capitalist," Bush replied pointedly, his eyes narrowing. "Aren't you?"

"Of course I am, but it just doesn't sound right when you say it that way."

"How would you prefer I say it?" Bush retorted mockingly, "given that I am a capitalist, and we live in a capitalist system where people risk capital—that's how our economy works."

Hughes suggested that Bush might discuss the virtues of the "free enterprise system" instead.

Then she listened in alarm as Bush started reciting his basic stump speech, "I believe in the free enterprise system . . . "—but only *after* making his idiosyncratic declaration "I am a capitalist!"

In the meantime Hughes had figured out why, aside from being out-of-date, the phrase bothered her so much. It sounded exclusive, not inclusive like the rest of the speech. That night on the plane when Bush asked, "How was the speech?" she jumped to her feet.

"I am a capitalist!" she shouted, waving her arms for effect.

"I am a capitalist—*a rich business guy*, and you—why, *you* are *not!*"

Bush pretended to ignore Hughes, while other aides convulsed in laughter. But at the next stop the line was gone, and it was not resurrected.

Some of Bush's wordsmiths were discomfited by the idea of the poorly read Hughes playing the role of a kind of Everyman, scouring his speeches for phrases that sounded pompous or insincere. But even these quiet critics conceded that she had her moments. The morning of 9/11, Hughes, in Washington, was patched into a call to *Air Force One* where press secretary Ari Fleischer told her the staff was working on a statement for the president.

Fleischer began to read the draft statement, which her deputy, Dan Bartlett, was writing: "America today was the victim of—"

"We are *not* victims!" Hughes interrupted angrily.

"We may have been attacked," she continued, her voice softer, "but we are not victims."

Whatever her limitations as a prose stylist, in this instance Hughes had perfect pitch. It was not the only time, either, and for the 2004 run, she would be back on the plane. Bush, for one, was happy to have her there.

By the time the second campaign rolled around, the top circle had enlarged, too. Dan Bartlett, who had worked for Bush since age twenty-two, assumed a large and significant role in the Bush communications operation, as did chief White House speechwriter Mike Gerson. Other significant players included former Montana Governor Marc Racicot as "campaign chairman," a kind of ceremonial title; Mercer Reynolds III, a Bush family friend, as finance chairman; deputy RNC chief Jack Oliver as deputy finance director; former Rove employee Kelley McCullough as deputy campaign manager; Nicolle Devenish as communications director; Thomas J. Josefiak as general counsel, with Ben Ginsburg, a campaign finance law expert, brought in as outside counsel. Terry Nelson was in charge of outreach to various constituency groups, and Rove designated veteran Republican spokesman Terry Holt to be the campaign's mouthpiece.

Most of these people had long histories with Rove and Bush, and were given expanded responsibilities over the roles they played in the 2000 campaign. This was most true of campaign manager Mehlman, who despite being only thirty-six years old seemed sometimes to be the old man of the group. Further, of the top five aides—Rove, Hughes, Mehlman, Dowd, and McKinnon—Mehlman shared motivations most akin to Rove's—their origins were ideological.

McKinnon and Dowd were Democrats brought into the Republican Party through the Trojan Horse named George W. Bush. Likewise, Karen Hughes almost certainly would have drifted out of Republican politics—just as she had gravitated away from journalism—had Bush not come along. This was definitely not true of Ken Mehlman. He did not have a Rove-style boyhood infatuation with Richard Nixon—but that was only because he was six years old when Nixon resigned. Mehlman's boyhood hero was Ronald Reagan ("He's our FDR," Mehlman says today), and at age fourteen he canvassed precincts in his hometown of Pikesville, Maryland, for Reagan voters. A party man and lifelong conservative, he was brought into Team Bush by Rove, who met him in Texas. It is easy to visualize Mehlman working for other GOP candidates after Bush has left the scene.

Mehlman's value, then, is not to bring a cultish devotion to the Bush clan but to be a disciplined, superbly organized operative with a quick mind and unlimited energy. McKinnon has referred to him as the caffeine of the campaign, and he has always struck his cohorts this way. He attended Franklin & Marshall College in Lancaster, Pennsylvania, where he was his fraternity's president, and then went to law school at Harvard, where—as Bush did at Yale—he reacted against what he perceived as the pervasive smugness of liberal elites. In a career path different from that followed by most Jewish students who excel at Harvard Law School, Mehlman wound up working as chief of staff for Kay Granger, a House of Representatives member from Texas, who happened to be a Rove & Co. client.

Rove was immersed much deeper in the 2004 campaign as well, to levels not delved into by most journalists. In an election everyone both inside and outside the Bush campaign was handicapping as a close one, Rove wanted every edge. This started with his junior-grade campaign officer corps.

In Florida, Rove was counting on Jeb Bush to replicate his 2002 get-out-the-vote operation, but as both sides looked increasingly to Ohio as the likely Florida of 2004, Rove deputized a young Ohio phenom named Bob Paduchik to organize the Buckeye State for Bush. Paduchik had run the state in 2000, but the job then wasn't as tough as it might have been. Ohio Democratic Party chairman David Leland crisscrossed the state in autumn 2000 exhorting

Democratic Party professionals and volunteers that everything could depend on them. "You've been given a great gift," Leland told them. "You get to decide who will be the next president of the United States."

This could have been true, although the Clinton-Gore ticket had carried Ohio in 1996, Gore's campaign did not see the same opportunity in 2000. Polls showed Bush leading Gore by six to eight percentage points, and the Democratic campaign cut advertising money in the state by two-thirds in the weeks before the election and kept Gore out of the state for the entire month before Election Day. Election returns later showed this may have been a huge mistake. The headlines and attention afterward were all about the Florida recount, and if despondent Democrats second-guessed the results in other states, they tended to wonder why Gore did not dispatch Clinton to Arkansas, why Gore himself was unable to carry his home state of Tennessee, and how Ralph Nader clearly cost Gore not only Florida but New Hampshire as well. Any of those four states would have given Gore the presidency, but the same was true of Ohio, which tightened considerably in the last days of the 2000 campaign. In the end, Gore lost Ohio by fewer than 176,000 votes—out of 4.6 million votes cast. Bob Paduchik, who was dispatched to Florida to help out during the recount, noticed this pattern and speculated that if the Democrats had put the same effort into Ohio as they had into, say, Pennsylvania, he might be fighting a recount in Ohio instead.

In 2001, Paduchik came to Washington. A reticent person who avoids the media spotlight, Paduchik was given a civilian job in the Pentagon after Bush became president. The Army personnel office where he worked was destroyed in the 9/11 attacks, but Paduchik, who was buying a birthday gift for a coworker in the Pentagon entrance near the subway at the time the plane hit, was unharmed. Two of his office mates, Major Lacey Ivory and Captain Ron Milam, perished that day. Later, Paduchik was transferred to the Department of Energy. By 2004 he would be back in Ohio, running the state for Bush-Cheney '04.

Brian Lunde was another of Rove's unsung midlevel operators. After the 2000 campaign ended, Lunde had returned to work as a Washington public relations man for Edelman Communications, his work for Bush barely noted even in a town of political junkies. But Rove remembered his contribution, and in 2003 he had Mehlman call Lunde and ask, *Are you with us again?* The answer was yes, as it invariably was when Rove and Mehlman tapped the members of their old network. The recipients of such invitations were pleased to be asked back.

The defection of Brian Lunde in the 2000 campaign had been something of a Republican coup. A political consultant by trade, Lunde had worked with Bill Clinton, whom he admired, and had worked only for Democratic candidates. Indeed, in the 1980s, Lunde served a stint as executive director of the Democratic National Committee. But Lunde was a moderate who found Al Gore too stiff, his policies too liberal, and his manner of political speaking too strident. In the late 1990s, Lunde had several friends in the Texas Democratic Party who spoke glowingly of their state's governor, among them McKinnon and Dowd, and on December 22, 1999, Lunde surprised even himself by placing a call to a Republican he knew only by reputation—Karl Rove.

"I'm going to go with my heart over my history," Lunde told Rove. "I'd like to help out on your campaign."

Rove was unrevealing. He wondered if Lunde was looking for a job. When Lunde insisted that any work he did for the campaign would be on a volunteer basis, Rove's attitude softened; he even cautioned Lunde not to give away his services too quickly.

"You're a political consultant," Rove told Lunde. "That's how you make your living."

But Lunde was firm about helping only on a volunteer basis. He even had an idea of a role for himself: head of a "Democrats for Bush" division of the campaign. Rove was noncommittal about that as well, and when Lunde got off the phone he wasn't sure what, if anything, to expect. Three months later, however, after Rove had Lunde thoroughly checked out, the onetime DNC official found himself face-to-face with Rove in the law office of Akin Gump partner (and well-connected Texan) Jim Langdon.

Rove and Lunde hit it off easily, first learning that both their fathers were of Norwegian heritage. Each man also had something of a chip on his shoulder, despite significant professional success. "He's an outsider; I'm an outsider," Lunde said. "I know he's intense, but I found him warm, and easy to talk to." By June 2000, Rove had brokered a meeting between Lunde and Bush in Kentucky.

"What are we gonna call this thing?" Bush asked Lunde when they met.

Rove had convinced Bush that "Democrats for Bush" might be too hard-edged for a campaign that wanted to appeal to Democrats, not alienate them.

"Whatever you want," Lunde replied.

And so Brian Lunde, erstwhile Democrat, became head of a low-profile arm of the campaign known as "Americans for Bush-Cheney."

Four years later, Team Bush had no qualms about the name. This time when Lunde asked Mehlman what he had in mind for a name for his effort, the answer was straightforward: Democrats for Bush. "Mehlman was already ahead of me," Lunde recalled later. "They had already decided that they wanted to do it. Mehlman was very aggressive about the idea. He dedicated a staff person to it, and it became an official program of the campaign."

Inside America's voting booths, Democrats for Bush never figured to be a large demographic slice of the electorate, especially after the 2004 race shaped up as a "base" election, in which each side tried to maximize turnout among its core supporters while managing to influence enough of the dwindling pool of independents to cobble together a victory. But Lunde had an expertise that strategists on both sides thought would be crucial in 2004—how to target Republican-leaning voters opting for early voting in places such as Florida and Ohio.

Another point of entry into the American electorate for Rove was a conservative Catholic activist named Wyatt Deal Hudson. Although he was a Texan, which counted in his favor with the Bush crowd, Hudson was an unlikely conduit to the prolife wing of the Catholic voting bloc. Thrice married, Hudson was confirmed as a Southern Baptist and converted to Catholicism as an adult. He had also abruptly, and without explanation, abandoned a promising career as a Catholic intellectual by leaving a tenured position on the faculty at Fordham University in the mid-1990s for Washington, where he took over a sleepy conservative Catholic magazine called *Crisis*. Yet that is how he came to Rove's attention. In 1998, Hudson commissioned polling by Steven Wagner of QEV Analytics seeking to explain the steady migration of Catholics out of the

Democratic Party after the high-water mark of the 1960 election of
John F. Kennedy.

The report ran to twenty-four pages, but its gist was that a huge
pool of devout, regular church-going Catholics had been voting
Republican for some time—by design—and that this group,
together with Protestant evangelicals, formed the core constituency
for any social-conservative Republican presidential candidate. In
other words, the appeal Ronald Reagan held for ethnic Catholics
was a bigger phenomenon than his Irish charm. The "Reagan
Democrats" could become a permanent fixture of the GOP coalition, Wagner suggested.

Ralph Reed, an Atlanta-based Republican political consultant
and past executive director of the Christian Coalition, had been
preaching this message for some time. And here was polling that
seemed to prove it.

"Reed is literally correct," read Wagner's report to *Crisis* magazine, in which he noted that 15 percent of voters were "active
Catholics"—nearly as many as were evangelical Protestants (18
percent). "A candidate for president espousing a socially conservative agenda can win every born-again, evangelical and fundamentalist vote there is, but without the support of Catholics, that
candidate is going nowhere."

Rove saw this report as soon as it came out in November 1998
and immediately called Hudson.

"You gonna be in Austin anytime soon?" Rove asked.

"I can be," replied Hudson.

In January 1999, Hudson met with Rove in his Austin office to
discuss the *Crisis* research. Hudson stressed to Rove that the most
important factor for correlating Catholic votes to the Republican

Party was regular church attendance. In 1996 Clinton won 53 percent of the Catholic vote—in a three-man race. But even that year Bob Dole narrowly won among "active Catholics." Also, for the first time since 1960, in 1996 half of active Catholics identified themselves as conservative.

To Hudson, the implications were obvious: If George W. Bush was running for president, he needed to court religious Catholics actively. These voters, Hudson said, would certainly support a Protestant from the South, but only if he was unshakable on what Hudson called "the life issues"—basically, opposition to abortion. Rove did not disagree, and he deputized Hudson to galvanize support among religious and socially conservative Catholics. In 2000, Bush outperformed Dole among Catholic voters, but he still did not win a majority of them, losing Catholics to Gore 53–47 percent.

Rove believed Bush would have to improve this number in order to be reelected, and in 2003, Mehlman called Hudson to make sure he was still on board. Oh yes, he said. Absolutely.

The selection of these three midlevel operatives to key commands demonstrated the multiplicity of thinking inside the Bush campaign. Getting to 50.1 percent was not just a chess match; it was a three-dimensional chess match. Making sure the talented Bob Paduchik was still on the team demonstrated how important Rove and Mehlman considered the get-out-the-vote ground effort in battleground states, especially Ohio. The overtures to Brian Lunde—and, later, to Georgia Senator Zell Miller—were tacit recognition that no matter how much one turned out the base, ticket-splitting independents were still important. Reaching out to Deal Hudson was an acknowledgment that, for better or worse, in the twenty-first century the Republican Party was the home of conservative

Christians, no matter where they worshiped, and that GOP success in national elections depended on them accepting that fact.

Rove had known it all along. In a December 2001 appearance before the American Enterprise Institute (AEI), he had asserted that one of the disappointments of the 2000 election was that the Bush campaign failed to realize the level of support "among the base" that he expected. He then defined "the base":

> If you look at the model of the electorate, and you look at the model of who voted, the big discrepancy is among self-identified, white, evangelical Protestants, Pentecostals, and fundamentalists. There should have been nineteen million of them, and instead there were fifteen million of them. Just over four million of them failed to turn out and vote. And yet they are obviously part of our base. They voted for us, depending on who they were and where they were, by huge margins, seventy and eighty percent margins. And yet four million of them didn't turn out to vote that you would have anticipated voting in a normal presidential election year. I think we may have failed to mobilize them.

In the aftermath of the 2004 election, commentators would make much—probably too much—of an exit poll showing that one-fifth of the electorate cited "moral values" as the most important issue facing the country. By then, a whole spate of difficult ethical questions were front and center, not all of them "conservative" issues. They included gay marriage, embryonic stem cell research, war in Iraq, and the morality of torture.

As 2003 gave way to 2004, these issues unfolded in ways that made it unclear which side would benefit. Most of the nation's Catholic bishops, following the lead of Pope John Paul II, were opposed to the Iraq invasion; and in the middle of the election year, the pontiff himself dressed Bush down—in person—over the prisoner-abuse scandal at Abu Ghraib. Moreover, polls continued to show support among swing voters for John Kerry's position on stem cell research, not Bush's. On the other side of the ledger, abortion continued to be a defining issue for church-going Catholics, even as gay marriage emerged as a classic wedge issue for conservative Christians of every denomination.

In his pursuit of Deal Hudson, Rove proved himself to be ecumenical, at least after a fashion. Do religiously conservative Roman Catholics really have more in common with Baptists or the members of sprawling nondenominational evangelical congregations than they do with, say, members of more liberal denominations such as Episcopalians or Congregationalists? That's an interesting question, but Rove was not interested in the theology of it, only the politics. In a campaign awash in money and resources, there was little risk involved. If Hudson said he needed a couple of dozen paid staffers and a few hundred volunteers to roust conservative Catholics to the polls, what was the harm? God knows Rove was already planning to do this with Protestant evangelicals.

Voter turnout was the real issue involved in 2004. The dirty secret of the Bush–Gore campaign was that *both* sides left millions of votes on the table—and not all were evangelical Christians. It was a low-turnout election in which roughly 105 million Americans went to the polls. Bush got only 50.5 million of them, and it was an article of faith at Bush-Cheney '04 headquarters that the ticket would need at least 5 million more votes—and maybe 10 million more—to reelect the president.

Matt Dowd was not convinced that Catholic parishes were necessarily the first place Team Bush should look for these votes; or, more precisely, he wasn't sure that appealing to swing voters on the basis of their Catholicism was the ideal way to reach them. "He had an honest intellectual disagreement with me about this," recalls Hudson. "He didn't think there was a Catholic vote you could move as a bloc."

Plenty of people agree with Dowd, including Joseph Bottum, an influential writer with the conservative *Weekly Standard*. These skeptics believe that the reason the Catholic vote looks so decisive is that it is so diverse and so large—27 percent of the electorate—that its number simply reflects the nation as a whole. But Matt Dowd certainly did agree that Bush would have to improve his performance among discrete demographic blocs to win reelection. In fact, in a statement that received less attention than Rove's declaration at AEI about undervoting evangelicals, Dowd bluntly told Republican operatives on Capitol Hill in 2001 that if Bush were to win the same percentage of minority votes in 2004 that he did in 2000, he would lose the presidency by 3 million votes.

Dowd was talking primarily about Latinos. Bush garnered roughly 35 percent of the Hispanic vote in 2000, a showing that was considered respectable for a Republican. Changing U.S. demographics meant that this number would be insufficient for the future. Dowd said that if Bush did not increase his support among African Americans to double digits and his backing among the nation's Hispanic communities to above 40 percent, he could not win—no matter what Christian conservatives did. Rove concurred. Two days before Bush was inaugurated the first time, Rove proclaimed that making inroads among Latino voters "is our mission and our goal."

Rove may harbor dreams of a gradual and vast realignment toward Republicans, but in the four years between Bush's two campaigns for president, both he and Dowd acknowledged that the "fifty-fifty" nation epitomized by Red America and Blue America was a reality, and that Bush's reelection would probably be close. A year before Election Day 2004, Dowd predicted in a two-page memo aimed at grassroots Republican activists around the country that "this race is likely to be very tight and go down to the wire" due to the "nature of a divided and polarized electorate."

"After the Democratic nominee is all but certain [to be known] in the late winter/early spring, it would not be surprising for us to fall behind for a bit," Dowd's memo cautioned. Rove agreed with this assessment as well. But he already had a plan to counteract it—and he telegraphed his strategy in a little-known meeting of Texas Republicans on June 25, 2003.

"Our object is not to defend our own turf," Rove told the GOP activists gathered at the Fort Worth Club. "Our goal is to get the other side to defend *their* turf."

Ostensibly, Rove was talking about the Electoral College map. What he was also alluding to, however, were his aggressive plans for helping the Democrats introduce their nominee to the country—and not in a favorable light. He did not promise to "take the bark off" the Democratic candidate, as Rove's mentor Lee Atwater once had decreed for Michael Dukakis. But that was the plan, regardless of who got the Democratic nomination. And that was the question, as 2003 turned into 2004. Who would the Democrats choose to challenge George W. Bush and the campaign juggernaut being assembled by Karl Rove?

17

In Their Heads

Rove certainly knew which Democrat he desired as Bush's opponent: Howard Dean of Vermont. In the summer of 2003, at an annual Fourth of July parade in his neighborhood, Rove was standing along MacArthur Boulevard near his home when a dozen Dean supporters marched by.

"Yeah, that's the one we want!" Rove said with a laugh.

Getting into the spirit of the thing, Rove added, "How come no one is cheering for Dean?"

He then began exhorting others in the audience, and even the parade. "Come on, everybody! Go Howard Dean."

Later he claimed to have been joking around, but he was kidding on the square: Convinced Dean was too liberal, too unknown, too volatile, and too much of a lightweight to give the president a serious run for his money, Rove began pulling for Dean openly, and e-mailing friends when Dean made news or went too far in appealing to his youthful liberal base.

Dean did go far at times. "We've allowed [ourselves] to become the slaves to the bottom-line of multinational corporations all over the world," Dean told a youthful crowd at Grinnell College just before Christmas 2003. "We are not cogs in a corporate machine. We are human, spiritual beings who deserve better consideration as human beings than we're getting from this administration."

But New Age rhetoric or not, in the last half of 2003, Dean emerged as a wild card—and an unorthodox front-runner. Nobody in the Democratic Party hierarchy seemed to believe he could beat Bush, but he was leading in the head-to-head polls, in money raised, in volunteers signed up, in major endorsements—including the backing of Al Gore and the Democrats' most prominent labor unions.

Dean appeared on the cover of *Time* and *Newsweek* before the summer was out, and as 2003 gave way to 2004, the media's herd mentality began to take root within the Democratic Party as well. Rove, who should have known better, was not immune. He began betting burgers with colleagues and friends that Dean would be the nominee. This was wishful thinking, as Rove's boss realized—even if the boy genius did not: One of those who bet Rove a hamburger at the White House mess that Dean would not be nominated was George W. Bush.

In an October 2003 meeting of the campaign staff, Rove dismissed Joe Lieberman's and John Edwards's prospects as "Nowhereville," said General Wesley K. Clark had "imploded," and insisted that John Kerry had already "pissed away every advantage of the front-runner." It was early yet, but Rove believed Dick Gephardt had the most plausible chance of overtaking the streaking Dean. A few days after Gore's endorsement of the former Vermont governor, Rove convened the first of what would be many Saturday "Breakfast Club" meetings at his house in the Palisades neighborhood of Washington.

In delicious anticipation of running against a guy who spoke first and considered the implications later, Team Bush had compiled a thick dossier on Dean's rhetorical flights and policy positions as governor. The cover included thirteen photographs of Dean looking overexcited. McKinnon had already produced a spot called "When Angry Democrats Attack!" starring Dean in full rant. That piece was posted on the Bush-Cheney '04 website, and the angry-Democrat theme became a standing feature of RNC press releases whenever some Democrat spoke of Bush in severe language.

But if Rove considered Dean an easy foil, the feeling was mutual.

Out on the campaign trail, Dean began invoking not just Bush's name but Rove's too. One of Dean's messages was that Democrats should not fool around with centrist positions—or even swing voters. He said the key to victory was for Democrats to fire up their liberal base, and he claimed to get this inspiration from Rove himself.

"Somebody who is pretty smart figured this out before we did," Dean told the kids at Grinnell. "His name is Karl Rove. The reason the president is behaving in such a right-wing way is because he knows the way to win elections is to give your base a reason to be proud to go out and vote, so they don't have to vote for the lesser of two evils anymore. Well, we're going to do that with the Democratic base."

By 2003, Rove had become a convenient target among the Democratic Party faithful. Rove's string of successes in Texas, the results of the 2000 race, and the unexpected victories in the 2002 midterms had brought him a blitz of attention. This included two biographies of Rove (including the first edition of this book), a documentary, and a great deal of coverage in the daily press and on television and radio. The coverage had an edge to it, however. The focus on Rove's role in transfiguring Texas into a Republican stronghold dredged up the hardball tactics of those early campaigns, which tended to invigorate the Democrats' rage anew. And the dominant story line of Rove's great national election successes—that the "boy genius" was really "Bush's brain"—did not exactly endear Rove to the president or vice president. Asked even before the 2002 midterms what he thought of a *National Journal* cover story about Rove, Dick Cheney grimaced and said tersely, "grossly excessive."

If he saw it, the vice president would have really detested a January 2003 piece in *The Cleveland Plain Dealer.* "Last week, I had coffee with the most powerful man in America," wrote Washington columnist Tom Brazaitis. "I'm speaking, of course, about Karl Rove."

Tensions between Rove and Bush over Rove's press notices had been there from the beginning: Bush is grateful to Rove, respects his supple intellect, and even likes him. At the same time, Bush is always on guard that Rove's ego doesn't overinflate. In February 1999, then-Governor Bush publicly chastised Rove for discussing the governor's presidential ambitions with the national press before briefing the Texas media about them.

"Maybe Mr. Rove should have talked to me before he talked to the press," Bush said pointedly. Later the same year, Bush passed by a gaggle of reporters gathered around Rove, who was holding court. "Is the Karl Rove press conference over yet?" cracked Bush. The governor was not smiling when he said it.

In April 2001, Rove's voice mail at the White House informed callers they had reached "the senior adviser to the president." It

may have been true, but when Howard Fineman wrote about it—
and put the first "the" in capital letters, the voice mail was quickly
changed in hopes Bush would not see the offending *Newsweek* reference.

A year later, when approached by another magazine writer for
National Journal regarding a profile piece, Rove described himself
"as one of many aides in service to the president," and tried to talk
the journalist out of writing it at all. When the journalist mentioned
Rove's "career," the interviewee interjected, "I have no career! My
only existence is a lowly member of Team Bush."

This style of talk is more to Bush's liking. Even when Bush is
kidding, the "Turd Blossom" quips can sting. After Hughes
decamped back to Texas, taking her leavening influence with her,
Bush would occasionally dismiss a suggestion he disliked by crack-
ing, "That idea's so fucking bad, it sounds like something Rove
came up with."

As Election Day neared in 2002, Rove encouraged Bush to make
one last stop in Iowa to give a boost to Republican candidates in
that state. Bush, who was tired, said no, but Rove kept at him.
Finally, as *Air Force One* headed from South Dakota to Indiana,
Bush said, "You better have a parachute, Karl, because when we get
over Iowa, we're throwing you off the plane."

On the 2004 campaign plane, Laura Bush, who is more charitable than her husband in her assessments of people, told a
Newsweek reporter that she thought Rove got too much credit
around the Bush White House—and too much blame.

"I love Karl," she said. "I love to call him for the scoop. I love to
gossip with him.

"He's fun to be with. He reminds me of Pigpen," she added in an allusion to a "Peanuts" cartoon character who walks around all day in a cloud of dirt. "Ideas come off of him (like) the dirt . . . you know, his hair kind of all stands up at the top."

At the outset of the 2004 campaign, Pigpen attempted to lower his profile a bit. The interviews he gave journalists were mostly off-the-record; his public speeches rare. But no matter what Rove did, he managed to attract attention from the other side of the aisle. The level of obsession could be pathological. In the run-up to the invasion in Iraq, former envoy Joseph C. Wilson IV managed to stretch his fifteen minutes of fame into a year or so after he challenged the White House on weapons of mass destruction and his wife subsequently was outed in a Robert Novak column as a CIA agent. That column prompted a special counsel's investigation that continued into 2005. (It is a crime under certain circumstances to name an undercover U.S. intelligence operative.) Several of Wilson's assertions have since been debunked, including his claim that his wife had nothing to do with his being sent on a CIA mission to Africa to determine if Saddam Hussein had attempted to buy uranium illicitly from Niger. Still, Wilson's gleeful proclamation upon learning that he had sparked a criminal investigation was telling: "Wouldn't it be fun to see Karl Rove frog-marched out of the White House in handcuffs?"

This was not a unique reaction. As the presidential primary season unfolded, it became clear that Rove was something of a fixation among prominent Democrats.

At one of the earliest candidate forums, a May 20, 2003, event sponsored by Emily's List, a Democratic political action committee, House member Richard Gephardt was discussing the prospect of even more Bush tax cuts when he revealed the prevailing Democratic Party mind-set.

"If we're to believe Karl Rove, who probably really is president, we're going to get another half trillion [tax cut] next year," Gephardt told the group.

Just over a month later, in an address at the National Press Club, Patrick Leahy, the highest-ranking Democrat on the Senate Judiciary Committee, suggested that Rove would be picking the next Supreme Court nominee.

"Republican activists are reported to be consulting closely with presidential adviser Karl Rove," Leahy said. "If they convince the president to choose a divisive nominee in order to tilt the ideological balance on the Supreme Court, they will not prevail without a difficult Senate battle."

There was hardly any issue that Democrats didn't see Rove's hand in. On September 10, 2003, Ralph Hall of Texas, the ranking Democratic member on the House Science Committee investigating NASA's response to the independent review of the space shuttle *Columbia,* twice asked NASA administrator Sean O'Keefe if Rove was part of an interagency executive-branch team involved in this issue. When O'Keefe answered no, Hall seemed disappointed. Hall, at least, had an excuse to level the charge: He was one of the Texas Democrats targeted by DeLay and Rove (and would soon change parties).

But the day before, at a September 9, 2003, Senate hearing on spending for homeland security, South Carolina Democratic Senator Fritz Hollings also clearly had Rove on his mind while embarking on a jag about how the administration was playing politics with money that Congress had already appropriated.

"We'll hold at $20 billion until next year's campaign, and then Karl Rove will dish it out," Hollings said. "But in the campaign [year] $20 billion will go around all over the darn countryside."

"Thank you for that optimistic overview," Senator McCain, chairman of the committee, replied wryly.

The same day, in another Senate hearing room, West Virginia Democrat Robert Byrd went further. Byrd launched into a diatribe against the war in Iraq, which he seemed to blame Rove for starting. Byrd could be idiosyncratic, but he was not the only such voice. In a Democratic presidential primary debate in Iowa on January 6, 2004, Howard Dean asserted without qualification (or sourcing) that the timetable for an Iraq constitution and Iraqi elections was "mostly driven by Karl Rove's political advice."

On January 14, 2004, Senator Edward M. Kennedy basically accused Rove of instigating the war in Iraq for partisan political reasons. "Prior to the terrorist attacks on September 11, President Bush's approval rating was only 50 percent, but with his necessary and swift action in Afghanistan against the Taliban for harboring bin Laden and Al Qaeda, his approval soared to 86 percent," Kennedy said. "Soon Karl Rove joined the public debate and war with Iraq became all but certain."

Kennedy's implication struck top White House officials, including Bush, as a cheap shot. But maybe it wasn't: In March 2004 a grand jury subpoenaed documents pertaining to the White House Iraq Group, which dealt with communications issues relating to the war. As reported by *Newsweek,* the task force was created in August 2002 to develop a strategy for publicizing the proposition that Saddam Hussein constituted a threat to the United States. Among its members? Karen Hughes, Mary Matalin—and Karl Rove.

Ultimately, however, the president squandered, rather than enhanced, his high job approval rating by going to war in Iraq—as

Rove could be the first to attest. Moreover, in ascribing such vast powers to a presidential underling, Democrats proved they were not only underestimating Bush but also not thinking clearly about what it would take to defeat him in November. In sports parlance, Rove had gotten into the Democrats' heads. And no one was more obsessed with Karl Rove than John Kerry.

On October 9, 2003, at a Democratic candidates' debate in Arizona, Kerry credited Rove with "exploiting national security" in a way that allowed the Republicans to regain control of the Senate in 2002. On November 18, 2003, at an AARP-sponsored debate in New Hampshire, Kerry again singled out Rove as being responsible for devising a Medicare prescription-drug bill that inoculated the president for the upcoming election, but did not provide tangible benefits to seniors until two years *after* the election.

"Karl Rove met on Capitol Hill," Kerry said. "Who did he meet with? He didn't meet with the legislators; he met with the lobbyists . . . to plot the victory for this bill."

In a December 3, 2003, speech to the Council on Foreign Relations in New York, Kerry made headlines by offering his sharpest criticism of Bush so far, accusing the president of pursuing "the most arrogant, inept, reckless, and ideological foreign policy in modern history." It was a catchy line. Indeed, it was so catchy that Kerry repeated it three days later in a speech to the Florida Democratic Convention—this time incorporating Rove's name into the sentence.

And in a December 10 town hall meeting in New Hampshire, Kerry alluded to Bush's appearance on the USS *Lincoln:* "I look forward to reminding Karl Rove and the Republicans that I know something about aircraft carriers for real."

Rove had wanted to run Bush against Howard Dean, but instead he drew a Democrat even more preoccupied with Rove than Dean was. Kerry won the Iowa caucuses on January 19, and took the New Hampshire primary eight days later on January 27. Dean made one last stand in Wisconsin on February 17, but Kerry won there, too, and the Democratic Party's nominee was all but chosen.

That night, as the crowd in Madison chanted "Kerry! Kerry! Kerry!" the presumptive Democratic nominee revealed what—and who—was on his mind.

"If George Bush, Karl Rove, and Ed Gillespie and company want to make national security the central issue of this campaign," Kerry shouted, "we have three words for them [that] we know they understand: 'BRING. IT. ON!'"

The audience repeated the refrain: "Bring it on!" Back in Washington, Rove and the team he had assembled watched the scene on television. One of them recalled thinking, "Well, big boy, we're fixin' to do just that."

18

The Machine

On Labor Day weekend, two months before Election Day 2004, Bill Clinton spoke for ninety minutes to John Kerry. Aides to both men said afterward that Kerry, befitting Clinton's status as the only Democrat to win two terms as president since Franklin Roosevelt, did more listening than talking. And Clinton, as is his custom, gave a lot of advice in that conversation. Not all of it was good advice. For one thing, Clinton suggested that Kerry endorse the various state measures seeking to codify a ban on same-sex marriage—and go around the country talking about it. If Kerry had agreed to demagogue on this subject, he simply would not have been believed. He was, after all, one of eight U.S. senators who voted against the Orwellian-named Defense of Marriage Act signed by Clinton in 1996, and by switching on this issue Kerry would have had to explain another "flip-flop"—while coming across as cynical to boot.

But some of Clinton's counsel was perceptive. He insisted that if the 2004 election was allowed to devolve into a debate about all the votes Kerry had cast in his Senate career and everything he ever said about Vietnam, the Kerry-Edwards ticket likely would lose. The campaign, Clinton insisted, had to be a referendum on Bush's four years as president—and nothing more. If you are the issue in the case, you lose, Clinton advised. If Bush and his record were made the primary issue, Kerry would win.

This was sound advice. The only trouble was that it came about six months too late.

Back in the spring, Kerry emerged quickly as the Democrats' official standard-bearer, but the consensus candidate was actually an entity known in the party by its initials: A.B.B.—"anybody but Bush." Rove, monitoring this emerging sentiment, warned his troops that they definitely must not allow the A.B.B. narrative to unfold in 2004. The Democratic challenger would have a past, a voting record, a personality, points of vulnerability. The race would be a contest between two politicians who would both be carrying baggage with them into November, Rove told the troops.

"We wanted this to be a choice, not a referendum," noted McKinnon succinctly. "And we made it a choice. That's hard for an incumbent to do."

The first step included ads that began airing in March 2004. Set to ominous-sounding music, they warned that Kerry would raise taxes "by at least $900 billion" immediately upon assuming office, and would undermine the war against terrorism by emasculating the USA Patriot Act.

For dramatic punch, McKinnon moved the McCain/Feingold-required disclaimer ("I'm George W. Bush, and I approve this ad") to the beginning of the spot. It ended with a narrator intoning, "John Kerry: Wrong on taxes. Wrong on defense."

Mehlman and McKinnon justified this preemptive sortie by pointing out that the opposition party had been beating up Bush in their primary debates for the better part of nine months, and that the news media had never felt constrained to get the Bush-Cheney side while covering this intramural Democratic Party discourse. Bush campaign officials added that Democratic Party–affiliated "527" groups (numbered for the pertinent tax provision), such as Move On, had gone negative much earlier, even posting on its website amateur attack ads comparing Bush to Hitler.

Nonetheless, this was early in the campaign cycle for negative ads to be issuing from a campaign—especially an incumbent president's campaign—and their presence on the airwaves upped the level of ill feeling on both sides. The ads also seemed to knock Kerry off stride.

"The Bush campaign launched a negative advertising campaign against me," Kerry complained in a written statement—as though that would be a surprise. The following day, March 10, while shaking hands with factory workers in Chicago after a speech, Kerry blurted out that the current crop of Republicans were "the most crooked, you know, lying group I've ever seen."

Kerry's remarks were caught by a National Public Radio boom microphone—and derailed the Democrat's attempts to position himself on the high road. Indeed, the following day, the Kerry campaign, in keeping with its "rapid response" philosophy, issued an attack ad of its own questioning Bush's veracity.

Matt Dowd issued a memo to the GOP faithful encouraging them to remind people of Kerry's outburst. A week later, Dowd had more fodder: While snowboarding in Ketchum, Idaho, Kerry collided with a member of his Secret Service detail, took an awkward spill—and promptly blamed the agent.

"I don't fall down," Kerry snapped. "That son-of-a-bitch ran into me."

This was an uncharitable comment—and inexplicable besides—since the reporters accompanying Kerry had witnessed him falling on his own a half dozen times the day before. The Bushies seized on it instantly.

"It is perfect material showing that Kerry will say anything," one Bush-Cheney operative told the press.

A pattern had been established: Kerry would say or do something that played to type—and the Bush campaign would pounce on it, reinforcing a negative image that they had helped to create. It was circular. When Kerry claimed to have spoken with foreign leaders who told the senator they preferred him over President Bush, the Bush campaign pointed to his travel schedule—he hadn't been abroad in a long time—and demanded that reporters ask which leaders he had in mind. "Is it Fidel Castro? Kim Jong Il?" one top Bushie quipped. It was a legitimate question; Kerry, just as legitimately, would not get dragged into naming names.

But within a day, the Republican National Committee had released a web video spoofing Kerry with an Austin Powers theme, dubbing the senator "the international man of mystery" for declining to identify the foreign leaders he said favored him. "Who are you, honestly?" the web piece asked.

To Team Bush, there was little downside to going negative on Kerry. For one thing, their first spate of ads produced by McKinnon's group—which began airing a week before the "wrong on taxes, wrong on defense" ads—were positive, feel-good ads portraying Bush as a strong leader in a time of national crisis. This is as positive as it gets in politics—yet the Bush campaign was still roundly criticized for them. One of the images in McKinnon's ad was of New York City firemen carrying a flag-draped coffin. At a

March 3 screening of the ad, several journalists seized on the 9/11 imagery, suggesting that Bush was exploiting tragedy for political gain. The networks and major newspapers, with encouragement from a handful of 9/11 survivors, played this exploitation angle up strongly, generating a controversy that lasted more than a week.

At that Saturday's Breakfast Club, McKinnon and Dowd expressed delight at the flap, telling their colleagues that generating "free media" this way was a bonus. Rove and Mehlman weren't so sure. To them, it suggested that they were in for a long war of attrition with the "liberal media." Since when, they wondered, can a wartime commander-in-chief not show images of the flag? And the 9/11 survivors who criticized them were a small minority of politically active people, some with established connections to the left wing of the Democratic Party—an angle only a few conservative news outlets bothered to report. Which side was truly exploiting personal grief?

Mehlman told Rove that it was only March of an election year and tempers were as raw as they usually get in October. Outwardly, Rove was upbeat as he cooked eggs that morning for the gang. But his inner reaction was even more pessimistic than Mehlman's. Rove later recalled thinking that the flap over the positive ads showed that in the long campaign ahead, the establishment media simply would not treat Bush fairly.

For their part, the nation's political reporters, especially the White House press corps, were catching grief from both sides. Conservatives have been convinced for a generation that the media are out to get their candidates. In 2004 this was a beginning point for all conservative radio hosts and bloggers. But this conservative oldie was countered by a thousand liberal bloggers—and a few prominent liberal commentators—who maintained on virtually a daily basis that Bush was so dim-witted and venal that he could be a viable candidate only if the media were shilling for him. In such a loaded atmosphere, the media resorted to chronicling nearly anything smacking of controversy. This defensive posture led to some dubious calls about what was newsworthy. Thinly sourced gossip about a nonexistent Kerry love affair? Why not? A bizarre conspiracy theory that Bush wore a wire (the odd bulge under the back of his suit coat) during the first presidential debate—so that he could take instruction from Rove? Naturally.

Rove was more likely to see liberal bias at work. But he could do nothing about that; what he could do was figure out how the media's quick-on-the-draw impulse in 2004 could be used against Kerry. He would need help from the Democrats, of course, but there was reason to believe they could be baited.

Rove and his group did not believe they should respond to every allegation aimed at the president. For one thing, they had no easily articulated answer to why the economy had lost private-sector jobs during Bush's presidency, why no weapons of mass destruction were found in Iraq, or why that country was more dangerous for U.S. soldiers and Marines a year after the occupation than it had been during invasion.

Nor did Republicans completely subscribe to the Democrats' theories of presidential campaigning: *Let no allegation go unchallenged. Win every news cycle*, the Democrats told themselves. *If the other side needles you, slap them; if they slap you, punch them; if they punch you, punch them harder.* Democrats formulated this creed after Michael Dukakis lost in 1988, a defeat they attributed to his supposed lack of agility in responding to Lee Atwater–framed finger-pointing over such issues as Dukakis's veto of a Pledge of Allegiance bill, his state's failure to clean up Boston Harbor, and abuses in the Massachusetts prisoner-furlough program while he was governor.

Many veterans of the Dukakis campaign drifted into Bill Clinton's 1992 campaign and, employing their new, hard-ass approach, helped elect Clinton to two terms as president. By the time Clinton left office, "rapid response" was a Democratic Party article of faith.

The Republicans in the White House considered this a simplistic way to view the practice of politics. Dick Cheney, for one, had long believed that neither presidents nor vice presidents could possibly respond to all the criticism leveled at them—and that some of it was best ignored anyway. Rove himself believed Mike Dukakis lost not because he failed to respond quickly to the accusations Atwater hurled at him, but because those accusations accurately reflected his actual (and too-liberal-for-the-rest-of-the-nation) policies as governor. George W. Bush seemed to think the lesson of his father's successful presidential campaign was even more basic: that the better, more conservative candidate won.

John Kerry, who had served as Dukakis's lieutenant governor and whose campaign was awash with Clintonites, bought in fully to the let-no-charge-go-unchallenged mentality. As the 2004 campaign unfolded, it dawned on the Bush brain trusters that they could use this theology as leverage. If Kerry believed he could let no provocation go unanswered, he was not really in control of the campaign agenda.

Ken Mehlman expressed this thought to his staff with this evocative imagery: "If the rabbit runs, he'll chase it."

Team Bush decided to test this hypothesis early on, ambushing

Kerry as he campaigned in the Appalachian Mountains. It was there that Kerry uttered his soon-to-be-infamous explanation of why, after voting in October 2002 to give Bush the authority to invade Iraq, he was one of only twelve senators who in October 2003 voted against the administration's $87 billion budget request to fund the venture.

Many of Kerry's own political advisers wished the senator's voting record could be reversed on the two Iraq votes, but as Team Bush itself knew full well, campaigns worked with what they had. Kerry's rhetorical struggle to reconcile his Iraq war votes could be painful to watch, however. On January 4, 2004, in an appearance on CBS's *Face the Nation,* Bob Schieffer asked Kerry to explain his thinking:

SCHIEFFER: That raises another question that I'd—I'd like to hear you explain because frankly I don't understand it. And that was you did vote to give the president the authority to go to war. Yet you voted against the resolution, that $87 billion, that was needed to fund the troops there.

KERRY: Yeah.

SCHIEFFER: Would you have voted for that money had your vote been needed?

KERRY: Yeah.

SCHIEFFER: Because it passed by a big margin. And they didn't need your vote to pass that.

KERRY: I would have. Bob, I made it absolutely clear that I support the troops. I support our being successful in Iraq. It is vital to the war on terror. It's vital to our international interests that we are successful. It's vital to Europe. It's vital to the Middle East. But

I also know from my own experience in Vietnam that when something is going wrong, it's important to fix it. What I was voting for was a better way to be successful in Iraq, by bringing the international community to the table and by doing what's necessary in order to minimize the cost to the American taxpayer.

McKinnon had a visceral response to this exchange: He felt Kerry was hiding a squirrelly nature behind Senate jargon. McKinnon told friends he found Kerry's entire approach to the legislation "irresponsible and reckless." Rove's reaction was similar. "It was one of the many instances," he recalled later, "where he indicated his willingness to bend himself into a pretzel." At the time, Rove had another thought as well: He was beginning to envision the possibilities if Kerry turned out to be Bush's opponent.

Ten weeks later, having emerged as the presumptive Democratic nominee, Kerry arrived in West Virginia for a campaign tour. The date was March 16, 2004. As Kerry landed, he was greeted by McKinnon-produced "wrong on defense" radio and television ads that highlighted his vote against the Iraq funding request—and listed some items the $87 billion was for, including body armor and combat pay for the troops. True to the rapid-response playbook, Kerry reacted to the ad before most West Virginians had even seen it.

"I understand that the Republican attack machine has welcomed me to West Virginia today, with another distortion and misleading statement," Kerry told an audience of veterans at a noon session at Marshall University.

One member of that audience had seen the ad, too, and he goaded Kerry about it during a question-and-answer session.

Kerry explained that he had offered an amendment to the president's supplemental funding request that would have provided the Iraq money by paring down Bush's previously enacted tax cut for the top 2 percent of taxpayers. The man in the audience answered that this begged the question of why, after his amendment failed to pass, the senator did not vote for the $87 billion on final passage.

"I actually did vote for the $87 billion, before I voted against it," Kerry blurted out.

After it was over, some Kerry staffers wondered about the "weird heckler" who asked the questions—without focusing immediately on the damage Kerry had done to himself. The traveling press recognized it at once. NBC's Norah O'Donnell called it "a tortured defense" on the air. John F. Harris of *The Washington Post* referred gingerly in his daily story to Kerry's "less-than-crisp statement defending the nuances of his position."

At Bush-Cheney '04, "nuance" wasn't the word that came to mind as the text of Kerry's faux pas was e-mailed around the office.

"This is manna from heaven," McKinnon told his crew. "And we're gonna need a new ad."

But George W. Bush had vulnerabilities, too, and Kerry's advisers thought they had an ace or two up their sleeve to exploit them. One pressure point was Bush's long-standing feud with John McCain, who had never forgiven Bush for the smearing he took in South Carolina in 2000. McCain's staff still considered the Bush staff— make that Karl Rove—responsible for spreading that slime. It was not quite true that Kerry and McCain were close friends, as Kerry kept insisting publicly, but they certainly did have a solid and cordial working relationship of long standing. It was easy to see why Kerry wanted to stress their association: McCain continued to register remarkable "favorable" ratings with American voters, roughly 70 percent with Republicans, Democrats, and independents alike—unheard-of numbers for a partisan politician.

And so, the presumptive Democratic nominee made a private overture to this maverick Republican senator and former Navy war hero: *Come be my running mate. We'll make history.* From a candidate who would be criticized for being unable to make a decision, this was a marvelously bold gambit. Alas, it was doomed. McCain rejected the offer, which leaked out. McCain was not interested for varied—or rather, multiple—reasons, but the most basic was that a great deal had happened since the South Carolina primary.

After 9/11, McCain had emerged as the staunchest voice on Capitol Hill in support of Bush's decision to decapitate the Taliban in Afghanistan. McCain had also given unwavering support to Bush in the run-up to the invasion of Iraq, and he had remained steadfast in this support, even as a bloody urban guerrilla war took hold there and the headlines turned from the toppling of Saddam Hussein statutes to the abuses at Abu Ghraib prison. In short, it was Bush, not Kerry, who more closely shared McCain's worldview.

Kerry's wooing of McCain shook the Bush camp, however, as it should have, but neither Rove nor Bush was quite sure what to do about it. Every campaign needs a bit of good luck, and it was at this time that McKinnon received a fortuitous call from McCain's Karl Rove—John Weaver.

The bad blood between Weaver and Rove predated the 2000 presidential race and became toxic afterward. The South Carolina episode drove Weaver out to California—and out of the Republican

Party altogether. Weaver even handled Democratic candidates, though he still considered himself first and foremost a McCain guy. To friends, when Weaver said "we," he still meant Team McCain.

Weaver had battled leukemia and had decided life was too short to be carrying around grudges. He had rid his body of cancer; now he wanted to rid his life of it as well. Rove was not the cancer Weaver had in mind—it was his feud with Rove.

"Karl and I have a lot of baggage," Weaver told McKinnon. "But I'm seeing things in a bit of a new light, and I want to leave all that behind."

McKinnon relayed this to Rove, who agreed to meet Weaver. It was the first week of May 2004. McKinnon offered his Washington apartment and was surprised when the two old antagonists chose a public place instead, the Caribou Coffee Shop at 17th and L Streets in downtown Washington. After getting their coffee, they surprised McKinnon again by deciding to sit outside—it was a nice spring day—even though they were somewhat concerned about being spotted. They were seen, too. Norah O'Donnell walked by and waved.

"We're going to see this on MSNBC tonight," McKinnon quipped. They didn't make the TV news though, and the rest of the meeting also went well.

"Karl, we've been at this a long time—and I'm tired of it," Weaver said. "I hope you are, too. Let's put our guns down."

"I appreciate that, " replied Rove. "I feel the same way."

Near the end of the session, Weaver said casually, "Anything we can do to help, let us know."

He meant anything McCain could do. This was not an idle offer—and Weaver knew something Rove didn't: McCain was eager to help Bush. A few weeks later, Rove telephoned Weaver to see if the offer of an olive branch was real. Could McCain meet the president in Fort Lewis, Washington, and appear with him there before the troops?

The answer was yes.

"All they ever had to do was ask me," McCain confided to Mark Salter, his top Senate aide.

At Fort Lewis, McCain introduced the president to a loud crowd of 6,000. Warm-up speakers on the Bush campaign were under strict orders to keep their introductions to one minute. McCain, a former Navy fighter pilot and Vietnam prisoner-of-war, talked for eight minutes. No one in the Bush camp stirred. McCain began by speaking evocatively about the "miserable business of war" and "the sublime love of those who sacrifice everything on our behalf."

The commander-in-chief "understands all this, and understands it very, very well," McCain said. "He heard the call to action on that terrible morning in September and summoned the rest of us to this long and difficult task. He has led this country with moral clarity about the stakes involved and with firm resolve to achieve unconditional victory."

When he walked onstage, Bush milked the moment for all the drama it was worth. The president strode over to McCain and hugged him as the soldiers whooped it up. "Both candidates in this race are honored to be the friend of John McCain," Bush told them. "Only one of us gets his vote, and I am proud that it is me."

If the public rally was mostly cheers, the closed-door event afterward was mostly tears. Accompanied by McCain, Bush met with the families of soldiers who had died in Iraq and Afghanistan. But with the images of Abu Ghraib fresh in their minds—and reports of daily roadside bombings in Baghdad on the increase—the emotions of the loved ones were raw. Later, aboard *Marine One,* Bush was silent. To McCain, he appeared almost heartsick. McCain put an arm around the president and squeezed his shoulder to buck him up.

"I'm proud of you," McCain told the president. He added that he would do whatever Bush needed in the reelection effort.

And so by August 2004, Karl Rove found himself having coffee not with John Weaver but with John McCain himself. The locale was Bush's ranch; the president was on one of his manic mountain-bike rides. By then, McCain had campaigned several more places with Bush, and during those trips Rove and McCain had discovered, incongruously, that they got along. On a trip that week into Pensacola, McCain regaled Rove with ribald stories of his wild days as a fighter jock based in the Florida panhandle. McCain also signaled in a very McCain sort of way that he had put the 2000 campaign behind him: He began referring to Rove as "staff scum," a tag that carried a perverse badge of honor inside McCainville.

McCain's steadfastness was tested in the summer when an anti-Kerry collection of former Vietnam Swift Boat crewmen—though none who served with Kerry—began running ads accusing Kerry of fudging his war record and making life tough for American servicemen still in Vietnam after he returned home and protested the war. Nearly everything about the approach taken by the "Swift Boat Veterans for Truth" offended McCain, and when asked by the press if Bush should disavow the ads and tell the vets to desist, McCain answered flatly in the affirmative. Bush did not follow this advice. The Bush campaign's position was tactical: It pointed out that the media—let alone Senator Kerry—had not objected to the anti-Bush ads being run by the liberal 527 groups, organizations far better funded than the Swift Boat vets, and with closer ties to Kerry than the Swifties had to Bush.

Bush's line of argument ran up against some inconvenient facts. One problem was that Benjamin L. Ginsberg was the legal counsel for the Swift Boat Veterans for Truth—and for the Bush campaign. Ginsberg stepped down from the campaign, but his departure hardly ended the controversy. Another problem was that Karl Rove had long-standing ties with several individuals connected to the Swift Boat Vets, most notably Texas developer Bob J. Perry. Rove and Perry were active together in Texas politics dating back at least to 1986 when both worked for Bill Clements. Perry donated $46,000 in total to Bush's two gubernatorial campaigns—and some $4 million to Texas Republicans over the years—and contributed $200,000 to the Swift Boat Vets.

Rove also did nothing to dispel suspicions he was pulling the strings behind the Swifties when, in an interview with the Associated Press during the Republican National Convention in New York, he blithely attached himself to the Swifties' most incendiary assertion: that Kerry's 1971 and 1972 antiwar speeches served to "tarnish the records and service of people defending our country and fighting communism and doing what they thought was right."

The controversy about the Swift Boat vets put McCain in an awkward position for another reason as well: His legislation on campaign finance reform was partly responsible for the mud flying back and forth. The statute prohibited a 527 group from endorsing a candidate by name, but because it did not prevent *criticizing* a candidate by name, it virtually legislated negative attacks.

Kerry had trouble of his own with the Swifties. Still smarting over how he was ensnared in West Virginia over the $87 billion, the Kerry campaign approached the Swift Boat vets apprehensively. It is not true, as many Democrats asserted after the campaign, that the Kerry team did nothing. The rapid-response members moved quickly but surreptitiously. They lined up friendly vets and historian Douglas Brinkley, and worked extensively with *The New York Times, The Los Angeles Times, The Washington Post,* CBS, and other outlets to discredit the Swifties and debunk their claims. Did this work? Maybe. Polls conducted by Gallup and Pew during the summer showed that contrary to conventional wisdom, Kerry's poll numbers did not decline in places where the Swift Boat ads aired. Yet strategists from both campaigns believed those ads had a corrosive effect on Kerry that showed up later in the electorate—even if it was hard to measure.

But by August, Team Bush was ready to spring yet another trap.

On July 29, 2004, at his acceptance speech at the Democratic National Convention in Boston, Kerry had said, "I will be a commander-in-chief who will never mislead us into a war." The line had stuck in Bush's craw. On August 6, in the conference room on *Air Force One,* the president discussed it with Rove and his other top advisers. According to *Time* magazine, the president himself was insistent that they toss out another rabbit—and make Kerry chase it. Specifically, they were going to force Kerry to answer a single question: Did he stand by his vote authorizing the war in Iraq, or did he regret it?

"I'm going to keep after him," Bush told his aides, "until he answers it."

The speech that day was in Stratham, New Hampshire, and there Bush laced the trap. "Now, there are some questions that a commander-in-chief needs to answer with a clear yes or no," Bush said. "My opponent hasn't answered the question of whether, knowing what we know now, he would have supported going into Iraq. That's an important question. The American people deserve a clear yes or no answer. I have given my answer: 'We did the right thing and the world is better off for it.'"

Three days later, at a photo-op while Kerry was campaigning at the Grand Canyon, a journalist asked him if he stood by his vote. "Yes, I would have voted for the authority," the senator replied. "I believe it was the right authority for a president to have."

Kerry went on to critique Bush's handling of prewar intelligence, the postinvasion planning, and his inability to persuade many other nations to bear the burden of the fighting. Kerry's advisers were pleased. They believed the real pitfall for Kerry was if he said he regretted the vote—because then Bush would quickly reduce the answer to: *If Kerry were president, Saddam Hussein would still be in power.* Instead, the Kerry campaign had refocused attention on the Bush administration's ineffectual execution of the war.

But the Kerry team was slow to realize that being nimble was in itself a pitfall for the senator. In giving these carefully constructed answers, Kerry seemed to be acting out his internal arguments with himself. The trap was in answering Bush's question at all.

"We couldn't believe he went for it," said White House communications director Dan Bartlett.

Aboard *Air Force One* that Monday—it was August 9—Bartlett received an e-mail on his BlackBerry from *Time* White House correspondent John F. Dickerson asking whether Kerry had given the Bush campaign "a gift."

"Yes," Bartlett text-messaged back, "and my boss is about to open it."

Rove, Hughes, and Bartlett immediately began drafting new

wording to stick in Bush's basic stump speech. Inserted was a section tracing the evolving Kerry position on Iraq, culminating in the punch line "I want to thank Senator Kerry for clearing that up."

In the aftermath of the 2004 campaign, Rove and the rest of the Bush brain trust congratulated themselves on neutralizing Iraq. That is not quite what happened, however. They may have made the best of a bad situation, and Kerry may have squandered his chance to draw bright lines between himself and the president, but exit polls after the November 2 vote showed that the Iraq issue hurt Bush. Fifteen percent of Americans chose Iraq from a list of seven choices as the most important issue facing the nation. Kerry won those voters by a handy three-to-one margin.

Iraq was not the only potential swamp for both candidates. There were other contentious issues, such as gay marriage.

On November 18, 2003, the Supreme Court in Kerry's home state ruled, on a four–three vote, that gays and lesbians had the right under the Massachusetts Constitution to have not only civil unions but to marry as well. The court gave the Legislature six months to rewrite state law to conform to its decision.

In San Francisco, a bastion of gay-rights activism, newly elected Mayor Gavin Newsom was not waiting even six months. Newsom had attended Bush's January 20 State of the Union Address and listened, his dander rising, as Bush reproached the "activist judges" who were redefining "one of the most fundamental, enduring institutions of civilization."

Bush, of course, was being whipsawed from his right flank. The bearer of this news was Rove, who informed him that gay marriage had galvanized religious conservatives. Bush, believing he was walking a fine line, was not ready to do their bidding—yet.

"If judges insist on forcing their arbitrary will upon the people," Bush said in his speech, "the only alternative left to the people would be the constitutional process."

Moreover, the president consciously struck what he believed was a tolerant tone. "The outcome of this debate is important—and so is the way we conduct it," Bush said. "The same moral tradition that defines marriage also teaches that each individual has dignity and value in God's sight."

This was Bush doing his best John Kerry, and—as each candidate would learn—2004 was not a year in which style points were being awarded for nuance. In late December, Bush had raised suspicions of leaders on the religious right by telling ABC's Diane Sawyer that he would support an anti–gay marriage ban "if necessary." Some evangelical leaders noticed after the State of the Union speech that the word "if" was still in Bush's formulation, and realized Bush had stopped short of what they were demanding, which was unequivocal White House support for a constitutional amendment banning gay marriage.

At the same time, Bush's call for a dignified debate won him no cover on the left. Most liberals and gay activists ignored Bush's rhetorical plea for tolerance; they found Bush's words patronizing—or, worse, disingenuous, given the policy he was advocating. As members of Congress cheered Bush's declaration to defend "the sanctity of marriage," Newsom recalled feeling he must be "on another planet." He returned to Planet San Francisco determined to do something, and on February 12, acting in his capacity as the top-ranking official in City Hall, the young mayor authorized the marriage of two well-known Bay Area lesbian activists. It was the first of many: City officials issued 4,100 such licenses in San Francisco during the next month—until the California Supreme Court halted them—but for four weeks, the network news carried nightly pictures of gay and lesbian couples lining up around the block to get their marriage licenses at City Hall.

Meanwhile, Karl Rove was having trouble fending off evangelical leaders, who warned that this issue had energized the conservative Christian base as no other—even abortion. James C. Dobson, head of Focus on the Family and, with his 7.5 million radio listeners, perhaps the most influential of the right-leaning pastors, had fired a shot across the White House bow with a fundraising letter to his vast donor base of conservative Christians saying that "the homosexual activist movement is poised to administer a devastating and potentially fatal blow to the traditional family and sadly, very few Christians in positions of responsibility are willing to use their influence to save it."

Dobson, ignoring the conditional language in Bush's State of the Union Address, praised Bush's speech and got on board. But others in the conservative Christian firmament were not satisfied. They tried to plant a vision in Rove's head of his great base of 15 million evangelicals not growing on November 2, 2004, but dwindling. They knew, and he knew, that if those Americans evaporated into the great ether of nonvoters, so would Bush's chances of reelection.

On February 3, 2004, some of these evangelicals, the most prominent of whom was Southern Baptist leader Richard D. Land, put it to Rove directly in a conference call. Would the president support the amendment? Rove assured them that he would. Two days later, Senate Majority Leader Bill Frist gave Land the same assurance at the National Prayer Breakfast meeting.

Neither Rove nor Bush has ever revealed exactly what the strategist said to the candidate, but it is a matter of history that on February 24, Bush did embrace the ban. Those who were there when Bush made the announcement were struck by how uncomfortable Bush looked—how little his heart was in it.

"After more than two centuries of American jurisprudence, and millennia of human experience, a few judges and local authorities are presuming to change the most fundamental institution of civilization," Bush said. "Their actions have created confusion on an issue that requires clarity. . . . Marriage cannot be severed from its cultural, religious and natural roots without weakening the good influence of society. Government, by recognizing and protecting marriage, serves the interests of all."

One journalist who knows Rove called him the following day.

"Congratulations, you managed to make your guy sound like an intolerant bigot."

"No way, man," Rove replied. "That view—what you just said—is what's intolerant. That may be the view in the Washington media, but not in most of this country. Two-thirds of the people in the country are bigots? Two-thirds of the country's deeply held, entrenched views out the window because of a four–three decision by an unelected court? It's undemocratic! The people will agree with us. You'll see."

Karl Rove does not pretend to be a theologian, but he is aware that to the Catholic bishops, the "life issues" that Rove pal Deal Hudson talked about include not just abortion, euthanasia, and embryonic stem-cell research but also capital punishment, AIDS funding, "just" war theory, and feeding the poor. Rove is familiar with this litany, even if his boss is only comfortable with about half of it, and Rove has discussed the implications of the bishops' beliefs not only with chief White House speechwriter Michael Gerson but also with a respected member of the "Christian left," Reverend David Beckmann.

Beckmann, president of Bread for the World Institute, a Washington-based hunger-fighting organization, revealed during the campaign that Rove had asked him for polling collected by anti-hunger groups. One such survey revealed to Rove that 78 percent of Americans would prefer to hear candidates expound on their ideas for fighting poverty than on their view of gay marriage. Beckmann, a liberal, said that after he shared that information with Rove, he noticed more antihunger references creeping into Bush's public remarks—call it the half-loaf strategy.

Just before going to Normandy for the sixtieth anniversary of D-Day, Bush made a stop in Rome. The ostensible purpose of the visit was to show homage to Italian President Silvio Berlusconi, but Bush paid his respects to Pope John Paul II as well. This was a visit in which the public relations could have gone badly: Indeed, even before it took place, the European correspondents on the trip were writing their stories about the pope's impending rebuke of Bush over the war in Iraq. And, true to the papal press release handed out before the visit, the pontiff read Bush a prepared statement reminding the president that the Vatican had opposed the war in Iraq and declaring that the "deplorable events" at Abu Ghraib were troubling to the conscience of the world.

As the U.S. delegation prepared to leave in its motorcade, Rove boarded his assigned van, then abruptly jumped out, grinning madly, to take a snapshot of the Swiss Guard, which protects Vatican City. Outwardly, it was the move of a rube, particularly since the banner headlines in Europe's newspapers the next morning did indeed read "Pope Rebukes Bush on Iraq." His tourist-type behavior was hardly the stuff of political genius, but Rove had reason to be thrilled after all. He knew what had happened inside the meeting. After the pope read his prepared text to Bush, the president plunged ahead, praising John Paul as a "son of Poland who became the bishop of Rome and a hero for our time." Rove knew his perky photo of the plumed and lance-carrying Swiss guards paled in significance to the poignant images beamed back home of Bush awarding a Presidential Medal of Freedom to the spiritual leader of the world's Roman Catholics, especially those in the battleground states of Ohio, Missouri, and New Mexico.

Rove also knew that word would get back to Roman Catholics in the United States that after the pontiff read his prepared statement, he warmly thanked the man he supposedly had just admonished, and ended the meeting with a benediction Bush often uses himself: "God bless America!"

There was one more twist ahead in Rove's 2004 Catholic strategy. It came from an unexpected source—Rove's handpicked emissary to conservative Catholics. Early in the year, Deal Hudson wrote in *Crisis* that Ono Ekeh, the moderator of the Catholics for Kerry website, was employed at the U.S. Conference of Catholic Bishops. This publicity made it difficult for the bishops group to retain Ekeh, who was making postings to the political website from his office at the U.S. Conference. Ekeh had well-connected friends, however, and after he was dismissed, it was Hudson's turn to be scrutinized.

Soon, the independent *National Catholic Reporter* newspaper learned why Hudson had left academia so abruptly. Fordham University revoked his tenure in the wake of a serious sexual harassment lawsuit filed by an eighteen-year-old freshman, a case Hudson settled for $30,000. He announced on August 18, 2004, even before the NCR piece was published, that in anticipation of its publication, he was resigning from his unpaid position in the Bush-Cheney campaign. Soon, he was forced to give up his editorship of *Crisis* as well.

A month before he left, however, Hudson teamed up with Rove for one last strategic decision. Finding resistance within the campaign and the RNC to hiring the three dozen paid staffers Hudson thought were needed to coordinate the volunteers in the Catholic get-out-the-vote drive he envisioned, Hudson put in a call to Ralph Reed, now an influential Republican consultant based in Georgia, and told him the trouble he was having. Within days, the campaign authorized Hudson to hire thirty-three people for the job.

"Ralph called Karl," Hudson said later. "Of course, Rove did it."

Such events were what passed for turmoil in the Bush campaign. The whole operation was reminiscent of the dog that didn't bark. Even when friction occurred, it was kept inside the family. While the Kerry campaign was turned upside down in a power struggle over whether director of communications Stephanie Cutter would be removed or demoted, her counterpart at Bush-Cheney '04, campaign spokesman Terry Holt, was quietly fired without a single story being written about it. He was transferred to the RNC to work for Ed Gillespie, it was announced. He continued to take calls about the campaign and sounded upbeat. Even after the election, not a soul in the campaign, including Holt, would say what happened.

This phenomenon was what made David Frum's observations about Rove and Karen Hughes so fascinating: these two very different types working together since 1998 *without a single known example of friction ever arising.*

The Bush acceptance speech these two brain trusters produced, with Mike Gerson's help, for the 2004 Republican convention in New York City was a case in point. Nobody's ego is evident in the address, with the possible exception of Bush's, who quipped that he knows some people look at him "and see a certain swagger, which in Texas is called . . . walking.") Otherwise, Bush said little about himself.

"Compare Bush's acceptance speech to Kerry's," said one White House adviser. "Kerry's was about him—Bush's was about the electorate.

"From a literacy standpoint it was a mess—it didn't hang together at all, but there was a method to it," the aide added. "The first thirty minutes were very gentle—that's Karen's target audience in mind—and it gets tougher and tougher, and by the time you're done he's talking to Karl's people."

The adviser said the speech was not organized logically but rather around the premise that swing voters and softer Bush supporters would watch the first half hour, while the hard-core Bushies would stay tuned until the bitter end. "That's how the game is played at the highest levels," the source said. "And it shows how Karl and Karen complement each other."

Whatever their differences, Rove and Hughes also share an important trait. They do not fool themselves, and consequently they do not mislead their candidate. In the last week of the campaign, Kerry's top advisers were telling one other and their friends that they were utterly confident Kerry was going to win. One can only assume they told their candidate the same thing.

By contrast, Matt Dowd, authorized to speak for the Bush campaign, said he believed Bush would win Florida, was pretty optimistic about Ohio, was worried about Pennsylvania—and believed they were ahead in the popular vote by roughly 51 to 48 percent. Dowd was asked about the so-called incumbent rule, which postulates that undecided voters break overwhelmingly in the last days of the campaign for the challenger. He said he had researched the question, discovered that in most presidential years the last-minute undecided voters split about evenly (with many of them staying home), and believed the same would happen this year. Dowd added that the campaign's polling showed Bush running better with women and Latinos than he had four years previously.

One day before the election, Rove fleshed this out. "We're going to win," he told reporters traveling with the campaign. "We will win Florida and Ohio. We will take at least two or three or four states that were won by Gore in the last election."

That all of these predictions came true is not necessarily the point. Rather, the point is that the Bush advisers did not deceive themselves.

"This is the main thing to give Karl Rove credit for," said one former Bush adviser. "He is very cold-eyed about his chances. He never spun himself—or his candidate—about where they were. This was in such contrast to the Kerry people. The Kerry people couldn't help but think that by the end of the election cycle, the American people would recognize Bush for the worthless bastard they think he is. Look, Karen Hughes and Karl Rove really love Bush. They *really love* him. But they understand why others might not. They don't kid themselves, and they plan accordingly. It's the best kind of loyalty."

As the 2004 campaign wound down, that loyalty would be tested one final time. It came after Bush fumbled the first debate in Coral Gables, Florida, by giving long-winded, repetitive answers, and by affecting a sarcastic, impatient, and belligerent tone—all of it complemented by slouching posture and annoyed facial expressions.

Bush had been prepped to a fare-thee-well, and as he went into the September 30 session at the University of Miami, his aides were confident to the point of cockiness. An hour before the debate began, McKinnon and Dowd sat on a stoop outside the hall, each smoking a cigar. Dowd, who was slated to be paired opposite Democratic spokesman Michael McCurry on cable TV afterward, was trying out humorous lines on passersby.

"I've decided *not* to say 'Bush was better tonight than Cicero,'" Dowd quipped with mock solemnity. "I'm just going to say he's *as good* as Cicero."

That mood was about to change.

In the sprawling media work space where journalists watched the debate on monitors, the electronic feed showed only the person speaking. Both Kerry's and Bush's debate negotiators—Vernon Jordan and James A. Baker III, respectively—had insisted on that condition. This insistence only made the networks determined not to follow it, which the Presidential Debate Commission had warned each campaign about. Viewers watching on network television, however, noticed Bush's piqued cowboy act immediately.

As the debate began, top Bush aides focused on their respective pet concerns: McKinnon had advised Bush about not using up the time allotted, so he watched the clock; Dowd was interested in how Bush characterized John Kerry; Rove was monitoring to make sure Bush made no gaffes or factual mistakes. But Hughes, watching the debate the way a swing voter would watch, was the first to deduce that the key to the debate was Bush's behavior when he wasn't speaking. She told them to watch the split screens.

"Oops," said McKinnon.

Dowd sighed and buried his face in his hands.

"This could be a problem," Hughes said softly.

Rove tried to keep them upbeat, but that was difficult. When it was over, all aides headed out to spin alley to say how great their guy had performed, but when the first round of instant polls came in, their worst fears were confirmed.

Bush was one of the last to face the fact that he had not done well. The president's impulse was to tell his aides that they were losing "the spinning war." They knew otherwise, but they were so accustomed to Bush's mannerisms—his habit of leaning into the lectern, of grimacing when he heard something he disliked—that they weren't sure what to tell him. "Just be yourself" didn't sound quite right; that may have been the problem.

It fell to Hughes to confront it. The woman who had told Bush to ditch the corny talk about being a capitalist all those years ago now told him over his cell phone that he had come across as irritated.

"I was not irritated," Bush said, according to an account in *Time*.

"Sir," replied Hughes, "you were."

The next debate was Vice President Dick Cheney's face-off against John Edwards in Cleveland. There, the debate debacle qui-

etly righted itself as Cheney remained calm and unflappable—
showing rather than telling Rove and McKinnon that, for instance,
if you had a good ten-second answer, you just gave a ten-second
answer. By the time Bush debated Kerry in St. Louis at a town hall
format on October 8, he had learned to relax again. At the last
debate in Arizona, he was steady and in command. When that
debate ended, what lay ahead for Team Bush was mainly to execute the ground game that Karl Rove had been planning for four
years.

The get-out-the-vote operation had a thousand components to
it, and Rove seemingly had his hand in all of them. He would go
through four dozen direct-mail pieces in a half hour, making stylis-
tic and substantive changes to all of them; he would pore over
spreadsheets of voter registration, precinct by precinct, in key counties in a dozen battleground states; he would coordinate with the
Catholic voters outreach and the evangelical team in signing up volunteers to go door-to-door—at 1,500 churches in Pennsylvania
alone—and he monitored the computer-driven effort to turn out
voters early.

This last effort was a relatively new wrinkle in modern campaigning. Brian Lunde had originally been brought aboard to
appeal to Democrats. As it turned out, Lunde had a more practical
talent that had nothing to do with bringing in voters from his former party—and everything to do with mining for Republican votes
in Democratic areas.

One aspect of this was identifying Republican voters who
wanted to vote early—70 percent of Americans now have the right
to do so—and facilitating that preference by letting them know how
and where to do it. One way he did so was working through busi-

ness groups, ranging from the U.S. Chamber of Commerce to individual companies such as Raytheon, Kodak, and Boeing—sending e-mails to their workers instructing them on how to vote absentee. Not all of these e-mails went to Republicans, of course, but most of them did, especially on lists like Americans for Tax Reform and the National Rifle Association.

Lunde was also adept at retrieving and electronically cross-referencing voter lists in ways that identified possible Republican voters living in Democratic strongholds, and who, for that reason, might not have seen Bush television ads or been privy to a phone call or a direct-mail piece. The campaign called such voters "Republican persuadables" or "unreliable Republicans," and Lunde's efforts constituted a surgical attempt to pluck them out of Democratic wards in Ohio, Florida, Pennsylvania, and other contested states.

The whole microtargeting effort was based on looking at voting as a rolling process. "In Wisconsin, 'Election Day' is thirty days long," said Lunde, who would frantically merge computer files searching for "discerning Democrats" or "Republican persuadables" to bombard with e-mail. "Shame on us if we can't pluck that 'sometime Republican' out of the data and persuade him to go out for us just once in thirty days."

Lunde called it the "quiet campaign" because the work was done below the radar in growing rural areas hard to reach by traditional methods. As Karl Rove studied all these data, he became convinced of two things: One, it was all coming down to Ohio. Two, he would need every piston in the machine to work properly in the Buckeye State: the "quiet" campaign, the African-Americans the Republicans target on school vouchers, the network of conservative Catholic volunteers galvanized by gay marriage and encouraged by antiabortion bishops, the thousands of evangelicals going door-to-door in towns in western and southwestern Ohio that journalists had never visited. It all had to come together.

In recent years, a Democrat wishing to carry Ohio in a statewide election would have to win Cuyahoga County (Cleveland) by 150,000 votes, win narrowly in Franklin County (Columbus), and hold the Republican to less than 60 percent of the vote in Hamilton County (Cincinnati). That was the recipe in the Democrats' cookbook, and they hit their targets in all three of those metropolitan areas. If that formula had remained good, John Kerry would have been president: On November 2, Kerry won Cuyahoga County by a whopping 217,000 votes, won Franklin County by 40,000 votes, and held Bush to 53 percent in Hamilton County. But Bush still won the state by 119,000 votes. The old Ohio blueprint did not work.

One-third of labor households—Democratic persuadables—voted for Bush. A surprising 16 percent of African-Americans in Ohio voted for him, too. Huge majorities of Bush votes poured in from the western and southwestern counties with their sprawling nondenominational churches. This contraption that Rove had constructed in Ohio had no name, but it had flown.

David Beckwith, a former *Time* magazine correspondent who had entered Republican politics as a spokesman for Vice President Dan Quayle, arrived to help out in Ohio in the waning days. Beckwith was once fired by Karen Hughes—back in the 2000 campaign—after being hired by Rove. But that power play had long been put in the background by the principals, even Beckwith himself, who later landed a job on the Senate staff of Texas Senator Kay Bailey Hutchison, a former Rove client.

Beckwith parachuted into Columbus expecting the typical chaos of a big, contested state. Instead, he found an efficient, well-running engine.

"I kept looking around for something to constructively criticize, or even help out with," Beckwith recalled later. "But they just had it under total control. I was along for the ride."

In the last days of a close campaign, everything spins out of control. It is too noisy; people give conflicting orders; volunteers flood the place, ratcheting up the confusion; there aren't phones for everyone.

Not in Columbus.

To Beckwith, it seemed as though everything got quieter, eerily quiet. The volunteers showed up, were given their assignments, and dispersed. The professionals made their calls and talked to reporters, field volunteers, and the bosses at headquarters. The voting was tantalizingly close all night long for those who had a stake in it. When it was over, no one could argue with Beckwith's assessment:

"The machine built by Karl Rove—it worked."

Epilogue

On November 1, 2004, George W. Bush made his last speech of that year's presidential campaign at Southern Methodist University in Dallas, Texas. As the event ended, Karl Rove joined the cadre of presidential aides for the fifteen-minute van ride from the SMU campus to Love Field. The president and first lady were flying on *Marine One* to their ranch in Crawford; the rest of the president's party was headed to Waco to spend the night there.

Seated in the van, Rove exchanged e-mails with the campaign pollsters on his BlackBerry. After a moment, he turned to Dan Bartlett and Mike Gerson, smiled, and said simply, "We're winning."

Bush had made a similar claim in his speech to the raucous Republicans gathered at SMU's Moody Coliseum, but inside the bubble is a spin-free zone, and the rest of the group was reassured by whatever intelligence Rove received—he still has not revealed exactly what it was—and by his easy confidence.

"When Karl said that, it put me completely at ease," said one White House aide present on that ride to the helicopters. "I slept like an angel that night."

The following day, Rove's prediction came true. It all came down to Ohio, which he had also predicted, and where the machinery he and Mehlman had put into operation gave the president a narrow 119,000-vote victory—out of some 5.6 million votes cast. Team Bush thereby claimed Ohio's twenty Electoral College votes, giving Bush-Cheney 286 electoral votes to 252 for Kerry-Edwards, and a second term in the White House.

Nationally, Bush won thirty-one states, to nineteen plus the District of Columbia for Kerry. Bush carried all the states in 2004 that he carried in 2000 except New Hampshire, while winning two states carried by Al Gore in 2000—New Mexico and Iowa. And this time, Bush carried the popular vote. The totals of the raw vote were 60.6 million for Bush-Cheney to 57.3 million for Kerry-Edwards, a margin of 51 percent to 48 percent.

Election Day 2004 gave the Republicans a scare when the first, erroneous exit polls showed Kerry comfortably ahead in several swing states, including Ohio and Florida. As *Air Force One* reached Andrews Air Force Base that Tuesday afternoon, Rove got on his cell phone and began jotting down the exit-poll numbers, state by state. His brow furrowed, just as the phone went dead. But Rove had heard enough to be concerned. "Not good," was his terse comment to Dan Bartlett.

"I was sick," Rove later confided.

After they arrived at the White House, Rove set up shop with his computers in what he called "the bat cave"—actually the White House family dining room—awaiting returns. From there, he communicated furiously with Dowd across the river at campaign headquarters. "These numbers make no sense," he told Dowd, studying a poll showing the Republicans losing Pennsylvania by seventeen points. The exit polls were clearly wrong. Or were they? By midday, the Bush brain trust realized that the exit-polling sample was inexplicably off. For one thing, the pool of respondents was composed of nearly 60 percent women—skewing it toward the Democrats. McKinnon e-mailed a friend that "either exits totally fucked up or the demographics in America have completely changed." By evening, Rove was convinced it was the former, although no one was completely sure. At the very least, in Rove's calculation, it was going to be a long night. At the peak of the evening's activity, Bush stayed in the room a while with his parents and other family and friends and staff—thirty people in all—but the party petered out as night gave way to morning. The television networks, spooked both by the early polls and their disastrous performance in 2000, would not declare Florida until virtually all votes were in—and would not officially call Ohio until the following morning.

Rove thought the networks were being too cautious. As more and more of the raw vote in Ohio and Florida was counted, Rove saw that it favored the president. He compared the results from individual counties in those two states with the 2000 election returns and became convinced Bush had won both states. At 10:30 PM, he called over to the Roosevelt Room to express this conviction to the senior staff. The shouts and applause were audible down the hall in the White House press briefing room. Still, Rove did not go home or even grab a nap. Ohio law called for setting aside questionable ballots in a "provisional" pile and recounting all of them if the election was too close. The question, in both camps, as the night dragged on was whether Bush's margin would exceed the stack of provisional ballots.

At 5:15 AM on November 3, Rove told Susan Ralston, "I'm

going to bed." After forty-eight sleepless hours, his only certainty was that teams of Republican lawyers had been dispatched to Ohio and Nevada. He was correct about the faulty exit polls, but John Edwards had addressed the Democratic faithful at Kerry headquarters just before 2 AM in a speech that was anything but a concession, and Rove was bracing for the worst.

He returned to the White House a couple of hours later, shaved, showered, a bit rested—and much more upbeat. Rove was in the Oval Office with Bush when the wire services moved stories saying Kerry had scheduled a concession speech. Rove walked back to his office. Those who saw him say he seemed dazed. His staff saw the emotion on his face—and for once he couldn't speak. Rove was joined in his office by Ralston and two other longtime assistants, Israel Hernandez and Barbara J. Goergen. The four listened to Kerry's speech at Boston's Fanueil Hall.

"Well, I can finally give you a hug and congratulate you," Ralston said.

First Goergen, and then Hernandez, expressed similar sentiments.

"I couldn't have asked for a better team," Rove responded, his voice husky with emotion. All four were in tears.

Not only did Bush prevail in his reelection effort, but the 2004 results demonstrated how Rove was continuing to put his stamp on Capitol Hill as well. Mel Martinez, Rove's handpicked candidate from Florida, won election to the U.S. Senate. Rove's decision to throw the weight of the White House behind liberal Republican Senator Arlen Specter instead of his more conservative GOP challenger also paid off, as Specter won reelection easily. The best news for Republicans came from South Dakota, where Rove, with help from the president, had convinced Republican John Thune to run again for a Senate seat he sought unsuccessfully in 2002. This time Thune won, upending a Democratic Party icon, Senate Minority Leader Tom Daschle, who had battled the White House on much of its legislative program. Rove took particular delight in the waning days of his campaign as a desperate Daschle ran ads showing him literally hugging the president.

The upshot of all this activity was that the Senate roster, split evenly fifty-fifty by party when Bush arrived in Washington, would have a ten-seat Republican majority when the new Congress convened in January 2005.

In the House of Representatives, the Republican Party continued to pad its lead as well. After the last two congressional contests were decided in Louisiana on December 4, 2004, Democrats were left occupying only 203 of the 435 seats in the House. The GOP gains in 2004 were entirely due to the redistricting engineered by Rove and Tom DeLay. Of the seven House incumbents in the entire nation who lost on November 2, four were Texas Democrats whose districts had been eviscerated by the Texas gerrymander. Of the seven white Texas Democrats targeted by the Republican apparatus, only Chet Edwards managed to survive.

✦ Rove was responsible for much of this Republican success—as no less an authority than George W. Bush himself volunteered during a press conference at the Ronald Reagan building on November 3. After thanking his family, Bush expressed gratitude to his "superb campaign team," singling out Marc Racicot, Ken Mehlman, Ed Gillespie—and "the architect, Karl Rove."

Thus did King Karl acquire yet another nickname. Certainly the real king, George W. Bush, had reason to be grateful. Bush also had reason to be proud of his own accomplishments. Every four years produces a winning candidate, and it was Bush—not his campaign manager—who pulled off a feat no American had ever achieved in the nation's history. No son (or daughter) of a U.S. chief executive has ever outperformed his ex-president father. But in winning a second term, the son Bush Forty-one affectionately called "my boy Quincy" had done just that. In so doing, Bush reached heights that Theodore Roosevelt Jr., James Roosevelt, David Eisenhower—even John Quincy Adams himself—never attained.

How much of the result was due to Bush and Kerry, how much to their campaign aides—or how much to deeper historical forces outside the scope of either campaign—is hard to say. The results of November 2 were not inevitable. If John Weaver and Karl Rove had not reconciled in the Caribou Coffee Shop, and if McCain had not contributed his support, would George W. Bush have lost? Possibly, if barely so. What if the Massachusetts Supreme Court had ruled four–three *against* gay marriage, a shift of one judge; would John Kerry be president? Somewhat more likely.

Sweeping international issues were also at play in 2004. John Kerry's aides told their candidate that every time President Bush alluded to Saddam Hussein being in irons, Kerry should counter by mentioning Osama bin Laden, the mastermind of the attack on the Pentagon and the World Trade Center, who was still at large.

Kerry faithfully followed that advice, asserting time and again that Bush had "outsourced" the job of capturing bin Laden to untrustworthy Afghan warlords. Yet Kerry was not helped—and may have been hurt—when bin Laden issued his latest videotape a few days before the election. Excoriating Bush in an address aimed directly to the American people, bin Laden appeared to make a crude attempt to influence the election. In this sense, his video message probably failed, as it did not directly harm either candidate. But it may have reminded Americans, for better or worse, that some issues are too important to be viewed through the prism of partisan politics—and this realization may have left swing voters who were not passionate about either candidate less inclined to change commanders-in-chief during wartime. In addition, how Americans defined the term "war" seems to have played a role in how they viewed the candidates.

In the exit polls, three-quarters of Americans who listed Iraq as the most important issue voted for Kerry. But 86 percent of those who named terrorism as the most important issue chose Bush. Taken together, these two numbers suggest that if Bush had not invaded Iraq, he might have won reelection easily. Conversely, if 9/11 had never happened, the numbers indicate that he might well have been a one-term president like his father.

But those events did happen, and Bush managed to win a second term at a time the economy was just keeping itself above water, the United States was bogged down in a foreign war, and Americans were pessimistic about the direction of the economy. This election also took place in a polarized political climate in which a huge percentage of Americans doubt that Bush has the capabilities to do the job. Despite all that, or maybe because of it, many American opinion-makers are still loath to give Bush his due.

This was not true of Karl Rove. He garnered plenty of credit. After Bush called him "the architect," longtime Washington Democrat Jack Valenti—a veteran of Hollywood and the Lyndon Johnson

White House—called him "a political genius." Donna Brazile, another Democrat (and manger of Al Gore's 2000 campaign), pronounced Rove "the master of the game."

Those on Rove's side of the political divide regarded such laudatory talk with skepticism. "Saying Karl Rove is a genius is a way for people who don't like the president to say, 'Bush is stupid,'" said Rove confidant Grover Norquist, president of Americans for Tax Reform, a conservative group that worked closely with Rove for Bush's reelection. "It gives neither Bush nor Rove the credit they deserve."

In Norquist's view, the most impressive aspect of Rove is his adaptability. In 2000, Rove devised a campaign inspired by Ronald Reagan's 1980 model: Run as a conservative, but as an empathetic, nonthreatening conservative who tries to sound reasonable during the general election while rhetorically steering clear of the most divisive issues. In this kind of campaign, Bush could stay above the fray, and most of the campaign's heavy lifting could be done with national television ads.

When the 2000 election returns did not pan out quite as Rove expected, he orchestrated a sharper-edged 2002 campaign, which drew bright lines between Republicans and Democrats and featured an incumbent president literally rolling up his sleeves and stumping for GOP congressional candidates. For a movement conservative such as Norquist, this was a desirable development. In the generation since Ronald Reagan swept to power, the two major political parties had gradually effected an almost complete polarization along ideological lines. In such an environment, the feel-good candidacy of Reagan in 1980—and of Bush in 2000—no longer was an effective approach. A few prominent Republicans, among them

Norquist, Ralph Reed, and Morton C. Blackwell, head of the Leadership Institute in Arlington, Virginia, insisted to Rove that in this changed political landscape, Republican presidential candidates could no longer run a Reagan-style airwaves-dominated national campaign while leaving grassroots organizing and get-out-the-vote efforts to Democrats.

Indeed, Rove called Blackwell after the 2002 midterms and said, "You were right—and did you notice? We took your advice."

They did it again in 2004.

"This showed a tremendous learning curve," Norquist said. "If Bush had run as Reagan one more time, he'd have been swamped. In 2000, Rove and Bush were content to go to the Republican base—to home-schooling evangelicals, gun owners, whomever— and tell them: 'We know what you want. You want to be left alone by government. We'll do that.' In 2004, they said, 'We know what you want . . . but if you want us to win, talk to your friend, have him talk to his friend, who talks to his friend—and make sure they all go to the polls.' This was Rove's vision, and he deserves credit."

And he got it. He got it from Bush—and from Bush's critics. In a postreelection reprise of Tom Brazaitis's old *Cleveland Plain Dealer* column, *Saturday Night Live* lampooned the president in a skit that begins with Bush in the Oval Office taking a call from a relaxed-looking John Kerry, who is vacationing with his wife on an unnamed Polynesian island.

BUSH: Hello there, John.

KERRY: Hello, George. I just wanted to congratulate the man who ran the most ruthlessly efficient campaign in the history of the nation.

BUSH: Thank you. I'll tell Karl Rove.

It's a joke that never seems to get old, just as it never stops putting Rove in the same awkward position vis-à-vis Bush. But it begs the question of what Kingmaker Karl does now. Bush can never run for chief executive again, and his political legacy as the two-term son of a president is set.

But what of Rove's future?

In the flush of the 2004 victory, Rove met with some four dozen Washington political writers at a *Christian Science Monitor* luncheon to field some of those questions. Facing reporters he had mostly avoided during the campaign, Rove was clearly in an expansive mood. He was, by turns, self-satisfied and self-effacing. At one point, Rove admitted to having a "reputation for being a hothead, occasionally." And when asked about the plight of the Democratic Party, he replied, "I barely understand the Republicans and the electorate. I claim no divine understanding of Democrats."

Rove was asked, inevitably, about the 2008 presidential campaign. "I am focused on 2005, 2006, 2007—and 2008 is going to be left to someone who has a little bit more energy and interest than me," he replied. "This will be the last presidential campaign I'll ever do."

The first part of that was certainly right. At a staff meeting two days after the election, Rove only half-kiddingly told his staff, "Now we have to turn our attention to 2006!"

Indeed, Rove was already at work doing just that. One day, he was brainstorming with Ohio Republicans on how to ensure congressman Bob Portman a higher profile in Ohio politics. The next, he was delicately exploring a way to pick up another Republican

Senate seat in Nebraska, perhaps by sticking conservative Democratic Senator Ben Nelson in the cabinet. Then there was the week-long job of helping Bill Frist walk Arlen Specter, the incoming Senate Judiciary Committee chairman, back from his provocative statements about the need for Bush to appoint prochoice judges. On his right flank, Rove was attempting to placate the evangelical Christians Specter angered—and who made no bones about their view that they want a seat at the table.

Rove was also more of a target than ever before, particularly as the White House purged one cabinet official after another and solidified even further its hold on the various agencies of the executive branch. As Homeland Security czar Tom Ridge was on his way out the door, someone in the federal government saw fit to pass on to *The New York Times* a fascinating—and frightening—tidbit about Rove. It seems that in 2002 Ridge was asked to work with the Environmental Protection Agency in formulating safety regulations designed to protect the nation's chemical plants and oil refineries from a terrorist attack. "But after the oil and chemical industries met with Karl Rove and other senior aides," reported the December 1, 2004, edition of the *Times*, "the White House quietly blocked those efforts, current and former officials say."

Thus was Rove casually accused of putting thousands of American lives in peril to placate an industry supportive of the Bush administration. On the other side of the coin, Bush's 2004 victory so solidified Bush's power that Rove could extend a quiet hand of conciliation to the NAACP, an organization that had worked tirelessly for the president's defeat. On November 30, Rove called outgoing NAACP chairman Kweisi Mfume and offered the president's best wishes. "I don't know what will come of it," said NAACP chairman of the board Julian Bond. "But we do want to have a relationship with the Bush administration."

But the second part of Rove's answer at the *Christian Science Monitor* lunch—that he didn't expect to be involved in the 2008 campaign—was more problematic. This promise, if kept, would make Rove an instant lame duck, and it was clear during that lunch why that is not the mantle Rove wants. He brought along his big binder of election returns and flipped it open to recite some of the results by way of rebutting a contention that Bush's victory was sufficiently narrow so as not to constitute a mandate. On the contrary, Rove said, Republicans now "need to focus on delivering" on Bush's campaign promises, among them, reforming Social Security, simplifying the tax code, and winning the war in Iraq.

Rove clearly expects to help Bush accomplish all this—and more. Rove's dreams of a historic realignment between the two major political parties existed before he latched onto George W. Bush as a gubernatorial candidate, and they continue. "There are big swaths of the country where Democrats are becoming less and less acceptable," Rove said after the election. "You have seen it already happen in the prairie states and in the South."

Maintaining this trend will entail getting the next Republican presidential nominee to duplicate Bush's success with evangelicals, married women, and Latinos while keeping the Republican lock on the "red states" in the American electoral map. For all those reasons, Rove soon began regretting his off-the-cuff remark about hanging up his spurs, and over the Thanksgiving holiday weekend he summoned Howard Fineman to his office to retract it officially.

"I said that in haste," Rove sheepishly told the *Newsweek* writer. "A lot of people in the White House told me that that was a really stupid thing to say. So let me say that I can't imagine spending two years away from my wife and son again, the way I did this time. But besides that, who knows?"

Who knows indeed? In 2002, in a ninety-minute interview with *National Journal*, Rove mused aloud about returning to Texas after the Bush administration ended and teaching school. It always required a leap of faith to imagine a person of such high energy being content behind the tenured walls of academe, but the 2004 election ratcheted up the stakes for Rove and his party. If George W. Bush made history in 2004 by winning the second term that neither his father nor John Quincy Adams won, Rove could make history, too. No man has ever been the brains behind two presidents.

It already appears that Rove will have first pick from among a large stable of eager Republican presidential candidates in 2008, a potential list that includes Jeb Bush, Bill Frist, Rudy Giuliani, and two Pennsylvanians, Tom Ridge and Senator Rick Santorum. Rove has worked most closely with Frist, so even four years out, it's not hard to imagine Rove going up against his old *compadre* John Weaver once again—should Senator McCain make another White House run. After the 2004 election returns were in, Weaver himself gave Rove measured praise for the progress toward Rove's stated goal of making the Republicans a majority party.

"He gets three feet here, three feet there, constantly eroding the other side and grabbing turf," Weaver said. "He has proved his point that you can expand the base, and not just among white males, without drifting or modifying either language or policy. I'm not sure it would work with any other candidate, at any other time. But it worked, and he proved the skeptics wrong."

Those skeptics, even if they disagreed, could no longer dismiss

Rove out of hand when he said—as he did after the 2004 election—
that America is undergoing "a rolling realignment."

Even if Rove is not solely responsible for this phenomenon, he
certainly believes in it, has helped it along—and wants to be a part
of it in the future. At the *Christian Science Monitor* lunch, Rove
was asked if the president will be inclined to work with congressional Democrats. "Texas politics is like Friday night football—a
blood sport," he replied. "But after you get it done, you sort of put
it aside for a couple of years and try to find some ways to work
together."

Rove is not a sports fan, and although "blood sport" is a dramatic image, his football analogy is all wrong. What you do after a
Friday night football game—win or lose—is replay the game in
your mind all weekend, then report to practice Monday determined
to do violence to the next opponent. That's the better comparison
to politics, a sport you can play long after your knees give out. Karl
Christian Rove turned fifty-four on Christmas Day still practicing
politics. And as his successful 2004 turned into an uncertain 2005,
Rove was busy with his "strategery," dreaming up game plans for
campaigns yet to come.

Sources and Acknowledgments

Our colleague John Ratliff's patient and skilled work as a researcher, interviewer, and copy editor was indispensable in the completion of this book. The chapter on South Carolina is largely his work. Elizabeth Esfahani's skillful research got us off to a fast start. PublicAffairs editors Lisa Kaufman, Paul Golob, and David Patterson have many hours of hard work invested in these pages. As does publisher Peter Osnos.

Working under extraordinary time constraints, we could not have completed our Texas reporting without relying on the diligent work of journalists at *The Austin-American Statesman*, *The Austin Chronicle*, *The Boston Globe*, *The Dallas Morning News*, *The Dallas Observer*, *The Houston Chronicle*, *Texas Monthly*, and *The Texas Observer*.

Profiles or long features including Miriam Rozen's exceptional Karl Rove profile in *The Dallas Observer*, Robert Bryce's early work in *The Texas Observer*, and the work of Paul Burka and Skip Hollandsworth in *Texas Monthly*, Melinda Henneberger in *The New York Times Magazine*, and David Shribman in *The Boston Globe* were particularly useful. The reporting of Sam Attlesey and

Wayne Slater in *The Dallas Morning News* was extremely helpful. As was the work of Robert Bryce in *The Austin Chronicle* and Frank Bruni in *The New York Times*. The reporting of Richard Fisk and Thomas M. DeFrank in the New York *Daily News* informed our chapter on the South Carolina primary. As did the reporting of Jacob Weisberg in *Slate* and Jake Tapper in *Salon*. The thorough and thoughtful coverage of Lena Guerrero by Lori Rodríguez of *The Houston Chronicle* was also useful. As was Tim Russert's July 2002 CNBC interview with Karl Rove.

Subjects interviewed by the authors and John Ratliff are identified within the text. Interviews done by the authors for earlier stories and other works in progress are quoted throughout the text or used as background. Material from the authors' previously published work, and from the authors' notes and transcripts, was also used.

—LD and JR

I am indebted to my colleague on the White House beat, Alexis Simendinger, who is not only a good partner, but a diligent political observer. It was Alexis who noticed quite early in the Bush administration that Karl Rove was an influential policy, as well as political, adviser in the West Wing. She and I interviewed Rove for ninety minutes in the spring of 2004, and went to his house together for the accompanying photo shoot, where she gleaned such details from him as the precise number of boxes of books the Roves brought north with them. While I'm at it, I'd like to thank my editors at *National Journal*, Charles Green and Steve Gettinger, as well as our publisher John Fox Sullivan and owner David Bradley, for putting out a magazine that allows reporters the time to find out what a key White House aide is doing and the space to write about it. I'm also indebted to several others among my New Jersey colleagues, especially our top political writer James Barnes, and our intrepid Charlie Cook, author of the *Cook Political Report.*

Like Lou and Jan, I also benefitted mightily from the hard work of many journalists working for other publications. It was *The New York Times* that unearthed the story of the 2001 dinner with Rove and the restive Republicans. Fred Barnes' work in the *The Weekly Standard* is the primary source about Jim Gilmore's truncated tenure at the RNC—and Fred has written insightfully about Rove's relationship with the Republican Party as well.

Those are but two of dozens of examples of good work that helped inform my own reporting, for even though I cover the White House myself, I learn something about the beat on almost a daily basis from my colleagues and competitors. Those who helped me greatly include Ed Chen and Maura Reynolds of *The Los Angeles Times.* I'd also like to tip my hat to the good work of Elizabeth Bumiller, Richard W. Stevenson, and David Sanger of the *New York Times.*

Sanger has Texas family roots, but I'd be remiss if I didn't acknowledge the help of several reporters working in Washington for Texas newspapers. Lou and Jan noted Wayne Slater's contribution. I've also learned much from the White House coverage of Wayne's *Dallas Morning News* colleagues David Jackson and G. Robert Hillman. The same is true of Bennett Roth of the *Houston Chronicle,* and that paper's lively and outsized columnist, Cragg Hines. The coverage of Knight-Ridder's Ron Hutcheson has been informed by his background in Texas journalist—as have Ron's readers. The same is true of the well-sourced and hard-working Ken Herman of the *Austin-American Statesman*; I've also been enriched by reading the White House coverage of Bob Dean, Herman's colleague in the Cox Newspapers Washington bureau.

Mike Allen and Dana Milbank of *The Washington Post* wrote about the Bush White House with skill and insight every day for four years. Their *Post* colleagues Bob Woodward and Dan Balz also did much of the ground-breaking work on the Bush presidency. I tried to give credit for others' work along the way, including theirs, but some recapping is in order: It is Woodward's book on Bush the wartime president that revealed the delicacy of the relationship between Rove and Colin Powell. And the behind-the-scenes details of election night 2000 first appeared in a 40,000-word *Post* series later published into a book, *Deadlock: The Inside Story of America's Closest Election*, written primarily by David Von Drehle, a peerless journalist and a friend, who provided encouragement for this book. Speaking of others' books, it is a happy coincidence that PublicAffairs Books not only published *Deadlock*, but also *Election 2004*, by Evan Thomas and the staff of *Newsweek*—a riveting insider account of the Kerry and Bush campaigns. The author learned a great deal from the excerpts that appeared in *Newsweek*, and by a *Time* magazine's exhaustive 2004 election post-mortem as well. Kudos to *Time* correspondents Matthew Cooper, John F. Dickerson, John Carney and Karen Tumulty for their reporting.

For help in getting this book in publishable form, Jan, Lou, and I owe much gratitude to editors Lisa Kaufman, David Patterson, Paul Golob, and Robert Kimzey. Also to the top gun at Public-Affairs, Peter Osnos, a New York publisher who finds a home for so many books about serious subjects.

I'd be remiss if I didn't thank my family for letting me disappear without complaint—well, the nine-year-old complained a bit—for much of the holiday seasons of 2002 and 2004. Another family member, my father Lou Cannon, supplied moral support—along with fact-checking help. He is a former White House correspondent himself, as well as a writer of the very best political books.

After covering national politics for twenty years and the White House for nearly ten, the sources whose interviews I used are too numerous to cite, but I will mention a handful: On a flight from Washington to my hometown of San Francisco, Les Francis showed me the paper he'd written to try and get the Democrats to think regionally. I also interviewed the late, great Paul Tully about this in 1991, along with Democratic National Committee chairman Ron Brown and a young governor from Arkansas named Bill Clinton. I also had long conversations about it with numerous California Republicans, including Pete Wilson, Ed Rollins, and Stuart K. Spencer, an original Reaganite. Those three also helped me focus on the uneasy truce within the Republican firmament of the economic and social conservatives. The late Lee Atwater, Rollins's onetime deputy in the Reagan White House, as well as Michele Davis, another talented Reagan administration ex-pat, also assisted me in making the big mental leap from a GOP dominated by Californians to one dominated by Texans. It was a Democratic political consultant with Louisiana and Texas roots, Jim Duffy, who first predicted for me that George W. Bush would be president someday, even though he hadn't yet run for governor. Duffy had been working on a nonpartisan campaign in Texas—something about a new ballpark in Arlington, Texas—and came away grudgingly impressed. Jim told me this in Memorial Stadium in Baltimore on a cold April day while we watched the quintessential Texan Nolan Ryan mow down Oriole hitters. Duffy also mentioned that Bush had a real pistol working for him, a guy with my same first name, although he spelled it with a K. It was at a racetrack in New Jersey that Mark McKinnon, the Texas Democrat turned George W. Bush loyalist, first talked to me about the heretofore unchronicled human side of Karl Rove. Last, and he probably won't like this because he's chary about the publication of this book, I'd like to thank Rove himself, as well as his deputy, Susan Ralston, who've dealt with me on a courteous and professional basis.

—CMC

Index

PublicAffairs is a publishing house founded in 1997. It is a tribute to the standards, values, and flair of three persons who have served as mentors to countless reporters, writers, editors, and book people of all kinds, including me.

I.F. STONE, proprietor of *I. F. Stone's Weekly*, combined a commitment to the First Amendment with entrepreneurial zeal and reporting skill and became one of the great independent journalists in American history. At the age of eighty, Izzy published *The Trial of Socrates*, which was a national bestseller. He wrote the book after he taught himself ancient Greek.

BENJAMIN C. BRADLEE was for nearly thirty years the charismatic editorial leader of *The Washington Post*. It was Ben who gave the *Post* the range and courage to pursue such historic issues as Watergate. He supported his reporters with a tenacity that made them fearless and it is no accident that so many became authors of influential, best-selling books.

ROBERT L. BERNSTEIN, the chief executive of Random House for more than a quarter century, guided one of the nation's premier publishing houses. Bob was personally responsible for many books of political dissent and argument that challenged tyranny around the globe. He is also the founder and longtime chair of Human Rights Watch, one of the most respected human rights organizations in the world.

For fifty years, the banner of Public Affairs Press was carried by its owner Morris B. Schnapper, who published Gandhi, Nasser, Toynbee, Truman and about 1,500 other authors. In 1983, Schnapper was described by *The Washington Post* as "a redoubtable gadfly." His legacy will endure in the books to come.

Peter Osnos, *Publisher*